Routledge Revivals

Migrants, Emigrants, Immigrants

Originally published in 1991, this book covers an usually long time – from the 17th to the 20th Century – and considers the impact of internal migration and immigration (primarily in Britain) as well as emigration to North America, South Africa, New Zealand and Australia. Population movements are now recognized to be an integral part of structural change within society and this book brings together a variety of approaches. Drawing on the findings of historians, geographers and sociologists, the essays highlight areas of concern and illustrate some of the directions research on migration was taking in the early 1990s.

Migrants, Emigrants, Immigrants

Colin G. Pooley and Ian D. Whyte

Routledge
Taylor & Francis Group
Routledge Revivals

First published in 1991
by Routledge

This edition first published in 2021 by Routledge
2 Park Square, Milton Park, Abingdon, Oxon, OX14 4RN
and by Routledge
605 Third Avenue, New York, NY 10158

Routledge is an imprint of the Taylor & Francis Group, an informa business

Publisher's Note
The publisher has gone to great lengths to ensure the quality of this reprint but points out that some imperfections in the original copies may be apparent.

Disclaimer
The publisher has made every effort to trace copyright holders and welcomes correspondence from those they have been unable to contact.
A Library of Congress record exists at LCCN: 91019817

ISBN 13: 978-1-032-00002-2 (hbk)
ISBN 13: 978-1-003-17291-8 (ebk)

DOI: 10.4324/9781003172918

Migrants, Emigrants and Immigrants

A social history of migration

Edited by
Colin G. Pooley
and
Ian D. Whyte

ROUTLEDGE

London and New York

In association with the Social History Society of the United Kingdom

First published in 1991
by Routledge
11 New Fetter Lane, London EC4P 4EE

Simultaneously published in the USA and Canada
by Routledge
a division of Routledge, Chapman and Hall, Inc.
29 West 35th Street, New York, NY 10001

Typeset in 10/12pt Times by Witwell Ltd, Southport, England
Printed in Great Britain by TJ Press (Padstow) Ltd, Padstow, England

British Library Cataloguing in Publication Data
Pooley, Colin G.
Migrants, emigrants and immigrants: a social history of migration.
1. Migration, history
I. Title II. Whyte, I. D. (Ian D.)
304.809

Library of Congress Cataloging in Publication Data
also available

ISBN 0-415-04976-8

Contents

Figures

Tables

Contributors

Kate Bartholomew is a research student in the department of Economic History, University College of Wales, Aberystwyth, Wales.

Stephen Constantine is Senior Lecturer in History, Lancaster University, England.

John C. Doherty is Senior Research Officer with the Training Agency (Sheffield) and was previously Research Assistant at the Department of Geography, Lancaster University, England.

Colin Holmes is Professor of History at the University of Sheffield, England.

Deirdre Mageean is Research Assistant Professor at the Department of Sociology, University of Maine, Orono, USA.

Colin G. Pooley is Senior Lecturer in Geography and Deputy Director of the Centre for Social History, Lancaster University, England.

Eric Richards is Professor of History at the Flinders University of South Australia, Australia.

Kevin Schurer is Research Fellow with the ESRC Cambridge Group for the History of Population and Social Structure, Cambridge, England.

Ian D. Whyte is Reader in Historical Geography, Lancaster University, England.

Preface

The chapters in this volume were all originally presented as papers at the annual conference of the Social History Society held in Oxford in January 1989. The theme of this meeting was migration and social change and some twenty-six papers were presented during the conference. Abstracts of all papers were published in the Social History Society Newsletter (14.1, Spring 1989). Having been asked to draw together and edit a coherent volume of essays arising from the conference we were faced with the difficult task of selecting a smaller number of papers for publication.

The contributions appearing in this volume were chosen on a number of principles. First, some papers were already promised elsewhere and thus excluded themselves. Second, we tried to select papers which covered a reasonably broad time period and range of migration themes: we have included material from the seventeenth to the twentieth century and cover internal migration, emigration and immigration. Although the main focus of the book is on the British Isles, several chapters consider the impact of emigration overseas including North America, South Africa, New Zealand and Australia. Third, we have tried to select essays which represent original and innovative approaches to the study of migration, or which put forward controversial and challenging views. Hopefully, the final collection is reasonably well-balanced (we found the bias towards the modern period unavoidable) and the volume will provide a springboard for further research on migration and social change. Hopefully, too, we have not offended anyone who has been left out!

We would like to thank the committee of the Social History Society for organizing the conference in the first place, all our contributors for delivering manuscripts reasonably promptly and bearing with us during the inevitable delays which seem to occur in the preparation of a multi-author volume. Most of the figures were redrawn for publication by Claire Jarvis in the Cartographic Unit at Lancaster, Sheila Hargreaves retyped substantial sections of the text and Claire L'Enfant of Routledge gave us helpful support during the production process. We hope that all concerned will feel that their labours have been worthwhile, and that new researchers will pick up at least some of the ideas and themes developed in this volume to initiate new research on the still relatively neglected topic of migration history.

Colin G. Pooley
Ian D. Whyte
Lancaster, May 1990

1 Introduction

Approaches to the study of migration and social change

Colin G. Pooley and Ian D. Whyte

PERSPECTIVES ON MIGRATION

Migration, undertaken for many reasons, over varying distances and on a range of timescales, is a fundamental feature of human societies today. Aspects of migration are continually in the news: the plight of the Vietnamese Boat People, the desire of many of the inhabitants of Hong Kong to settle in Britain due to unease about the impending Chinese take-over, and the efforts of East Europeans to reach the West are topical themes. Less sensational but still of considerable concern are influences which inhibit mobility in a free market economy: examples from Britain include regional variations in house prices and the difficulties of moving within the local authority housing sector.

Migration was also important in the past and, as well as being an interesting phenomenon in its own right, it is also an important diagnostic feature of the social and economic structures of past societies. Population movements have long been a focus of interest and study. The unrestricted migration of labour has been seen as an essential element in the development of capitalism as evidenced by large-scale rural–urban movements of population within industrializing nations, emigration from Europe to North America in the nineteenth and early twentieth centuries and the high degree of labour mobility within capitalist societies like those of the United States and Canada in more recent times. Any consideration of migration involves posing certain fundamental questions about the migrants and the nature of their movements: how many, who, where and why? These in turn lead to further questions probing the effects of migration on the socio-economic structures of both source areas and destinations.

DOI: 10.4324/9781003172918-1

THE DEVELOPMENT OF RESEARCH ON MIGRATION

Until the nineteenth century concern with migration was of a practical rather than an academic nature as societies and communities adjusted to inflows and outflows of people and authorities tried to impose controls on population movements which they considered undesirable for social or economic reasons.[1] Interest in the accurate measurement of migration and attempts to model the processes involved grew during the later nineteenth century with the development of better statistical sources, particularly population censuses, in different parts of Europe. In Britain this approach is exemplified by the work of Ravenstein, whose 'laws' of migration (more strictly hypotheses) were based on detailed empirical research and still provide a useful framework for analysis.[2]

There has been a growing body of research into migration in the modern world by geographers, economists, sociologists and other specialists and a variety of analytical techniques has been used, ranging from interviews and questionnaire analysis of individuals to sophisticated statistical analyses of large data bases derived from official censuses. Along with this there has been increasing interest in the nature and role of migration in past societies. Inevitably the study of migration is closely linked with demography and the development of more sophisticated approaches to the study of historical migration has been in part the result of important developments in historical demography in Britain, Western Europe and North America. In particular migration studies have benefited from the more rigorous evaluation of sources, the development of more sophisticated techniques of analysis and the formulation of new theoretical approaches by schools of historical demographers, notably the Cambridge Group for the Study of Population and Society.[3]

The work of early statistical researchers like Ravenstein and a wealth of readily available contemporary commentary on internal migration and patterns of emigration made it clear that migration was a pervasive element in European society during the era of industrialization in the later eighteenth and the nineteenth centuries. On the other hand knowing that migration had occurred on a large scale was only a start and, as some of the chapters in this book amply testify, we are still a long way from knowing in detail the scale, pattern, and nature of internal migration and emigration in the nineteenth and early twentieth centuries despite the apparent wealth of statistical information which is available for analysis.

Because of the range of spatial and temporal scales at which it occurs migration can be very difficult to measure and understand. Demographic events such as births and deaths are finite, having been recorded in England and Wales by the Registrar General since 1837 and before that as baptisms and burials in parish registers since the sixteenth century. Such events have at least short-term consequences which are reasonably predictable. In contrast migration is an imprecise event which can include anything from a short-distance move within a small community to emigration to the other side of the world, and from a move to a new location for only a few days before the migrant travels elsewhere to one that lasts a lifetime.

Partly because migration events are so ill-defined and sometimes transitory they are rarely recorded. Although some countries (notably in Scandinavia) keep central migration registers which go back to the nineteenth century, most information about migration comes from surrogate sources, all of which pose problems of interpretation. Migration is also an aspect of human behaviour which, to a much greater extent than other demographic factors, can occur for a variety of interrelated reasons and which can have many complex and unpredictable outcomes.

THE LIMITATIONS OF THE SOURCES

This combination of imprecise definition, poor recording and complex causes and effects creates particular problems for the historical study of migration. Inevitably research on migration in the past must begin with a careful evaluation of appropriate source material. A perennial problem with historical sources is that virtually none of them was designed with the specific intention of recording migration. They shed light on the process incidentally, incompletely and often obliquely. Rather than having access to a clearly defined data set with known parameters, such as records of births and deaths after 1837 or the detailed information about landholdings given on a tithe map in England and Wales, the historian of migration must often begin by constructing a data set gathered from many different sources. This may involve comparing evidence between sources, nominal record linkage of migrants from one time period to another, and the use of different evidence relating to various groups within the population. Inevitably the data set which is assembled will be incomplete and, as the total number of moves is not known, the researcher will not even know what is missing. At best the complete data set is only likely to give limited information about the moves undertaken and the characteristics of the migrants. From this limited evidence the historian must then begin to speculate about the reasons why a move was made and about the effects of migration on different members of a family. Research on migration is a little like trying to do an unfamiliar jigsaw in the dark!

The nature of the sources and the information that they contain determine the kinds of question which can be legitimately posed, the framework of analysis which can be used, and the kinds of result obtained. Similar kinds of source tend to occur throughout Britain and indeed are often closely comparable between different countries; for example registers of baptisms, marriages and burials, local population listings, settlement certificates, apprenticeship records, census schedules, emigration data. These often allow useful comparability of migration between different countries, a possibility which has been far from fully exploited.

Given these problems there is a surprisingly large volume of literature on migration[4] but it is, perhaps, not surprising that much of what has been written tends to be superficial and/or inconclusive. Given the complexity of the migration process it is also not surprising that the level of theoretical generalization which takes place has progressed little since the work of Ravenstein in the 1880s.[5] Research into migration has also often been more concerned with methodology than philosophy. Much of it has been overtly positivist in its approach, some of it more humanistic. A limited amount of research has tried to provide an alternative framework based on relating types of migratory movements to modes of production within a Marxist framework,[6] but most research has simply dived into the empirical analysis of available sources.

PROBLEMS IN MIGRATION RESEARCH

There are five main ways in which existing migration research is defective. First, a good deal of published material, especially that written by geographers, reports the aggregate analysis of migration patterns.[7] The development of increasingly sophisticated computer packages for statistical analysis has had an important influence on research. Geographers and economic historians have pioneered the application of statistical modelling and econometric analysis to the study of migration data.[8] Heavily quantitative studies using large data sets tend to produce an impersonal, dehumanized approach in which flows replace individual people and the motives for migration are assumed rather than proven, often being interpreted in a simplistic and generalized way to a point where they have little meaning. Such aggregative work can stretch the credibility of available sources to their limit without giving any significant additional insights to the migration process. In the process of aggregating the data, individuals, with their hopes, fears and aspirations, become lost. Although such work provides valuable information, and can clearly demonstrate patterns of inter-regional and international migration (which is what it sets out to do), the macro-scale analysis of migration tells us little or nothing about the processes of population movement or the causes and effects of migration.[9]

Second, too much migration analysis is static in nature, providing a cross-section in time rather than a dynamic view of an evolving process. This is particularly true of research that is heavily dependent on a single source such as the published censuses of the nineteenth century.[10] Census evidence simply gives place of birth and residence on census night, thus enabling something to be said about lifetime movement from birthplace to place of enumeration at a specific date. This, however, is not an accurate picture of migration experience, as it completely misses the sequence of events which fit together to make a lifetime move. Unfortunately many studies simply use such surrogate census evidence to describe migration.

Third, because the detailed study of migration requires the use of many sources and the linkage of individuals between records, such studies tend to focus on one fairly small community. Thus, through the work of local historians, we know something about migration into particular villages or small towns,[11] but we know much less about migration into and out of large towns and cities and very few studies have made a genuine attempt to compare different places and time periods. Very small-scale detailed studies with a humanistic bias, based on the evidence of the diaries and correspondence of migrants or on interviews, may inform us about the detailed experience of individuals or small groups but may not allow us to relate them to a wider canvas. Studies of this kind may be 'parochial' in the best tradition but they need to be set within a wider context for their full value to be realized.

Fourth, where there is explicit information about the motives for and effects of migration, this tends to be anecdotal and, possibly, unrepresentative of a wider community. Material from diaries and letters can shed considerable light on the individual motives involved in migration, as well as on the detailed processes operating. However, such evidence is limited in its occurrence and is heavily biased towards those who were literate. Diaries or oral histories[12] can include relevant information about migration, but few studies have sought to collect a large volume of individual experience on migration, nor have they tried to check the representativeness of this material. However, as Bartholomew's chapter shows, oral evidence can be used to provide detailed histories of individual migrants which highlight the context in which migration took place in a way of which few written sources are capable. Although the time period for which such evidence is available is limited, the evidence regarding the motives for migration, the conditions under which movement occurred, and patterns of assimilation in the receiving area, as well as the degree of contact maintained with the source area may provide useful insights into the processes which occurred in earlier times.

Undoubtedly the motives involved in migration in the past were complex, just as they are today; thus there have been many attempts to simplify these processes. Classifications of 'types' of migration such as 'push/pull' or the idea of subsistence and betterment migration are a useful shorthand device as long as we remember their conceptual limitations. Equally the division of migration studies into 'internal' movements and emigration is an artificial construct based as it is on flows within or across equally artificial and arbitrary boundaries. Not only were internal movements and emigration complementary, they were frequently elements of the same process.

Fifth, because more data are available for some periods than others, our information about migration is very time-specific. Temporal variations in the coverage of source material tend to lead to a concentration of research on periods for which data are relatively abundant and detailed regardless of their historical significance. Thus we know far more about migration in England during Tudor and early Stuart times than during the later seventeenth and early eighteenth centuries due to the superior quality of ecclesiastical court depositions for the earlier period. Thus, too, many studies attempt to study migration from census evidence in the period 1851–81, yet we know very little about population movement in the period 1780–1830. This is particularly significant as it is a period of rapid urban and industrial expansion when population movement was an important motor of social and economic change. Some countries, notably Sweden and Iceland, have far better documentation on population and population movements at an earlier date than their neighbours. Mishaps of survival, such as the destruction of the Irish census enumerators' books, limit scope for study in some areas. Furthermore, in general, we know relatively little about migration before the eighteenth century in comparison with later periods.[13]

It should be emphasized that most of these deficiencies are inherent in the data and are an inevitable outcome of the sources and methods used. It is not that previous studies have been done badly – indeed many have been done very well and have made a major contribution to the historical literature – but they all represent the problems involved in working on migration. The chapters in this volume also suffer from some of the problems discussed above, but many of them also make an attempt to overcome these difficulties and thus point towards new directions in migration research. Inevitably, these chapters do not fully overcome any of the fundamental problems which beset migration research. However, they do collectively demonstrate how, through careful attention to detail and the use of a wide range of sources, it is possible to construct much more complete evidence about migration and emigration than is often available. Using this evidence, the authors are in a position to make informed speculations about the motives for, and effects of, migration. As such the chapters are a major contribution to research on migration and social change.

APPROACHES TO MIGRATION RESEARCH

In recent years a wide range of approaches has been used in studies of migration in the past. At a micro-scale the detailed study of movement into and out of individual communities, whether rural or urban, using the widest possible range of sources, still provides the essential building blocks for more general studies. This scale of approach is as applicable to recent times as to the medieval or early-modern periods, and Schurer's chapter demonstrates how the integration of standardized census data with other local records can add new insights to the nature of migration even for a much-studied period like the later nineteenth century. For more recent periods archival data can be supplemented by oral evidence provided by migrants themselves. Data of this kind are particularly amenable to a more humanistic treatment which delves below the generalizations of motive and pattern to uncover the real experiences of particular migrants. Bartholomew's chapter exemplifies this approach.

An important direction in research on migration in recent years has been to begin probing back beyond the nineteenth century to the pre-industrial period with its even less satisfactory and more problematical source material. In the case of England it is now evident that high levels of mobility were not confined to the period of industrialization but were also characteristic of pre-industrial times. Initially this was demonstrated for the period from the late sixteenth century onwards, a period for which detailed demographic information is available in the form of parish registers and for which a range of other sources including parish listings, settlement records and ecclesiastical court depositions provide details of population movements.

A significant development in migration studies has been the study of population mobility in later medieval times based on manorial court records.[14] By assessing population turnover between consecutive views of frankpledge and other types of listings this work has demonstrated that levels of mobility were as high in the late fourteenth and fifteenth centuries as in Tudor and Stuart times.

In this high degree of pre-industrial movement England undoubtedly contrasted with some parts of Europe where the continued survival of a peasant society and strong feudal controls encouraged higher levels of stability. Macfarlane[15] has used these contrasts as one of the main elements in his argument about the nature of English individualism. Yet, increasingly, research is providing evidence of high levels of population turnover and movement in many other parts of Europe, indicating that in such areas movement was the normal expectation rather than the exceptional experience. Recent research on population mobility in Scotland, for instance, has demonstrated that levels of migration were comparable in many respects to the English experience rather than to the static model which had previously been suggested. Even in countries where substantial sectors of the population were less mobile, migratory flows were still important. In France the temporary migration of workers from impoverished upland regions like the Massif Central to lowland areas to help with the harvest, or transhumant movements from the Cevennes to the plains of Languedoc formed an important element in the economic system.[16]

Many different types of migration have been identified. Some classifications have been based on motive (subsistence/betterment), or on the positive and negative influences that lay behind mobility (push/pull). The nature of source areas and destinations allows certain types of movement to be isolated such as migration from the countryside to the towns, or in England from champion to wood-pasture regions or closed villages to open ones.[17] Other studies have focused on the mobility patterns of specific socio-economic groups including vagrants, farm and domestic servants, apprentices, and women at marriage. Many kinds of migration were purely temporary and short-term such as the frequent but extremely short-distance movements of young men and women in farm and domestic service, or the seasonal movement of migrant harvest workers from upland areas to the adjacent lowlands. A good deal of the mobility in pre-industrial

England and Lowland Scotland was accounted for by this kind of movement.[18]

Distinctions have been drawn between the frequent and generally short-distance movements which occurred within the countryside and longer-distance movements to the towns. Important changes through time in both the amount and the nature of migration have been identified; thus Clark has shown that movement in Tudor and early Stuart times was characterized by an emphasis on long-distance movement from countryside to town and from upland to lowland with a significant element of subsistence migration. In the later seventeenth and early eighteenth centuries long-distance movement became rarer and movement was overwhelmingly short-distance in character.[19]

Migration is an interesting phenomenon in itself but is also an important indicator of differences in the social and economic structures of different areas and regions. Variations in the social composition of migratory flows, temporal and spatial differences in the scale and pattern of movement, the motives involved in migration, the information flows and personal contacts which aided migration, the characteristics of source areas and destinations, the official and unofficial reaction to population movements (favourable and unfavourable) all influence and at the same time reflect the nature of society in the areas which send and receive the migrants.

Movement of population, within the country, from country to town, from underdeveloped upland periphery to industrializing lowland core, from Europe to the New World, was an important aspect of the process of industrialization in the nineteenth century, one whose characteristics illuminate many aspects of the rise of the Industrial Revolution. Similarities and differences in the mobility experience of different countries and different regions can highlight the contrasts inherent in their reaction to industrial, or pre-industrial economic developments.

The discovery and evaluation of new historical sources has often provided a series of landmarks in the historical study of migration. The advent of parish register demography,[20] the use of ecclesiastical court depositions for the late sixteenth and seventeenth century in England,[21] or the testaments provided by Scottish kirk sessions[22] and the exploration of the potential of late medieval manorial court records[23] have all heralded major advances in our understanding of migration in specific areas and at particular periods. New sources relating to migration are still being discovered and more sophisticated ways of analysing established ones applied. Much research on migration in later nineteenth-century Britain has developed using census enumerators' books. Despite the considerable volume of work which has been undertaken using this source[24] new techniques and new approaches are still being developed. The material contained in the enumerators' books can be used in new ways – as in the linkage of information in successive censuses for particular communities[25] or between different areas.[26]

A perennial problem with migration studies is that few sources, with the possible exception of oral evidence, provide full migration histories for individuals. Some contain information relating to specific groups – apprentices, servants, vagrants – but these may not be representative of the population as a whole and the migratory moves studied may not have been the only ones which these individuals undertook. Other sources provide complete listings of inhabitants – but only limited amounts of information on migration. This is a frequent problem but it is particularly highlighted by work on census records. Thus the British census enumerators' books of the second half of the nineteenth century contain details of the birthplace and present place of residence of virtually the entire population, but for any individual this only allows a simple comparison of movement between birthplace and position on census night, a completely arbitrary datum. The significance of such a move may be completely illusory. It says nothing about the timing or nature of migration or of intermediate stopovers between place of birth and place of census registration. As studies in this book show, linkage analysis of data in consecutive censuses can be used to provide more background information and considerable additional insight into migration. However, this can only be done for a minority of people and the amount of effort involved in establishing linkages between successive censuses is considerable.[27] A similar approach can be used, within a specific community, to look at the character of 'movers' and 'stayers' by using successive census data in a similar way to parish listings of population.[28]

THE AIMS AND SCOPE OF THE PRESENT VOLUME

The study of migration in the past is an interdisciplinary topic which has attracted the attention of geographers, sociologists and other specialists as well as social and economic historians. The diversity of approaches which this encourages is well shown in the present collection, which stems from papers given at a conference of the Social History Society at Oxford Polytechnic in January 1989. This volume does not aim to be comprehensive in its scope; rather, its function is to illustrate some of the directions current research in migration is taking in terms of themes, approaches and the evaluation of sources, and to highlight areas of potential concern for future scholars.

Three chapters (those by Schurer, Pooley and Doherty, Mageean) explicitly tackle the problem of static migration studies by trying to construct longitudinal migration profiles for a representative sample of migrants. By linking individuals between sources, and comparing the characteristics of individuals and families before and after movement, it is possible to build up a data set on migration which gives some clues as to the changes which the process of migration wrought in people's lives. Discussion of motives for movements and the effects of migration is still speculative, but at least the authors are speculating from a much more solid basis of evidence than many previous migration studies.

The two chapters by Richards and Bartholomew use individual evidence collected through oral testimonies, diaries and letters to build up a picture of the migration process. Recognizing the problem of producing a representative sample from such studies both authors stress the range of evidence available and Bartholomew, in particular, sets out to collect a large and representative sample of oral testimonies which focus on one particular migrant group. Although the evidence remains individual and anecdotal, collectively a much more reliable picture of individual migration motives and experience is revealed.

Two authors (Whyte, Constantine) tackle the problem of comparisons over time and space. In wide-ranging discussions Whyte reviews evidence relating to migration in Scotland and England during the early-modern period and Constantine examines Empire migration to New Zealand, Australia, South Africa and Canada in the context of social reform. Their chapters demonstrate the gains to be made and the problems encountered in trying to construct genuinely comparative studies of population migration. Finally, Holmes provides a critical review of research on immigration to Britain since the nineteenth century.

FUTURE DIRECTIONS IN MIGRATION RESEARCH

If these chapters begin to tackle problems inherent in many migration studies, what are the most significant directions in which future research should move? First, we believe that the historical study of migration can be most effectively tackled through a behavioural approach using individual level data. None of the chapters in this volume adopts a heavily quantitative methodology, and given the limitations of available data it seems unlikely that further quantitative studies will yield significant dividends. Even where good statistical data on migration are available, the quantitative analysis of migration flows tells us little about the migration process as it affected either individual migrants or the society in which migration occurred. Much more promising is the accumulation of individual longitudinal migration profiles for large samples of people drawn from different places and time periods, followed by the sensitive subjective interpretation of this evidence.

Second, in order to build up these migration profiles, it is necessary for researchers to utilize and compare a much wider range of sources than has often been used in the past. In particular, researchers must seek sources which reveal actual moves (rather than lifetime migration experience) and which span a wide range of time periods. We still do not know in detail how migration in sixteenth-century England differed from that in the eighteenth or twentieth centuries. Neither do we know in detail much about the different emigration experiences of those going to New Zealand, Australia and North America. For instance, did someone who moved from rural Scotland to London in the seventeenth century feel more or less alienated than an emigrant from Scotland to Canada in the late nineteenth century? Questions such as these can only be answered by researchers utilizing a wider range of sources and making genuine comparisons over space and time.

Third, it is essential that future studies of population migration in the past are clearly related to the social context in which they are set. Aggregative and quantitative studies in particular tend to represent migrants as independent beings who move within or between countries, with very little regard for the geography or history through which they move. Thus migration must be explicitly related to factors such as regional economic prosperity, variations in wage rates and employment opportunities, the availability and cost of transport and the topography over which a move took place, the availability of information through kin, friendship networks or propaganda, social and cultural barriers of language and culture which may have inhibited movement, and political controls on movement and immigration. The importance of such factors for the understanding of migration is obvious, but it is surprising how few studies have taken them explicitly into account.

Most of this introductory chapter has focused on the problems of accumulating a satisfactory body of empirical data about migration and on the difficulties of analysing and interpreting these data. Because of the paucity of good sources most migration studies are preoccupied with data, and research is essentially empirical in nature. Where migration theory has been developed it has been applied to the aggregate flow of populations between places of different size and economic attraction and has, in most cases, contributed little to our understanding of the migration process.[29] Historians have, by and large, been rightly wary of migration theories developed by demographers, economists and geographers because of their lack of realistic historical contexts.

The historical study of migration could, however, benefit from the use of social theory to inform the speculative interpretation of scanty migration evidence. In particular, structuration theory as developed by Giddens[30] provides a useful framework within which the individual decisions of the migration process may be related to the broader social context. Briefly and simply, structuration theory focuses attention on the social practices by which individuals cope with the constraints and pressures imposed by the underlying and often unobservable structures of society, and the ways in which individual actions may, over time, even modify and change the structures of society. Migration itself is one set of social practices which can be adopted when structural constraints place pressure on an individual or family: the migrant moves to a new location to modify particular structural constraints. In moving, however, a whole new set of constraints and problems will be encountered and the act of migration itself requires individual reactions to assimilate new circumstances. It is the interaction between structures in society, which produce both opportunities and constraints, and the reactions of individual people which is of greatest interest to social historians. One of the most common, but also potentially traumatic, reactions is migration or emigration. Population movement should thus be a central concern of the social historian, and is an essential element in understanding both the creation of, and effects which stem from, structural change within society.

NOTES

1 A. L. Beier, *Masterless Men: The Vagrancy Problem in England 1560–1640*. London, 1985; A. J. Youngson, *After the Forty Five*. Edinburgh, 1973.
2 D. B. Grigg, 'E. G. Ravenstein and the "laws of migration",' *Journal of Historical Geography*, 3, 1977, pp. 41–54.
3 For recent reviews of relevant material see P. Clark and D. Souden (eds), *Migration and Society in Early-modern England*. London, 1987; P. White and R. Woods (eds), *The Geographical Impact of Migration*, London, 1980.

4 Much of the material is cited in P. Clark and D. Souden (1987) and P. White and R. Woods (1980), op. cit.
5 E. G. Ravenstein 'The laws of migration', *Journal of the Royal Statistical Society*, 48, 1885 pp. 167–227; 52, 1889 pp. 214–301.
6 H. Jones, 'Evolution of Scottish migration patterns; a social relations of production approach', *Scottish Geographical Magazine*, 102, 1986, pp. 151–64.
7 R. Lawton, 'Rural depopulation in nineteenth-century England' in D. R. Mills (ed.), *English Rural Communities*, London, 1973, pp. 195–219; D. Friedlander and J. Roshier, 'A study of internal migration in England and Wales', *Population Studies*, 19, 1966, pp. 239–79.
8 A. A. Lovett, I. D. Whyte and K. A. Whyte, 'Poisson regression analysis and migration fields: the example of the apprenticeship registers of Edinburgh in the seventeenth and eighteenth centuries', *Transactions of the Institute of British Geographers*, New Series, 10, 1985, pp. 317–32.
9 But see D. Baines, *Migration in a Mature Economy*, Cambridge, 1986.
10 For a recent review of census-based work see D. Mills and C. Pearce, *People and Places in the Victorian Census*, Historical Geography Research Series, 23, 1989.
11 E.g. M. B. White, 'Family migration in Victorian Britain: the case of Grantham and Scunthorpe', *Local Population Studies*, 41, 1988, pp. 41–50. D. G. Lockhart, 'Patterns of migration and movement of labour to the planned villages of North East Scotland', *Scottish Geographical Magazine*, 98, 1982, pp. 35–47.
12 For instance, R. M. Jones, 'Welsh immigrants in the cities of North West England 1890–1930: some oral testimony', *Oral History*, 9, 1981, pp. 33–41; C. Erickson, *Invisible Immigrants: The Adaptation of English and Scottish Immigrants in Nineteenth-Century America*, London, 1972; J. Burnett, *Useful Toil*, London, 1974; D. Vincent, *Bread, Knowledge and Freedom: A Study of Nineteenth-Century Working-Class Autobiography*, London, 1981.
13 P. Clark and D. Souden (1987), op. cit.
14 R. M. Smith, 'Kin and neighbours in a thirteenth-century Suffolk community, *Journal of Family History* 4, 1979, pp. 219–56; Z. Razi, *Marriage and Death in a Medieval Parish: Economy, Society and Demography in Halesowen 1270–1400*, Cambridge, 1980. K. P. Field, 'Migration in the later Middle Ages: the case of the Hampton Lovett villeins', *Midland History*, 8, 1983, pp. 29–48.
15 A. Macfarlane, *The Origins of English Individualism*, Oxford, 1978.
16 O. Hufton, *The Poor of Eighteenth-Century France*, Oxford, 1974; F. Braudel, *The Mediterranean and the Mediterranean World in the Age of Philip II*, London, 1975, vol. 1 p. 75.
17 J. Thirsk, 'Industries in the countryside', in F. J. Fisher (ed.), *Essays in the Economic and Social History of Tudor and Stuart England*, Cambridge, 1961, pp. 70–88. M. Berg, *The Age of Manufactures 1700–1820*, London, 1985, pp. 103–7.
18 A. Kussmaul, *Servants in Husbandry in Early-Modern England*, Cambridge, 1981. T. M. Devine, 'Highland migration to Lowland Scotland 1760–1860', *Scottish Historical Review*, 72, 1983, pp. 137–49; E. J. T.

Collins, 'Migrant labour in British agriculture in the nineteenth century', *Economic History Review*, 2nd series, 36, 1976, pp. 38–59.
19 P. Clark, 'Migration in England in the late seventeenth and early eighteenth centuries', *Past and Present*, 83, 1979, pp. 57–90.
20 E. A. Wrigley, *An Introduction to English Historical Demography*, London, 1966; E. A. Wrigley and R. S. Schofield, *The Population History of England 1541–1871*, Cambridge, 1981, pp. 3–30.
21 P. Clark (1979), op. cit.; 'The migrant in Kentish towns 1580–1640', in P. Clark and P. Slack (eds), *Crisis and Order in English Towns 1500–1700*, London, 1972, pp. 111–63.
22 R. A. Houston, 'Geographical mobility in Scotland 1652–1811', *Journal of Historical Geography*, 11, 1985, pp. 379–54.
23 R. M. Smith (1979), op. cit. Z. Razi (1980), op. cit.
24 D. Mills and C. Pearce (1989), op. cit.
25 K. Schurer, chapter 6, this volume.
26 C. G. Pooley and J. Doherty, chapter 7, this volume.
27 ibid.
28 K. Schurer, chapter 6, this volume.
29 D. B. Grigg (1977), op. cit.; E. S. Lee, 'A theory of migration', *Demography*, 3, 1966, 47–57.
30 A. Giddens, *A Contemporary Critique of Historical Materialism*, London, 1981. A. Pred, 'The social becomes the spatial, the spatial becomes the social: enclosures, social change and the becoming of places in Skane', in D. Gregory and J. Urry (eds), *Social Relations and Spatial Structures*, London, 1985, pp. 337–65. D. Gregory, 'Areal differentiation and post-modern human geography', in D. Gregory and R. Walford (eds), *Horizons in Human Geography*, London, 1989, pp. 67–96.

Part I

Emigration from the British Isles

2 Voices of British and Irish migrants in nineteenth-century Australia

Eric Richards

INTRODUCTION

The rise of mass emigration from the British Isles to Australia began tentatively in the 1830s and developed rapidly in the middle decades of the nineteenth century. Apart from a few years in the 1850s and 1870s the immensely long-distance migration to Australia was always dwarfed by the much greater movements across the Irish Sea and across the Atlantic. Emigration to Australia was more expensive and much more awe-inspiring to the potential migrant. It required far more government intervention, more human engineering, and far more complex and expensive arrangements. Indeed the creation of a substantial flow of migrants to Australia was one of the great achievements of government and commerce in mid-century. It was also a victory of the imagination: the emigrations to Australia were not only a defeat of distance but were also a triumph over the old convict image of the southern continent. Australia became an acceptable, respectable and even fashionable place of exile and colonization. At the same time great changes occurred in the minds of the emigrants, for Australia required greater psychological preparation than short-distance destinations.[1]

Most of all, emigration to Australia was more selective and better documented than most other mass movements of the period. The extraordinary requirements of this migration called into life an elaborate governmental and commercial apparatus to promote the recruitment and delivery of migrants to the other side of the world. Very little could be left purely to private enterprise or to *laissez-faire*. There was a substantial framework in Britain itself, the Colonial Land and Emigration Commission, and each colony also developed its own bodies. Their purpose, of course, was to identify and tap the various reservoirs of potential migrants in Britain and to select out the best

DOI: 10.4324/9781003172918-3

available to suit the particular needs of Australia. It was their professional responsibility to know more than anyone else about the springs of British mobility. And in order to compete in the great market for migrants Australia needed more financial inducement, more propaganda and more organization than its transatlantic competitors. The consequence, in terms of historical sources, was that these Australian agencies generated relatively thorough documentation of the processes of migration – in terms of recruitment, selection and consignment. Migrants who were assisted to the antipodes were required to pass through a series of turnstiles before they reached Sydney, Melbourne or Port Adelaide, and they were well recorded at several points along the way. Hence Australian sources, both literary and statistical, are comparatively rich on questions such as origins, occupation, family, age and literacy.

The generosity of the official documentation of assisted migration to Australia is well known though still grossly under-exploited. However, we are now beginning to realize the complementary strength of the informal record – the evidence contained in the private papers of these migrants. In particular the emigrant letter, and other related testimonies,[2] are exposing the mental worlds of the people who constituted the longest-distance migrants in human history. Moreover, the requirement (both moral and practical) that virtually every migrant would write home an account of this extraordinary act of mobility, caused even the least likely and least literate correspondent to put pen to paper. Migrants were more likely to reflect on their condition and their lives than those who stayed at home. A surprisingly large number of these letters have survived, though few of them have been collected together. Emigrant letters from Australia contain testimonies from people who do not normally leave archival residue for posterity: through them one can read the painful prose, even hear the voices, of the least literate members of the immigrant host.

The reason for concentrating on this aspect of the record will be evident. The best collection of emigrant letters from anywhere, and the most sensitive general consideration of their strengths and weaknesses is, of course, Charlotte Erickson's *Invisible Immigrants*.[3] She points out that the poor and the least literate are not well represented in the surviving American evidence even though she tried to 'dig deeper into the social structure of the migrant population'. Similarly Patrick O'Farrell's collection of Irish-Australian correspondence is heavily weighted towards the well-heeled.[4] Erickson says that very few letters from former agricultural labourers have turned up[5] and O'Farrell experienced the same difficulty. In reality, of course, labourers and domestic servants constituted a very large proportion of all British migration in the mid-nineteenth century and they have so far mainly escaped the net of migration historians; proletarian migrants are yet to be rescued for posterity. The suggestion here is that some of the Australian sources are more promising than the American record and that they may have special interest for historians of British society.

It is important to avoid the claim that the Australian material provides a cross-section of Australian immigration in general, or a cross-section of the labouring poor of Britain. The first point is undermined by the fact that we do not yet know accurately the general composition of Australian immigration. The second has to contend with the highly selective character of the emigration. Emigration to Australia was in no sense a spontaneous response to general conditions. It was an artificial flow induced by government incentives though it may have drawn upon already existing pools and propensities for migration in Britain. Australian immigration schemes, and there were dozens of them, may have skewed the intake towards the lowest echelons of British society, towards the very poor and otherwise least able to emigrate. Certainly there were times when Australia drew upon the extreme peasant fringe and the worst urban and rural slums of the British Isles, accepting and subsidizing thousands of economic refugees. Some of these emigrant voices may be heard, indistinctly it is true, when in Britain itself these categories of people were almost totally silent. Moreover the Emigration Commissioners and their successors were instructed to obtain labouring people. There was therefore a built-in proletarian bias in the process, even though the Commissioners were supposed to cream off the best of them. We know that from Ireland the migrants tended to be better off than the average and were regionally concentrated. Although we are not yet in a position to make systematic comparisons of people going to North America and Australasia it is likely that a higher proportion of proletarians went south[6] and this may be reflected in the surviving documentation.

Two particular categories of Australian immigrant sources have considerable potential in the study of questions addressed in this volume. The recruitment of people for Australia required a small army of emigration agents to scour the British Isles and report back to the colonial governments with information on conditions and the probabilities of mobility. Often they offer Australian interpretations of British life and circumstances. Secondly, emigrants' letters from Australia, although frequently full of nostalgia and self-justification, also provide accounts of origins, career paths, expectations and direct comparisons of conditions in Australia with those in the original points of departure in the British Isles.

These thoughts lead towards a small conceit – that the usual flow of historiography might be reversed and that Australian sources could be used to help write British history. An old complaint about Australian history was that, too often, it was written from London from British archives, and from an Imperial viewpoint.[7] Now it is becoming possible to use Australian immigration materials to explore social change and economic conditions in the British Isles. Already there have been several explorations in this direction. Stephen Nicholas and Peter Shergold have analysed convict data to produce important propositions about labour mobility in the Industrial Revolution.[8] Keith Snell, in the *Annals of the Labouring Poor*, has employed published emigrant letters from South Australia, from rural labourers, specifically to cast a beam of light into the obscure agrarian world of Suffolk in the 1830s.[9] In another sector David Fitzpatrick, using Australian statistics, has argued that Irish emigration to Australia in the post-famine period was a highly specific process which drew upon a well defined regional zone so that Irish Australia reflected a particular reconstruction of that part of Ireland.[10] Patrick O'Farrell has made extraordinary deductions about the state of Ireland from his collection of Irish letters, suggesting that the scale and psychological devastation of emigration was so great that 'Ireland had virtually exploded, disintegrated'.[11] Already therefore these studies suggest that Australian materials offer a mirror of Britain, sometimes fragmented and sometimes distorted; they provide antipodean perspectives on various aspects of British mobility and social change.

My purpose, therefore, is essentially programmatic. It is to offer a brief illustrated guide to some of this Australian material (in the form of direct testimony), in order to indicate its particular potential, and also as a vehicle to carry a commentary on some of the specific characteristics of Australian immigration, categories of migrant behaviour and problems that reside therein. The greatest problem is the sheer underdevelopment of the subject. Australia has not been integrated into the systematic history of international migration. The Pacific sector has not been connected to the great work on the North Atlantic – for instance there is no Australian counterpart of Oscar Handlin, Alvin Hansen or Bernard Bailyn. But at least there is now, to use Banjo Paterson's phrase, some movement at the station.

INDIVIDUAL TESTIMONIES

As soon as we reach into individual testimonies of emigration we confront the awkward realities of people who fit only very uncomfortably into the simple categories of the subject. It is probable that most migrants to Australia were straightforward enough: that is, they were preponderantly assisted couples or young families from, to begin with, rural backgrounds, and recruited by migration agents into ships from Liverpool or Plymouth. Yet the first impression one absorbs from the individual accounts – especially where these are connected with longitudinal data over more than one generation[12] – is the sheer diversity of backgrounds, origins and mechanisms which brought these people to an Australian migration.

Of the materials available there is a simple distinction to be made between letters and reminiscences. The retrospective character of reminiscences, of course, removes the immediacy and adds the gloss of hindsight: it is a source also which filters out the least literate and least successful of the people. On the other hand reminiscences provide a longer perspective on the migrant experience than the odd surviving letter.[13] And among letters there is a further distinction to be made, between published and unpublished. Those that saw print were often laundered or doctored for the reading public, frequently for transparently propagandist purposes, usually to stimulate or retard further emigration. People at the time were probably aware of this danger and editors of letters tried to counter the suspicion by guaranteeing the authenticity and unadulterated condition of their material. Some, like Charles Dickens, published colonial letters partly for their exotic value, partly to poke fun, and partly also to indulge an Arcadian fantasy of Australia. Nevertheless even in the published material there is much data which is clearly beyond suspicion, adding to the rich seam of working-class documentation that is largely unexploited.

The rarest form of this documentation is the unpublished migrant correspondence from the lowest strata of British society, at the level at which even basic literacy was barely attained.[14] The chances of these letters being written, let alone surviving in the pure form, were small. One example only can be presented here, that of Benjamin Boyce, three of whose letters from Australia survive from the years 1839–44. They are written in the most extraordinary and painfully phonetic form, yet with no embarrassment or apology. Boyce was a young sailor, the son of a beer-house keeper in the village of Freiston in Lincolnshire. He was employed on the emigrant ship, the *Moffat*, which sailed to South Australia in the autumn of 1838, arriving at

Holdfast Bay at Christmas two years after the first colonial settlement. During the voyage he formed a liaison with one of the official emigrants, Louisa Thomson, one of a family of six from Heathfield in Sussex. They were both from agricultural backgrounds and they decided to marry on arrival. Now this, of course, required Boyce to desert his ship and hide until the *Moffat* departed from the new colony on the southern shores of Australia. During the interim there was a reward of £2 on his head.

His three letters, now a prime exhibit in the early colonial history of South Australia, vividly recount his journey, escape, and subsequent career in the colony. They were written back to Freiston in Lincolnshire and, in their semi-literate fashion, are full of the loneliness, bravado and self-justification of emigrant youthfulness, reminding us of the sheer vitality and carelessness of many migrants.

He reported back to his family that during the voyage thirty people had died and that Boyce himself was 'taken very ill and that i ad to giv hup all my games with the young whemen' as well as the 'dancing and sining on bord the ship every night'. On his recovery he became acquainted with Louisa Thomson and then planned his escape. In fact, on arrival, Boyce lived in the sandhills, living off fish for several weeks until it was safe to emerge. He then found various sorts of employment and fell into partnership with another unofficial – indeed illegal – immigrant, a man named William Holland, an ex-convict from Van Diemen's Land, who had served fourteen years after being transported from Boyce's own village in Lincolnshire. They worked at tree-felling and fence building, and within nine months Boyce was able to accumulate the remarkable sum of £40. But a succession of misadventures and a clear degree of prodigality soon parted him from his money: as he wrote 'i out to been making muny as fast as I culd count it but in stead of that i uest to spend it faster than i earnt it.' As he explained, he 'eust to go in town a bout every three munths and ava bit of a spree for ten pounds.'

At this time Boyce was prepared to move about from job to job even though he was a married man and his wife had already borne him a son. One of Boyce's employers remarked on the general status of labourers in the colony, making a direct comparison with conditions in England:

> you may think with these high prices that the labourer is little better off than in England, but I can assure you that he is a very independent fellow here, and you must be humble to him or you may do your work yourself. What a contrast to England where so

> many are in a state of starvation, for what does he care about the high price of provisions when he has them found him by his master, besides £1 or £1.10.0 per week and some even more.

Boyce's assertion of his independence, and his mobility, were evidence of these migrant realities even though he, unlike his emancipist colleague William Holland, was unable to haul himself out of his status as a labourer. 'Independence' is the word which reverberates through colonial testimonies such as Boyce's even though many (like Boyce himself) eventually settled for wage labour, albeit well paid. The prospect of independence, even of owning land itself, was the central goal in their minds.

Boyce was undoubtedly homesick for Lincolnshire, yet was perfectly enthusiastic in his recommendation to his friends and relatives that they too should emigrate:

> i am shure that if laboren people ad the least idea of the colney they would not work hard in Ingland to starve whear in the colnies thear is plenty for whe ave plent of wheat and mutton and biefe and evrey thinks that whe can whish for the onley thing is crossing the salt warter.

In these words we hear the clear voice of the labouring migrant, a testimony which carries complete conviction. But it was also mixed with a certain element of bravado, and a taunting refrain can be heard in the last of the letters. In this, Boyce boasted that, unlike his contemporaries at Freiston, he had not been 'a fraid to go from the smoke of my mothers chiminey', he had not been like 'a great many of your freistoners a fraid to leave home'. This of course offers the ring of prestige and glamour that was wrapped around the act of long-distance migration, especially for the very young – the sheer adventure and excitement of it all.

Had these three letters not survived and had Boyce not suffered a fatal accident, he would have experienced the essential anonymity of most of his class. But in 1846 he fell out of a tree, shattering a leg, and died sixteen months later despite extensive assistance from the local Independent Order of Oddfellows, which paid out £85. Boyce's story was one of exuberant mobility, one which is captured in none of the official statistics of Australian or British migration – in fact he is part of that great dark figure of nineteenth-century international migration. It is also evident that Boyce regarded himself as different from and better than his stay-at-home contemporaries in boring old Freiston.[15]

Some of the social priorities of working immigrants are clear and recurrent in such contemporary accounts. Listen, for instance, to Sarah Mundon who, with her labourer husband, departed from Poole in Dorset for Australia in early 1840. They were working people with a good knowledge of agriculture, strong constitutions and a small amount of capital inherited from Sarah's father. In a modest way they quickly raised their status: John Mundon became an overseer on a farm belonging to F. H. Brown, a gentleman immigrant and the eldest son of the Bishop of Ely. The Mundons were surprised that Brown was fully prepared to work beside them and even to share the evening meals with them – 'to dine and sit, indeed say his equal in living in everything'. Dissolving social barriers was often the first consequence of emigration. The Mundons' joint salary was £120 per annum together with 'the privilege of keeping what stock we manage to purchase'. This particular provision was critical for their forward upward mobility; it was the classic colonial path of social mobility because it gave them the means of accumulating their own stock of capital and the true fulfilment of the targets of emigration. Emigration, when fully successful, accelerated the rise in social status. John Mundon soon possessed the symbols and the substance of such success – he had a horse for his own use, and the authority to hire, discharge and pay Brown's labour force, subject entirely to his own discretion in the management of the farm. By 1841 the Mundons had bought half an acre of land and had accumulated wealth worth £130 derived entirely from their Australian savings. They remarked, 'this is the place for tradesmen and labourers; if they are industrious and sober they can live and save money.' But they also noted the erratic character of colonial life: 'People are gentlemen one day and all most begars the next'. By the end of 1843 they were well settled on eighty acres of land and living in a stone-built house, effectively set up as autonomous farmers. They employed their own servants, and now complained about their excessive independence and the terrible expense of domestic servants. Sarah Mundon reported that they had to pay labourers 6 shillings (30p) per day for which they did extraordinarily little, 'and if you do not like it you may do it yourself'. When the Mundons died in 1883 their son was described as 'a gentleman'.[16]

The Mundon story was an example of physical mobility operating as a mechanism to accelerate the improvement of social status. Its reciprocal, in the colonial context, was the erosion of old standards of social behaviour and the visible decline in social deference. Thus when the Mundons arrived in Australia, at the bottom of the ladder, they were happily impressed by the social openness and apparent egalitarianism of their employer; as they achieved their own social elevation they became distressed that their inferiors were less deferential to them than they had hoped to experience. Some of the gloss of upward social mobility was thereby rubbed off by their transmission to a colonial society in which the velocity of social movement was obviously more rapid than in England.

The acceleration of social mobility and rapid dissolution of social standards was a recurrent theme in the private correspondence of British migrants of all strata. Migrants had a heightened self-consciousness about their social attitudes and were apprehensive and talkative about how they might have to adapt themselves. Emigrants, more than most people, found themselves constructing their future mental worlds. Some, like William Calder, a printer from Edinburgh migrating in 1852, said 'I put on the resolution of leaving all caste behind, and putting my hand to anything. I was aware that we were going to a country where everything like stiffness or "starch" would be looked upon with the greatest contempt.'[17] Thus his social expectations were reconstructed in anticipation and such ideas inevitably reflected back on Britain since all this correspondence was couched in either implicit or explicit comparisons. Mary Thomas from Southampton and from the employing class remarked in 1839, 'the servants are becoming as saucy and independent as they are in America. Both servants and labourers being scarce, they get too much wages by half.' When John Church, 'a gentleman', arrived in 1853, he could hardly believe the sheer effrontery of the working people in Australia. Clearly his mental preparation for the emigrant life had been deficient.

But it was the voice of the labouring immigrant which carried the message furthest and clearest. When William Purling arrived from Plymouth in 1852 he was astounded at his good fortune:

> we were all paid every week, we get plenty of drink for nothing from our masters [who] give us drink for nothing to keep us from going to the gold digers . . . you are afraid to say anything to your masters in England but that is the other way hear they are afraid to say anything to you for they know you will go to the gold diggers and they cannot get men to do their work.

His only complaint was the lack of marriageable women. He was particularly astonished that labourers could hire themselves to whomever they wished 'for they are at liberty to go where they like'. He added, 'this is a free country, you are not obliged to move your hat to your masters for a man is as good as his master and all set at the same tabel'.[18]

The reciprocal of these endlessly repeated remarks was, of course, the deference, the immobility, the caste system, the restricted social horizons, and the poverty of the British Isles which had been left behind.

THE CASE OF WILLIAM CLAYTON

The general category of migrant reminiscence, as already noticed, tends towards self-justification and a clear selectivity. Migrants on the whole had a more dramatic tale to tell and perhaps for this reason felt more enthusiasm and energy for writing their memoirs – their per capita level of reminiscence is probably greater than that of non-migrants.

The best example I know of is that of William Clayton, whose career encompassed an extraordinarily long life of mobility in both England and Australia. He penned his memoirs in 1910 but in fact was a child of the Industrial Revolution, an authentic voice of British urban mobility in the age of colonization. William Clayton was born in Manchester in 1833, son of a Catholic sawyer from Yorkshire who had married a Protestant woman from Selby – this itself indicating a record of mobility, inter-county and rural-to-urban, some time before Clayton's birth. Clayton himself began work in Manchester before he was 7, working as an errand boy for a fishmonger for a shilling (5p) a week plus his dinners. He then helped a pastrycook until he began work at two shillings (10p) a week in a dyeworks at which he remained until he was 11. In 1844 his father was killed in a log-fall while at work and Clayton, now a veteran of three careers, was taken on in a weaving factory working fourteen hours a day for six days a week. At 15 he changed again – to his father's old employer making packing cases and trunks – and by the age of 21 he was earning 25 shillings (125p) a week. He had vivid memories of the great labour campaigns in Manchester and the excitement of Chartism.

Clayton was a footloose youth looking out for opportunity. At 16 he had thought of emigrating to America where friends had already gone. Instead he caught smallpox and almost died. In 1854 the idea revived when he married a woman employed in a Manchester cotton factory. At the time the Crimean War was disrupting trade in Lancashire – as he said 'Things were very slack of work owing to the Russian War. So my wife and I took it into our heads to emigrate to Australia.' They made arrangements for a free passage to Melbourne but in a farce of domestic chaos missed the ship at Liverpool and eventually gained passages to Port Adelaide in the following year, 1855. Clayton said that all they possessed was an Irish half-penny, though he earned £2 as a steward on the voyage, during which Mrs Clayton gave birth to twins.

In Australia the Claytons experienced various passages in immigrant life which included near destitution and a great deal of tramping from place to place, though by 1864 he had acquired a house and an acre of land worth £18, together with four children. He was proud to have commanded work except for a few periods of broken time, 'but it was never my own fault', he claimed. In 1864, however, the Claytons decided to return to England. The homecoming was a great mistake. Clayton had great difficulty re-establishing himself as a case-maker. More specifically there was a disastrous family reunion at Selby, which turned sour. It all seems to have turned on the fate of a cockatoo which, by request, Clayton had brought from Australia as company for his mother; however, she quickly sold the creature to a travelling show and Clayton was furious. This incident seems to have precipitated the decision to re-migrate to Australia in 1866. Astonishingly the colonial authorities approved the second round of free passages with a warning that it could never be done again. And so the Claytons returned to a further life, back and forth between Victoria and South Australia. His wife died in 1912; at 80 Clayton wrote his remarkable and unpublished memoirs in semi-literate prose that echoes through the mobile colonial world. Equally remarkable was the fact that he lived on for another twenty-one years, dying in 1933 of chronic bronchitis at the age of 100, still celebrated for his vivid recollections of the Chartist riots.[19]

The Claytons were examples of that large class of return migrants and the smaller class of double migrants. Clayton was an example also of the fully mobilized semi-skilled proletarian from a world in which mobility had become normalized and in which he became a colonial version of a tramping artisan. His own account of his migrant decisions suggests an inconsequential attitude, a great carelessness precipitated by relatively small disruptions to the social psyche. Emigration, as this case might suggest, almost certainly selected out people who were already experienced in mobility, though there are plenty of examples of people who went to Australia who had never previously been to sea. Patrick O'Farrell sees mobility – in his case Irish mobility – as a continuing psychology of restlessness – 'once released from the containment of a tiny Irish village, these immigrants became inveterate wanderers. Often they moved in search of betterment, but often it was for the sake of moving.'[20] Most, like Clayton, eventually came to rest at the sunset of their working lives. In his case he had never gained much economic betterment.

PUBLISHED MIGRANT LETTERS

Considerably more problematical as evidence is the category of published migrant letters. Many such collections were transparently propagandist in character, usually subject to editorial improvement and selection, often promoted by colonial authorities and emigration agencies. Others are more clearly authentic and efforts were made to preserve their credibility.[21] Of a large range of Australian material it is possible to choose just one letter by a Wiltshire labourer who arrived in late 1851. Jacob Baker was a farm labourer and carter from Hodson near Swindon, part of an emigration of 258 people promoted with the aid of Poor Law funds by the so-called Wiltshire Emigration Society under the leadership of Earl Bruce, eldest son of the Marquis of Aylesbury. Baker, described as a skilled and versatile labourer who was often unemployed in the winter months, emigrated with his pregnant wife and eight children, some of whom had reached working age. Before his departure he wrote a speech addressed to the local farmers and landlords in which he described the circumstances of his fellow labourers:

> And, you gentlemen, must know that our case is very bad, and that we have not near victuals enough. How would you like to sit down with your wife and young children four days in the week to not half bread and potatoes enough, and the other three days upon not half enough boiled swedes, and but with little fire to cook them with?

He described how he mended all the shoes of the family, made his own clothes, was greatly skilled in agriculture and occasionally earned an extra sixpence (2½p) by drawing teeth. He remarked how it was indeed possible to go into the Poor House but that 'thousands would rob or starve than go to the house'.

In September 1852 a letter from Jacob Baker, written in the Barossa Valley, South Australia, was published in the *Scotsman* (and probably elsewhere too), reproduced in full and in its original semi-phonetic form. It was addressed to his friends and neighbours back in Hodson and described the voyage and the settlement of his family. They were all now in employment, and his wife Anne 'can now get 1 shillen a day with her nidel'. Baker went on to express all the doubts, aspirations and vagueness of an agricultural labourer adrift in a new world. For instance he wrote:

> I could not think how it was for labren men to get a farm, but now I can see how it is. I can save money enofe in one week for to buy one aker of land; so it plese God we have got our health, by the time this year is out I think of getting a little land; if I do not buy some I can rent some at 5s per acre, and buy it for one pound later.

Here of course, was clear evidence of the land-centred thinking of many immigrants, obsessed with the idea of rural independence[22] even where the returns to labour from urban life were probably greater.

Baker was also concerned about the ultimate security of his large family. He urged his friends and kinsfolk to migrate to Australia on specific grounds. 'The longer the journey the better', he explained:

> All my children can make their own fortune if I should die tommorrow. Mary and Anne have got the refuse of 2 young farmers now, and there is another farmer and his wif who have got a farm of their own and only one daughter, and this daughter and her mother is very struck over our Fred, and all they have got is for their daughter. This is the country, my boys.

Baker offered other implicit comparisons with England which echo through so many other emigrant letters of this period. Thus he reported, 'I have bought a dog for shooting. Tim and me can take our guns and a dog and go out and shoot all we can without licences.' This was a taste of colonial freedom. And Baker was particularly proud to report that he had been asked to supervise other men while his master was absent, that he was placed in a position of authority. Living conditions, of course, loomed large in his account. Baker quoted wages and prices but he mainly conveyed the prevailing plenitude by examples – by the fact that the Bakers now ate fresh meat every day of the week, and by the fact that 'we do not put tea in the pot with a tea spoon but with the hand'. But it would be a mistake to depict Baker simply as a crass materialist, as the emigrant labourer on the make. Much of his letter, like so many others, was devoted to spiritual matters and to his own outdoor preaching in the colony.[23]

'OFFICIAL' DOCUMENTATION

Jacob Baker had arrived in Australia at the high-water mark of its popularity as a migrant destination. Gold had just been discovered and all the colonies were desperate for replenishments of labour. One of the most obvious determinants of the tone and content of migrant letters was, indeed, the time of arrival and its relationship to cycles of economic activity in Australia. Thus letters written in say 1841 and 1856 were almost certain to cast a decidedly gloomy view of Australia simply because the labour market was glutted and immigrants unwanted in the interim.[24] At such times other categories of evidence tend to be more useful, for instance the material generated in the reception facilities for incoming migrants as well as newspaper reports which investigated such problems. Once more the Australian data may be compared with parallel materials from Canada and the United States.

Australian Parliamentary Papers contain substantial though infrequent reports into migration questions, usually timed to deal with the effects of excessive or costly immigration, often into the origins and conditions of the immigrants. More than occasionally they deal with recruiting conditions in Great Britain and the precise circumstances of individual migrants on arrival in Australia. For instance a parliamentary inquiry in Adelaide in 1856 reported on the alleged Excessive Female Immigration in the previous few years. In its deliberations the Inquiry interviewed several dozen young female immigrants, mainly from Ireland of course. They were extraordinarily moving, direct testimonies of the Irish past and the antipodean future from women like Bridget Carroll from County Clare, pathetic survivors of the famine who had buried their parents in common graves in Ireland and witnessed the dispersal of their siblings to England and America.[25] Many of these colonial reports also expose the practical detail of the mechanisms of recruitment in the British Isles.

Within the general category of official materials we should notice the obligatory medical reports which often reveal the physical conditions of the immigrants. They tend to focus upon death and birth rates but these data are now being employed to investigate the international transmission of disease and immunities.[26] From such Australian records, for example, we find evidence of the laxity of smallpox inoculation in the Outer Hebrides in the 1850s and the prevalence of tuberculosis among middle-income British immigrants pathetically seeking a cure in Australia where tuberculosis death rates were actually worse than in Britain.[27] Of the relationship between health and emigration, the most affecting case I know is that of the people of St Kilda who arrived in Melbourne in New Year 1853. The St Kilda community was, of course, the most remote and most perfectly preserved peasant community in the British Isles. A third of them, thirty-six in all, were assisted to Victoria by the Highland and Island Emigration Society. During the voyage half of the contingent died of simple disease, mainly measles and scarlatina, demonstrating their tragic vulnerability to common disease in a manner rather similar to that of the people of Tristan da Cunha a century later.[28] Among much evidence of this type there is also material about the mental condition of the migrants; recent statistical work on shipboard mortality and morbidity had tended to neglect suicide and violence aboard the migrant ships. Mostly the Australian record is very good but some immigrant stories were, in reality, a sequence of hells on earth and water – for instance the people evicted from Harris and Skye who suffered the horrific passage to Adelaide by the *Hercules* in 1855. They arrived in the height of summer and found themselves unwanted in the overstocked colony: it was not surprising that their collective and individual mental states deteriorated in some instances into suicide and insanity.[29]

OTHER EVIDENCE

Finally I want to refer to a number of other categories of Anglo-Australian evidence which also reached into the lowest strata of the migratory population of the British Isles. Colonial migration agents, systematically reporting back to Australia, were needed to undertake direct investigation and evaluation of migrant source districts. They were professionally required to discover and tap the mobility patterns in Britain. In 1859 Francis Dashwood, on behalf of the South Australian government, was under pressure to recruit migrants but to reduce his Irish proportion. In November he travelled to the West Highlands where he was encouraged by a strong disposition to emigrate among the farming people. There was, however, a snag:

> wherever there is the slightest disposition to waver, they are overpersuaded by the landlords and employers of labour. I have also found this interference with emigration not only in Scotland, but in parts of England. The extent to which emigration has been carried on for several years past, has unquestionably very much thinned the ranks of the labouring classes.

Dashwood naturally was much aggravated by the interference of landlords who 'induced' the migrants to alter their intentions 'in exchange for a miserable pittance'. More generally Dashwood, proceeding from Tobermory to Skye and North Uist, repeatedly uttered in antipodean astonishment at conditions observed. From Tobermory he reported:

> when I compare the condition of the lower class of people in this part of Scotland with the same class in Australia, the only wonder to me is that they do not have a ship for themselves and exchange want, poverty and misery for wealth, plenty and comfort, this being literally the difference between the two conditions. They are a hardy industrious set of people, however, but they do not seem to have anything to do, but loiter about with their hands in their pockets.

There was no cynicism in these remarks and Dashwood genuinely believed in the philanthropic character of the work in which he was engaged. He also described in detail objective conditions in the West Highlands, including precise observations about the seasonal and financial factors which affected the success of his recruiting drive.[30] He, like other migration agents, knew the pulse of migration in the different parts of the British Isles.

Equally incisive observations on British conditions were also penned by another neglected group, the returned migrants and the Australian visitor. Here one could cite the example of Captain Charles Bagot, former estate agent in Ennis, County Clare, who established himself as a colonial leader in South Australia in the 1840s. He returned on a visit to Ireland in 1853 and was appalled by the 'fearful scourging' which Ireland had undergone since his departure. His solution, of course, was better leadership and emigration.[31]

This review should mention two other voices of Celtic Australia. Within Australia, migrants, usually *in extremis*, sometimes expressed themselves in petitions to government. There exists, for instance, a document, signed by crosses and translated from the Gaelic, of people from Harris and North Uist pleading for land in 1854, unaware that the entire immigration system was based on Wakefieldian assumptions designed to deny immigrants immediate access to land. A more direct public voice could be heard through newspapers, although there were surprisingly few specifically immigrant papers in colonial Australia. One exotic example, however, was *An Teachdaire Gaidhealach* (the Celtic Messenger), put out by émigré Highlanders in Victoria in 1857. In this, among other things, they resurrected old allegations of 'the tyrrany and oppression of Lords and Factors' back in the Highlands who had evicted 'our once numerous and hospitable inhabitants' from the 'Glens and Straths and converted them into sheep walks and deer forests'. As one correspondent said 'Pharoah is still alive and . . . his heart is as hard as ever'.[32]

In Australia one is most likely to find letters from home addressed to the migrants, sometimes describing conditions in the British Isles with stark immediacy. Some of the Irish survivals trace social and political change. Listen briefly to the voice of Timothy McAuliffe from Westmeath to his son in Port Augusta, South Australia, in January 1884. He reminded his son that he had promised to return to Ireland and that his mother was concerned that the promise be kept. They were emphatic that young Patrick should feel no obligation to send money home. But, in passing, McAuliffe recorded that:

> our agent and landlord come very hard – he has deprived me of my stock for the past four years. He has not left me a four-footed beast. . . . A deal of the people has left their homes and is turned out by the landlord . . . they are doing nothing in Ireland for the past three years but shooting and hanging people but now the landlords are coming to a settlement with the people.[33]

CONCLUSIONS

This guided tour of Australian sources may offer more promise than it can presently deliver. The task of assembling and analysing such material has hardly yet begun. Nevertheless evidence from individual testimonies may take us beyond the necessary but stark statistical series and simple correlations upon which we tend to depend. This is not to undervalue the central and prior importance of a quantitative view of migration. Establishing the basic dimensions and chronology of movement is obviously indispensable. Nevertheless deduction from statistical data is a limited exercise[34] and is best complemented by direct testimony from the migrants themselves, thereby putting flesh and blood about the statistical bones.

From the limited work already executed it is evident that direct testimonies often provide detailed accounts of the paths of mobility both before and after the central act of emigration. Clayton's story – which is probably far more peripatetic than most – shows more than a century of mobility in this family's wanderings and illustrates vividly several of our received hypotheses, from E. G. Ravenstein to Dudley Baines. More particularly, however, it shows how a canny urban proletarian can manipulate the bureaucracy of Australian immigration assistance schemes.

Australian immigration materials relate to virtually every level in British society from pauperism to aristocracy.[35] These testimonies repeatedly look back on the conditions from whence they departed, held up as it were for social investigation. The correspondence between home and Australia, as in the case of the McAuliffes, provides a commentary on rural transformation and its salience for family decision making. The clever taunts of Benjamin Boyce directed at his immobile relatives in Lincolnshire expose the tensions generated in the community by the exercise of adolescent mobility. The anger and stoicism of migrants evicted from the West Highlands is captured in the letters of the exiles from Skye written thirty years after their ejection. Such material, of course, needs to be set beside the sheer 'animal spirits' and carelessness of other accounts, as well as the confusion in the hearts of people swept across the globe by structural changes of which they had virtually no understanding.

The Australian evidence also exposes the methods by which migrants were able to wend their way through the mechanisms which conveyed them over very long distances. Their letters are particularly vivid in demonstrating the extraordinary patience and readiness required of emigrants – the long waiting, then the sudden frantic preparation, the selling of assets, the farewells, the rush to the ports, and then the waiting. In some cases emigration to Australia became an exercise in deception, a deliberate masking of occupation, age, marital status, etc., to meet the passage requirements. In others it involved a hasty marriage, even at the quayside, in order to qualify for assistance.[36] Migrant correspondence itself was the central link in chain migration. The statistics of Australian immigration already demonstrate clearly enough the differential propensity of various groups for this mode of migration, notably among the Irish. But the correspondence between the migrants reveals the mechanism at work in the network of kith and kin.

Migrant behaviour depended on expectations.[37] The central core of migrant psychology was the expectation of accelerated social mobility and its attainment was the *sine qua non* of continuing emigration. Much of the individual testimony is a commentary on this question which necessarily exposed perceptions of class and social relations about which the British migrant was both highly conscious and vocal. The question of social progress in the new environment was the recurrent theme in all plebeian letters from Australia, paralleled by endless concern about comparative living standards between the world lost and the world gained.

In a sense, therefore, migrants to Australia (as to elsewhere) offer an unusual commentary on the transit of British society in the nineteenth century. They and their letters are part of a faint but continuous dialogue between the two societies. For instance we can probably hear more direct working-class perceptions of the living standard in the Industrial Revolution from migrant letters than from any other single source. This sort of material, taken from all the strata of emigrant life, is also critical in the construction of a typology of mobility, that is a classification of social origins and migrant motivations which will eventually illuminate the patterns of selectivity in British mobility. As such a typology emerges it is likely to mirror the economic and psychological landscapes from whence the migrants departed. I am thinking, for instance, of such clear categories as the migratory tenant farmers of southern England in the 1830s, the economic refugees of Harris and St Kilda in the 1850s, the footloose young urbanites of Manchester, the extruded petty landlord class, doctors in the grip of an agrarian myth, and so on.[38]

It is hardly necessary to stress that the sound of the voices of the lowest strata of British society is a relatively rare thing. The fact that migrant letters derive from the less literate parts of the social structure suggests that this Australian material may be productively set beside the internal British data employed so effectively by John Burnett and David Vincent.[39] The fact that that evidence is direct, immediate and current renders it more interesting than retrospective accounts on which we tend to depend.

Most of all there is the question of individual and collective agency amid the great floods of Anglo-Celtic humanity across the globe. If we are to allow that most migrants were not merely flotsam and jetsam, not merely the hapless products of biological or economic forces; if we are to allow that they acted as rational creatures, that they possessed some measure of volition – then we should also listen to their voices, let them speak for themselves in their accounts of their origins and their reasons for emigation. The migrant voice should be given a hearing at both the British and the Australian ends of this, the greatest of all the migratory movements of the nineteenth century.

POSTSCRIPT

In a recent tutorial in Adelaide we were talking about the reliability of emigrant letters in the nineteenth century. We referred to Patrick O'Farrell's opinion that they were especially reliable when written back to places whence many people had migrated to the same place, like from County Clare to South Australia. After a while one of the students in the group objected to this assumption. She was a migrant herself, from Lebanon, and after about ten years, had recently paid a visit to her homeland to see her relatives, including her aunt. During this visit she had talked with her aunt especially about her friends, who had also migrated to Adelaide. The neighbour proudly pulled out a photograph sent by her own son in Adelaide. He was standing in front of a large building which he described as 'my shop'. There was no shadow of a joke about this, but the shop in question was a multi-million dollar emporium, Adelaide's equivalent of Harrods. My student, of course, claimed that this was a typical emigrant deception, to gladden the hearts of the old folks back home, and one which she made no effort to disperse.

Quite rightly the story cast proper doubt over this whole category of evidence. It also serves as a salutary warning over the content of this chapter!

NOTES

1 On nineteenth-century Australian immigration see Geoffrey Sherington, *Australia's Immigrants*, Sydney, 1980; R. D. Madgwick, *Immigration into Eastern Australia 1788–1851*, London, 1937; James Jupp (ed.), *The Australian People*, Sydney, 1988, which contains an extensive bibliography.

2 I am omitting the great number of shipboard journals kept by many British migrants to Australia. Sometimes they are revealing about the categories of migrant and inter-communal relations aboard ship, but generally they are a disappointing source. See, however, Don Charlewood, *The Long Farewell*, Melbourne, 1981.

3 Charlotte Erickson, *Invisible Immigrants: The Adaptation of English and Scottish Immigrants in Nineteenth-Century America*, London, 1972, Introduction, pp. 6–7.

4 Patrick O'Farrell, *Letters from Irish Australia, 1825–1929*, Sydney, 1984, p. 5.

5 Erickson, (op. cit., p. 20) seems to say that for all the rural labourers who emigrated to the United States in the nineteenth century – a vast category, as she emphasizes – only eight manuscripts can be traced. South Australia alone, with its minuscule population in comparison, can provide more than this.

6 Fifty years ago R. B. Madgwick believed that the migrants assisted to Australia were generally 'lacking in initiative and independence of mind, and inferior to those who emigrated to the United States and Canada'. This raw statement about the 'quality' of the immigrants has never been tested. See R. J. Shultz, review article, *Historical Studies*, April 1970, vol. 14, pp. 273–82.

7 See for instance the remarks of Peter Burroughs, *Britain and Australia 1831–1855*, Oxford, 1967, p. v.

8 Stephen Nicholas and Peter R. Shergold, 'Internal migration in England, 1817–1839', *Journal of Historical Geography*, 13, 1987; 'Inter-county labour mobility during the Industrial Revolution', *Oxford Economic Papers*, December 1987. Further research is published in Stephen Nicholas (ed.), *Convict Workers*, Melbourne, 1988.

9 K. D. M. Snell, *Annals of the Labouring Poor*, Cambridge, 1985, pp. 9–14. Snell uses published letters which, as a category of evidence, sometimes

arouses scepticism; see Erickson, op. cit., Introduction, and p. 484, footnote 11, p. 487, footnote 22.

10 David Fitzpatrick, 'Irish emigration in the later nineteenth century', *Irish Historical Studies*, vol. 22, no. 86, September 1980.

11 O'Farrell, op. cit., p. 6. O'Farrell has used his series of immigrant letters to construct an extraordinarily doleful picture of Irish settlement in Australia, a vision of inconsolable anguish and exile: '. . . they brought their kinship mentality to Australia, where it gradually fell apart, declining into a residual social atomism, marked by separation, isolation, loneliness and eventual alienation of society's individual parts.'

12 It is becoming clear that the best current migration research is of this sort, e.g. Jan Gjerde, *From Peasants to Farmers: The Migration from Balestrand, Norway, to the Upper Middle West*, Cambridge, 1985; Bruce S. Elliott, *Irish Migrants in the Canadas*, Kingston, 1988. An Australian variant is found in the most interesting work of S. Colin Holt, 'Family, kinship, community and friendship ties in assisted emigration from Cambridgeshire to Port Phillip District and Victoria, 1840–67', unpublished M. A. thesis, La Trobe University, 1987.

13 Erickson's anthology comprises collections of letters; much of the Australian material is in the form of isolated, random survivals of single letters.

14 Emigrant letters may, of course, contain a built-in bias. Patrick O'Farrell suggests that there is a tendency towards failure and that some migrants 'wanted to report success – which, if it ever came, might be in ten, twenty years'. O'Farrell, op. cit. p. 4. By contrast, W. A. Armstrong suggests that surviving sources 'may be suspected of having a Smilesian bias towards the successful', Alan Armstrong, review of R. Arnold's *Farthest Promised Land* in *Agricultural History Review*, vol. 32, 1984, pp. 106–7. The Australian sources appear to be unusually rich in working-class testimonies of the semi-literate, healthy, subsidized migrants. There are, of course, no records directly from the illiterate, none from paupers or dying migrants. Such difficulties may best be solved by longitudinal studies of groups of migrants and their documentation.

15 This section is derived from Eric Richards, 'A voice from below: Benjamin Boyce in South Australia 1839–1846', *Labour History*, no. 27, 1974.

16 Quoted in Eric Richards, 'Immigrant lives', in Eric Richards (ed.), *The Flinders History of South Australia. Social History*, Adelaide, 1986, pp. 145–8.

17 Quoted in Eric Richards, 'Australia and the Scottish diaspora' in John Hardy (ed.), *Stories of Australian Migration*, Sydney, 1988, p. 47.

18 Quoted in Richards, 'Immigrant lives', op. cit., p. 149.

19 MLSA D6424 (L) Reminiscences of William Clayton 1833–1933.

20 O'Farrell, op. cit., p. 8.

21 Charles Dickens used migrant letters in *Household Words* partly to depict Australia as an idealized Utopia which could solve all social problems. Samuel Sidney established the *Emigrant's Penny Magazine* as a counterpoise to the alleged monopoly of information exerted by colonial emigration agents and shipping interests. See Samuel Sidney, *The Three Colonies of Australia*, London, 1852, p. iii.

22 Cf. Snell, op. cit.

23 This section is based on Baker's letter published in the *Scotsman*, 15 September 1852, and Mark Baker, 'A migration of Wiltshire agricultural labourers to Australia in 1851', *Journal of the South Australian Historical Society*, vol. 14, 1986.

24 Published migrant letters tend to coincide with up-turns in the labour market which, of course, suggests an inherent bias.

25 South Australian Parliamentary Papers: *Reports of the Select Committee of the Legislative Council of South Australia into the Excessive Female Immigration*, Adelaide, 1856.

26 Ralph Shlomowitz and John Macdonald of Flinders University are studying mortality rates on immigrant voyages to Australia.

27 See, for instance, Robin Haines, 'Therapeutic emigration: Australia, the last resort', unpublished B.A. Honours thesis. Flinders University, 1987.

28 See, for instance, Ann Maclean Holahan, 'St Kilda: emigrants and disease', *Scottish Medical Journal*, vol. 31, 1986.

29 See Eric Richards, 'The Highland Scots of South Australia in the 1850s', *Journal of the Historical Society of South Australia*, vol. 4, 1978.

30 Public Record Office of South Australia, GRG 35/1 Crown Lands and Immigration Office, Inward Correspondence, *Dashwood to William Milne,* October 1859; *Dashwood to Wildman*, 15 July 1860; *Dashwood Papers*, PRO No. 721 *Dashwood to Davies*, 6 July 1860.

31 He observed: 'The natural resources of Ireland, by which an enterprising, industrious people might raise themselves and their country to an exalted position among the States of Europe, are in a large measure neglected. After years of residence among the active, intelligent and go-ahead occupiers of Australia, I have been much struck by the listless want of energy evidenced by the people of Ireland. The very poor houses contain a sufficient number of young females, full of intelligence and eager for employment, to supply labour for numberless manufactories if there was spirit among the people to start them with the incalculable waterpower to be seen wasted and neglected in every direction.' *A Holograph Memoir of Capt. Charles Bagot of the 87th Regiment*, Adelaide, 1942.

32 See Eric Richards, 'Highland Scots', op. cit.; *An Teachdaire Gaidhealach*, 1 August 1857.

33 Timothy McAuliffe to Patrick McAuliffe, 25 January 1884, belonging to Ms Pat Tedmanson of Adelaide, to whom my thanks are due.

34 There is a continuing tension between the famous injunction of Frank Thistlethwaite, that we study villagers and small groups rather than nationalities, and our reliance on quantitative data. In the British case we have the greatest difficulty reaching even to the county level let alone the parish, village or family. Thistlethwaite also, of course, insisted that migration be seen as a continuous process from origins to ultimate destination. See Frank Thistlethwaite, 'Migration from Europe overseas in the nineteenth and twentieth centuries', *Comité International des Sciences Historique*, XI Congress, Report V, 1974, pp. 32–61.

35 The differential consequences of migration on the various strata has been the subject of interesting hypothesizing. For example, referring to his collection of Irish letters, Patrick O'Farrell, op. cit. p. 7, remarks 'The experience of the middling migrant confirmed what they constantly contended: that Australia was a paradise for a capitalist and the working

man, and hell for anyone in between'.

36 See, for instance, Eric Richards, 'Problems on the Cromartie Estate', *Scottish Historical Review*, vol. 41, (1973), p. 154, footnote 3.

37 Often, of course, emigration was expected to be a temporary exile, perhaps as a means of repairing a decaying social status back at home. Listen to Mrs Rosina Ferguson, originally of Roxburgh, who had originally emigrated in 1836 to South Australia but who was still there in 1852. She wrote to her mother to wish her a happy New Year: 'This is the fifteenth since we parted. Many, many a change has taken place since then. At that time we did not expect to have been here till now, but it seems we must stay a little longer.' In fact she stayed on and died in South Australia in 1893 aged 81. William and Rosina Ferguson, pamphlet, Mortlock Library of South Australia; 1384/14.

38 Nominal records may be the only effective means by which to tackle the problem of accounting the unknown element of unassisted (i.e. private) migration to Australia.

39 I am thinking of David Vincent, *Bread, Knowledge and Freedom*, London, 1981, and John Burnett, *Useful Toil*, London, 1974 and *Destiny Obscure*, London, 1982. Many of the Australian testimonies echo to the sound of their British counterparts.

3 From Irish countryside to American city

The settlement and mobility of Ulster migrants in Philadelphia

Deirdre M. Mageean

INTRODUCTION

In the 1980s there was increasing recognition of the distinct regional differences in experience and in the different form and structure of Irish emigration over time. One of the problems with the regional study of Irish emigration has been finding sources which both contained data on the level of the individual and provided a run of information which allowed changes over time to be charted. Hence it has proved difficult to examine the process of emigration. Of course, this problem is not confined to Irish emigrants. The freedom of movement enjoyed by all emigrants from the British Isles and the consequent lack of information at a nominal level has meant that, special colonization schemes aside, it has been generally impossible to trace emigrants from their area and culture of origin to that of destination. This chapter reports on the results obtained from a unique set of sources which not only reveals information on migration from one area of Ireland – the north west of Ulster – but which, when linked to American shipping manifests and census data for the city of Philadelphia, traces the movement of people from their homes in the Ulster countryside to urban life in one of America's most thriving industrial cities.

The main sources used in the research are the shipping registers for the years 1847 to 1867 of a shipping firm which operated sailings from the port of Londonderry in the north west of Ireland.[1] The hinterland of this important emigrant port was the counties of Derry, Donegal and Tyrone along with adjacent areas of Antrim and Fermanagh. This hinterland was already well established in the eighteenth century for emigration from north west Ireland was not purely a 'famine phenomenon'. In common with the rest of Ulster the area experienced considerable movement of population overseas during the eighteenth

DOI: 10.4324/9781003172918-4

and early nineteenth centuries and over these years a tradition of emigration grew. Much of the early emigration from the area resulted from fears of religious persecution and in the late seventeenth and early eighteenth centuries many Presbyterian ministers from the Laggan area[2] led their congregations to settlements in New England. Although by the time large-scale emigration from Ulster began most of the measures against Protestant dissenters had been relaxed, this early movement of dissenters had engendered an emigration mentality in the region. The main causes of emigration in the latter half of the eighteenth century were economic – the burden of ever-increasing rents and tithes, short leases and insecurity of tenure, and periodic crop failures. The combination of such economic forces and a migration tradition fuelled emigration throughout the eighteenth century and into the nineteenth.

The regional economy played a role not only in creating local conditions conducive to this emigration but also in determining the destinations involved. Linen cloth had been produced for home consumption in Ulster from earliest times. Flax was grown in parts of the province to produce yarn and considerable quantities were exported throughout the eighteenth century. Flax could be grown remuneratively on the small farms predominant in the north west and as a cash crop it yielded a larger return from the land than any other. Farming–weaving households proliferated, sub-division of land increased and population grew. In the eighteenth century the growth in the linen industry resulted in rises in land prices and rents and competition for land increased. Gambling on linen profits to offset rising rents merely added the caprice of trade to the uncertainty of nature. As a result emigration rose and fell as the fortunes of the linen trade fluctuated. High prices of land intensified the emigration of unemployed linen workers but it often took the combination of linen and farming losses to cause emigration among the farming classes.[3] The subsequent decline in the linen industry, growing pressure of population on resources and a lack of urban and industrial centres to absorb the growing numbers of population and unemployed prompted further emigration to North America in the first half of the nineteenth century. Dissatisfaction and distress were fuelled by the information which flowed back from the United States.

Philadelphia featured prominently as a destination for eighteenth- and nineteenth-century Irish emigrants, particularly those departing from Ulster. Links between Ulster and Philadelphia go back to the early eighteenth century.[4] A combination of hostility in New England and the economic opportunities and religious freedom offered in

Pennsylvania diverted almost all Scottish–Irish emigration to that state from about 1725. The passenger trade between the Irish port of Derry and the port of Philadelphia grew out of commercial links. Flax seed from America was imported for the linen trade and, in the early spring, flax seed fleets from Philadelphia and New York arrived in the northern Irish ports. Rather than turn away empty, the ships took on passengers for America, a pattern which continued into the early nineteenth century. Philadelphia was the destination for 78 per cent of Derry ships sailing between 1750 and 1775[5] and its particularly strong connection with the port of Derry was to continue well into the nineteenth century, establishing a beaten path for successive generations of emigrants.

SOURCES

For the years 1800–20 United States shipping manifest records for ships from Ireland which sailed to Philadelphia show that 45 out of 137 ships came from Derry, making it the most frequent port of origin.[6] Most of the ships were American cargo vessels whose masters had advertised for passengers in the local newspaper, the *Londonderry Journal.* Information on sailings was also disseminated through agents in the small towns and villages of the north west. These agents were generally shopkeepers and publicans and they displayed posters advertising the sailings on their premises.[7]

The shipping registers used in the present study are of more than local significance for Irish emigration study. Derry was an important emigration port throughout the eighteenth century and into the first half of the nineteenth century. Local shipping firms controlled a significant amount of the emigrant trade. One of the two major firms operating in the nineteenth century was J & J Cooke, a firm which had been in the passenger trade since the end of the Napoleonic wars in 1815. The ship registers of J & J Cooke contain information on approximately 21,800 passengers who left the port of Derry for various destinations in the United States and Canada during the years 1847–67.[8] Thus they cover the immediate Famine period, the post-Famine exodus, and the smaller, steadier stream of the 1860s. The Cooke registers give the name of the vessel, its date of departure and port of destination and the name, age, residence, and (occasionally) occupation of each passenger. The registers also record the cost of the passage, when it was booked, and how the passage money was paid – pre-paid by agents in America, paid by the workhouse or by an estate owner, or paid by the individual himself (usually in instalments to local agents of the firm). From this information quite a detailed picture of the emigrants and their origins can be obtained.

Of the 21,844 passengers recorded in the Cooke registers, 8,624 sailed to Philadelphia. For 38 of the 48 ships listed in the registers as sailing to Philadelphia the US manifests were successfully located and the two sets of information linked by passenger name. This nominal record linkage allowed for comparison and cross-checking of the data and the combined information was entered into a large database.[9] The large body of quantitative data thus constructed made it possible to carry out detailed analysis of the migrant body and to examine the processes of emigration from the north west of Ireland to Philadelphia.

One of the strengths of the registers is the level of information on the areas of origin of the emigrants. In most cases addresses are available at the level of the townland, thus permitting analysis of the regional origins of the emigrants and changes in that distribution over time. Throughout the twenty years Donegal, Tyrone and Derry, in that order, were the largest contributors of emigrants. There were considerable spatial and temporal variations in the volume of emigration between baronies[10] and the origins of the migrants from within the north west varied markedly over time. Nevertheless the heaviest emigration came consistently not from the poor, congested areas of Donegal and parts of Tyrone, but from the fertile farming areas, the northern parishes of Tyrone and parts of Inishowen peninsula (Figures 3.1 and 3.2). Even in the immediate Famine period, when we might expect ecological forces to be at their strongest, not only did simple population pressure not provide an explanation but the pattern was actually the reverse of that which might be expected.[11] This is not to suggest that those who were emigrating were necessarily affluent but that they at least had access to sufficient capital to finance their passage. In contrast those in the poorest, over-populated areas were caught in a poverty trap.[12] It is likely too that the presence of a strong emigration tradition increased the likelihood of emigration from these more fertile areas. Only in the later years when fares became cheaper and the idea of emigration more diffused do we see a spread of emigration into the more remote, poorer baronies.

Cost was always a crucial factor in determining who could travel and when. As noted earlier the cost of emigration was simply too great for some. Landlord-assisted migration and assisted pauper migration from the workhouses were common, especially during the Famine years. However, assisted migration from the north west was almost exclusively directed to Canada. Important though landlord and

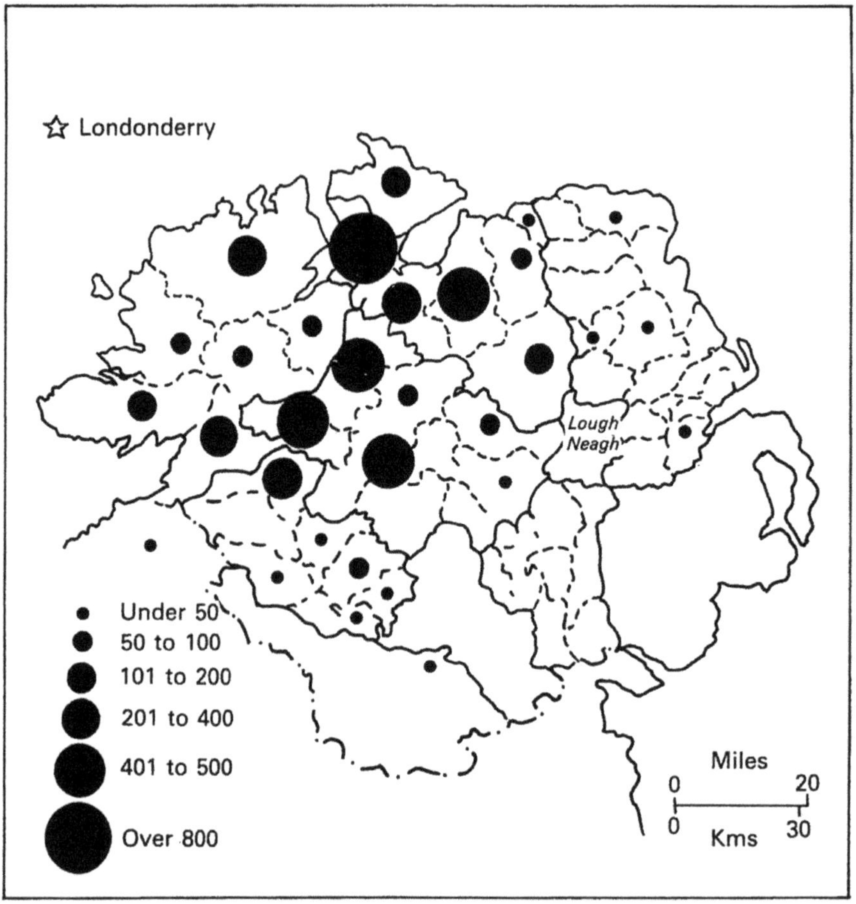

Figure 3.1 The origins of emigrants leaving Derry, 1847–51
Source: Cooke Registers, 1847–51

workhouse assistance was in providing emigration passages, assistance from those who had emigrated earlier was even more significant. Shipping firms relied considerably on passenger bookings made by Irish people who wished to bring out their friends and relatives. The importance of pre-paid bookings in Irish emigration had always been considerable and the practice was most prevalent in Ulster, particularly in Derry where it had the longest history and was most deeply rooted. During the years 1847–67 Cooke had two agents in Philadelphia.[13] These agents handled the Philadelphia bookings and passages booked through them are indicated on the registers. Their activities are reflected in the high proportion of pre-paid fares, a proportion which increased in the post-Famine years. This increase is not surprising under the cumulative impact of increasing numbers of

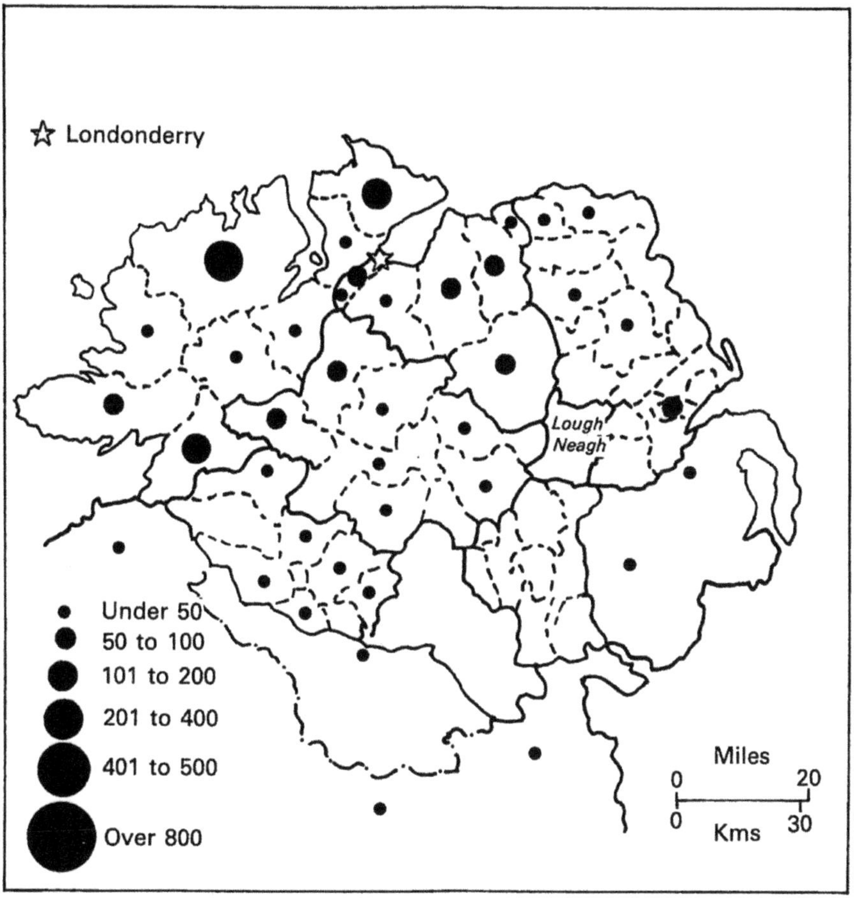

Figure 3.2 The origins of emigrants leaving Derry, 1857–61
Source: Cooke Registers, 1857–61

migrants arriving to settle in the United States and in turn sending for more migrants. This would be particularly true in the city of Philadelphia which had a large Irish population and which offered good opportunities for housing and employment.

Both the high percentage of pre-paid tickets emanating from Philadelphia and the long tradition of emigration from the north west region to that city suggested that there might be a considerable 'pool' of Cooke migrants in the city. Under normal circumstances the chances of locating these migrants would be all but impossible. The sheer size of the city's population and the mobility of a nineteenth-century population alone make such a task extremely difficult even when specific areas of settlement within the city are known. For the city of Philadelphia, however, the ethnicity files from the Philadelphia

Social History Project (hereafter referred to as PSHP) made the task of linkage considerably easier.[14]

From the outset it was obvious that the chances of successfully locating or identifying with certainty those passengers who travelled as unaccompanied individuals were extremely poor. Several factors accounted for this. First, the fact that there was information on only one individual who was not linked to other relatives made positive identification almost impossible. The John Doherty who sailed from Derry to Philadelphia in 1847 could be one of twelve John Dohertys located in the 1850 census or not present at all. Age was an uncertain link and even if information on the occupation of the passenger at the time of sailing was available this was likely to have changed in the city. The physical mobility of young men was extremely high at this time and many quickly moved out of the city after arrival in search of employment. Demographic tables for the city at this time show a drastic underrepresentation of young men in the Irish migrant population.[15] Single females were equally problematic and their situation was exacerbated by the fact that they were very unlikely to be listed in the head of household files. Many of these young women 'disappeared' into other households as domestic servants or might be found in boarding houses. Therefore I decided to try and locate only those who travelled in family groups. Of the 8,624 passengers recorded on the Cooke registers as sailing from Derry to Philadelphia, 1,229 sailed in nuclear family groups.[16] As such they constitute a sample of the total number of Cooke passengers sailing during the twenty years covered by the registers. From this sample 555 individuals were positively located. Living with them were a further 166 relatives. In addition to obtaining census information on those identified it was possible to plot the location of the families within the city using the grid system of the PSHP.[17]

RESULTS

Over the course of the nineteenth century the profile of emigrants from north west Ireland was changing. In the first half of the century it was dominated by young, single males. During the years 1803–6 the sex ratio of those sailing from Derry to the United States was 198 males per 100 females. By 1830–1 the ratio had fallen to 145 males per 100 females. Children constituted a small percentage of both populations and most emigrants were between the years of 16 and 30.[18] One of the dramatic changes which occurred in the composition of the migrant body as a result of the Famine was the shift to family migration. To a

Table 3.1 Cooke migrants travelling to Philadelphia

Year	No. of passengers	No. of passengers travelling in families	% of passengers travelling in families
1847–51	3727	713	19.1
1852–56	2943	277	9.4
1857–61	1299	129	9.9
1862–67	655	110	16.8

Source: Cooke Registers 1847–67

great extent this reflects the strong forces impelling emigration. The high percentage of families during the Famine years (19.1 per cent), is typical of mass migration consequent upon disaster. In the subsequent years the number of emigrants travelling in family groups never again reached the Famine figures but instead steadily declined (see Table 3.1). After the immediate Famine exodus, there was no longer a dominance of men emigrating. The proportion of women rose steadily and in the 1850s they were the dominant sex. The one constant factor throughout the twenty years is the concentration of young people.

After the immediate Famine period the number of Cooke passengers travelling to Philadelphia steadily declined, most dramatically in the late 1850s. This was a period of general business and trade recession which influenced the number of voyages made. More important, however, was the increasing competition from shipping lines outside Derry. In the local newspapers there were daily advertisements by Liverpool clippers to Australia, some of which even offered free passages to selected emigrants. At the same time Glasgow and Liverpool clippers to Canada increasingly sought passengers in Derry. The fares on steamships were considerably more expensive than those on the Cooke ships but the shorter passage and generally more comfortable conditions was a sufficient attraction to many.[19] It is probable that the cheaper passage by sail may have affected the nature of the migrant body, attracting those of lower socio-economic status compared to those travelling by steam.

Over the course of the twenty years that the Cooke passengers recorded here were coming to Philadelphia the city was growing and changing. The economic and physical changes which occurred over these years affected the physical and social mobility which they experienced as well as determining the strategies which they could adopt in their new world.

The years 1830–60 were years of rapid growth for Philadelphia, both economically and physically, when it changed from being a booming town to a thriving industrial metropolis. The pace of urbanization and industrialization were rapid. In 1830 the old municipality and adjacent boroughs contained 161,410 inhabitants. In 1860 the consolidated city was 565,529 inhabitants strong.[20] Philadelphia was second only to New York in terms of its social and economic diversity and was unique among American cities in terms of its geographical spread.[21] Most notable was its social and economic heterogeneity. Most areas were a mixture of occupations, classes, homes, immigrants and native Americans, although by 1860 one could see the beginnings of social and economic concentrations. The net effect of this diversity was that migrants arriving in the city encountered a much broader range of social and economic opportunities than those in other cities of the time.

The physical pattern of development and the nature of housing in the city further influenced the environment which met immigrants. Philadelphia had been planned on a strict grid system and as the population grew the grids were subdivided.[22] Rapid growth spurred on construction of new homes at a furious pace. According to Warner such construction for ordinary citizens followed a very simple set of alternatives.

> . . . shacks, shanties and back-alley two room houses for the poor; three room row houses or three rooms in multiple family row houses for the skilled working man and six to eight room row houses and flats for middle class managers, prosperous shopkeepers, professionals and downtown businessmen.[23]

The social geography of the city of Philadelphia into which the Cooke migrants arrived was a peculiar one. There were no segregated slums or tenements. Instead, there was an unusual mix of new housing often occupied by low-income families. This mix was to affect the pattern of settlement of the Cooke migrants in the city. Of those who left Derry and travelled in family groups during the years 1847–9, 212 persons were located in the 1850 census. Living with them were 50 other kin, including children born in the years between their arrival and the date of the census, making a total of 262 persons in 43 households (see Table 3.2 for figures and those for subsequent censuses). Slightly over half these families lived in houses by themselves. The remainder lived in houses with other Irish families and individuals or, in the case of one remarkably large family, were spread over two houses. There was

Table 3.2 Cooke migrants located in Philadelphia

Located in census	No. of migrants	No. of co-resident kin	Average household size
1850	212	50	6.1
1860	250	79	5.3
1870	93	37	6.2

Source: Cooke Registers; 1850, 1860 and 1870 Censuses, City of Philadelphia

no clear relationship between the level of skill of the head of household and whether the house was shared, the exception being those who were in the retail trade. Only the households of grocers, liquor dealers and milk dealers show the presence of servants.

Using the PSHP grid reference each household was plotted for the three census periods used. The patterns of settlement of those living within the city's boundaries thus revealed is shown in Figures 3.3, 3.4, 3.5.[24]

The Cooke migrants who arrived in Philadelphia in the late 1840s were part of the Famine Irish – the largest wave of emigrants ever to arrive in the city. As such, they formed part of an influx which strained the resources of the city. However, even in this period, when the Irish were flooding into the city, they did not concentrate into any one area. Rather than being concentrated into ghettos the Cooke migrants, like Philadelphia's Irish population in general, were dispersed throughout the city and lived in a variety of social and economic contexts. They did, however, settle in what were predominantly Irish neighbourhoods – Kensington in the north east of the city, Spring Garden to the west, Moyamensing and Southwark to the south and a few in the city centre (Figure 3.6).

By 1860 Philadelphia's population was 30 per cent foreign born and included 44,000 immigrants from Ireland. Of the sixty-two households located in the 1860 census most were within Irish neighbourhoods, but were more scattered throughout the city and now included the area of Port Richmond and a few who settled across the Schukyll river in West Philadelphia. The most interesting feature of the 1860 settlement pattern is that it shows the later migrants to be settling on the outskirts of those grid units occupied in 1850. Overall the settlement pattern of the Cooke migrants in 1860 correlates closely with the distribution of the general Irish population throughout the city's wards. In contrast the settlement of those located in the 1870 census shows a contraction to a few areas, namely Port Richmond in the north east, a few in

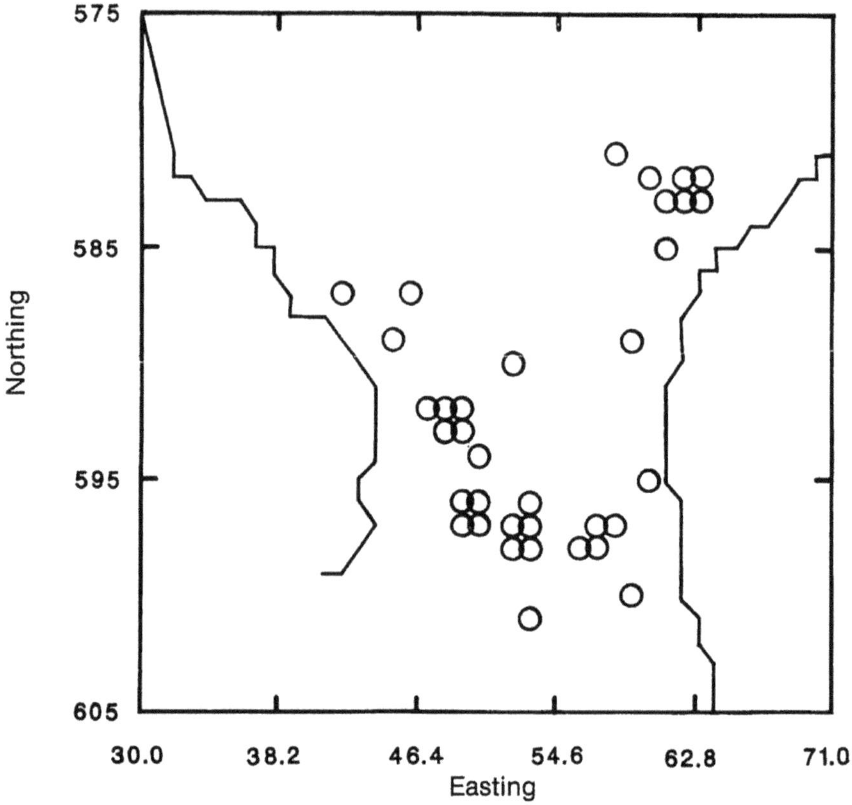

Figure 3.3 Residential location of Cooke migrant households in Philadelphia, 1850
Source: Cooke Registers and Censuses of Philadelphia

Kensington and the rest to the south of the city in Moyamensing and Southwark.

The socio-economic and occupational profiles of these Irish neighbourhoods varied greatly. Each area displayed a distinctive economic profile and, apart from the city centre, was dominated by one or two industries. In 1850 the Irish neighbourhoods ranged from Kensington, an older area many of whose residents were immigrants who arrived in the 1830s from Ulster in the wake of the collapse of the domestic linen industry and where three-quarters of the adult Irish male immigrants were employed in skilled trades or white-collar positions, to Port Richmond, where four-fifths worked in unskilled jobs, mainly labourers on the Reading Railroad wharfs. The Southwark and the Southwark docks areas displayed quite a diverse local economy. Some Irish worked on the docks but others occupied higher status jobs. According to Light:

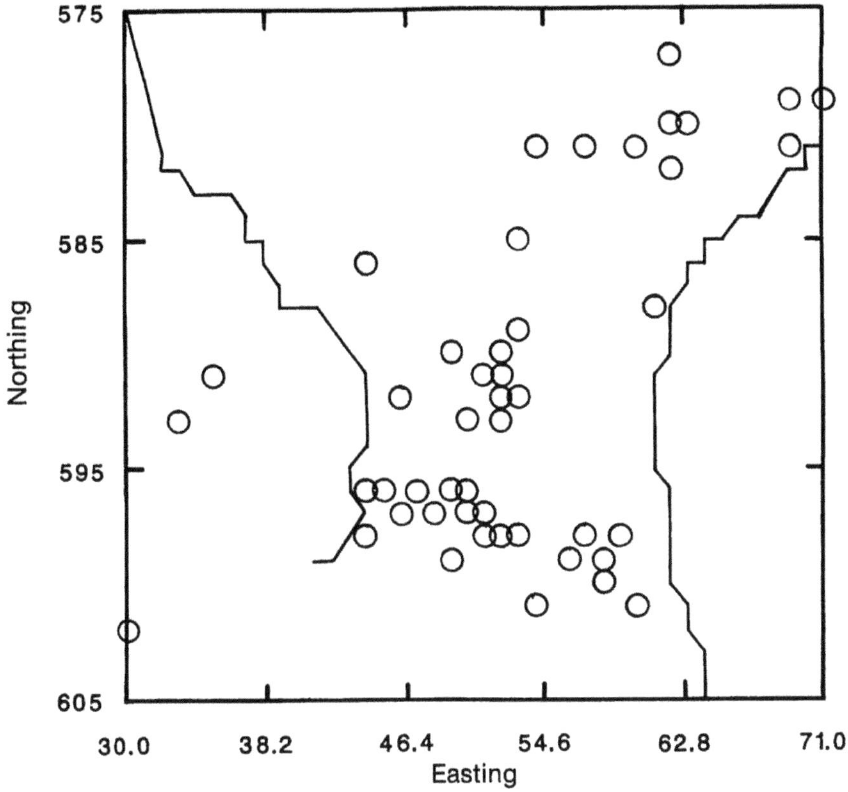

Figure 3.4 Residential location of Cooke migrant households in Philadelphia, 1860
Source: Cooke Registers and Censuses of Philadelphia

> A significant number of Irish in both of these areas were involved in general commerce and in the case of Southwark, this foreshadowed the emergence of a sizeable Irish middle class.[25]

In 1860 Philadelphia was still an agglomeration of old trades – labourers, clerks, carpenters, tailors, weavers, shoemakers, grocers, liquor dealers, butchers, tobacco dealers, cordwainers, blacksmiths and cabinet makers.[26] The occupations of the migrants largely reflected the occupational structure of the city at large. Of the heads of households for whom occupation was recorded, 54.7 per cent were unskilled, 38.5 per cent skilled and 6.8 per cent in retail employment. The majority of the unskilled were common labourers, with the rest of this category composed of porters, drivers, carters and draymen. Among the skilled the most significant occupation, representing one-third of this category, was weaver. Most weavers lived in Kensington,

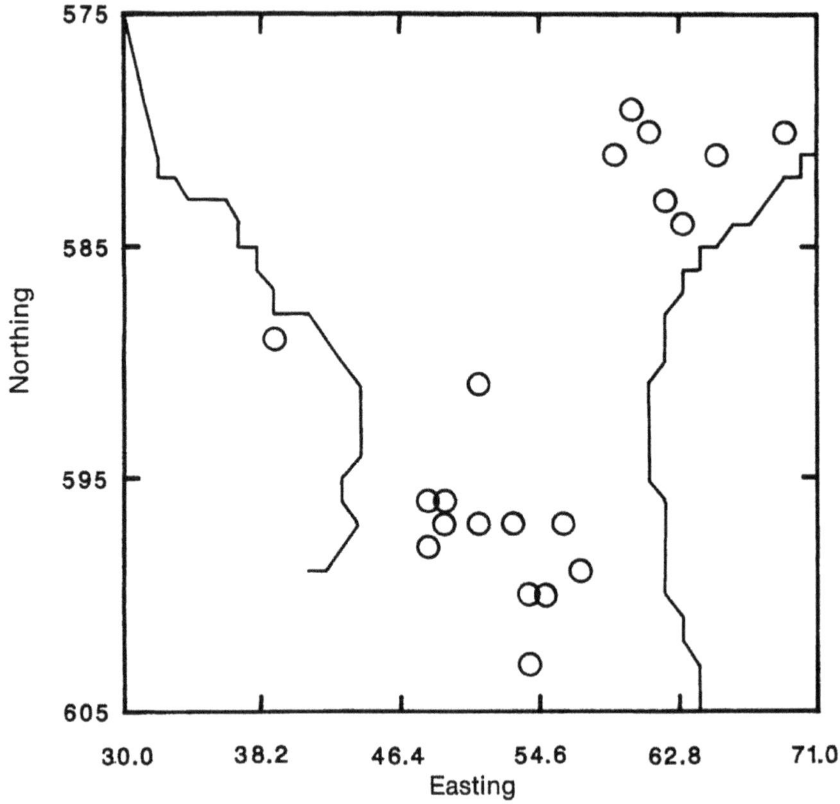

Figure 3.5 Residential location of Cooke migrant households in Philadelphia, 1870
Source: Cooke Registers and Censuses of Philadelphia

the weaving district of the city, with the remainder in the south west of the city where there was a small but significant textile manufacturing trade. Because of the paucity of information on occupations in the Cooke registers it is impossible to compare the occupations of the migrants before and after their settlement in Philadelphia. However, given the history of the domestic linen industry in the north west of Ireland, it is very likely that many of these migrants would have had weaving or spinning skills. What is of importance here is that these skills of cloth production were among the few transportable skills which migrants from this region of Ireland could have employed in an industrial urban setting in the New World.

The nature of the textile industry in Philadelphia greatly facilitated this situation. Philadelphia's textile manufacturers specialized in smaller-scale, handloom production. The city was the greatest seat of hand weaving in the country. Much of this production was 'domestic'

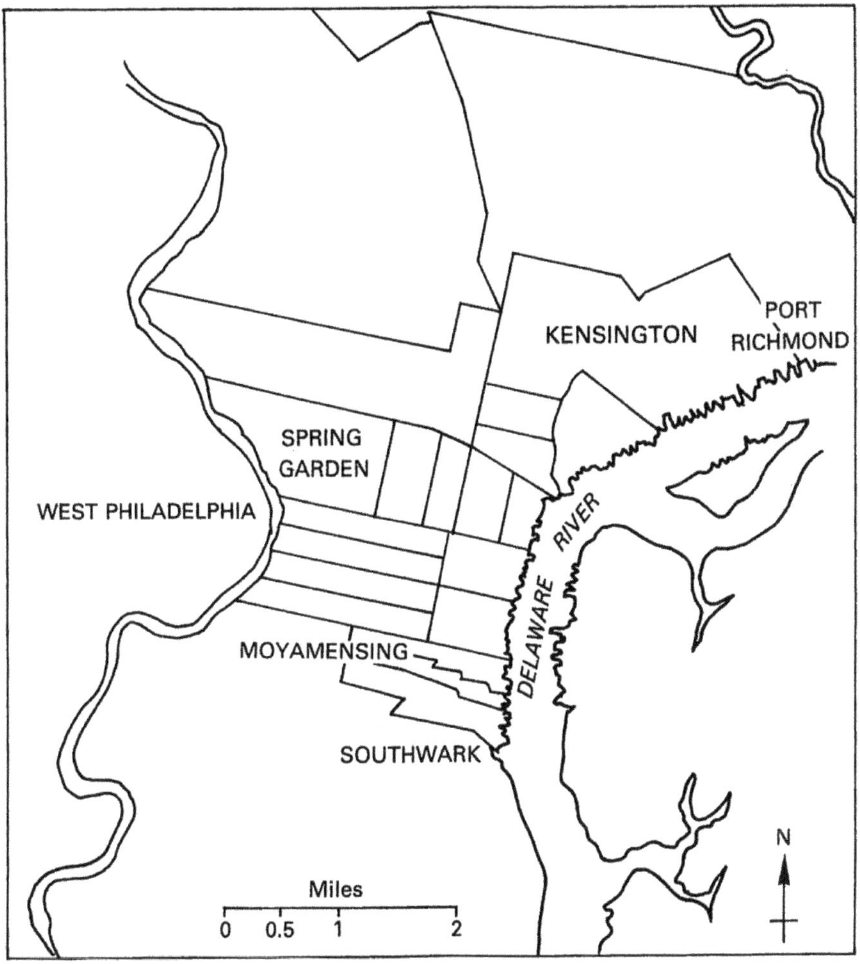

Figure 3.6 Philadelphia in the mid-nineteenth century
Source: Based on S. B. Warner 1968

based – effectively a 'putting-out' system to small, home-based workshops.[27] Significantly, over half the weavers from the Cooke sample shared their houses with other families or individuals engaged in weaving. Typical of such arrangements was William Chambers who lived in Kensington with his wife and six children, having arrived in Philadelphia in 1852. The 1860 census shows none of the children working but the house is shared with six male weavers and one female, all from Ireland and all single and in their fifties. Chambers' house, which he owned, was effectively a small workshop – a situation which was not uncommon at the time. Indeed, many trades such as shoemaker and tailor were carried out in small shops based in the home. William Chambers' workshop was quite successful, for he is

Table 3.3 Number of migrants with recorded wealth (Philadelphia 1850–70)

Value	Real estate	Personal
Above $5,000	2	1
$1,500–5,000	4	1
$501–1,500	4	3
$1–500	2	25

Source: 1850, 1860 and 1870 Censuses, City of Philadelphia

recorded as having $2,000 in real estate and personal estate of $500. However, the pay and position of hand weavers was beginning to decline as competition from factories grew. For the time being at least these migrants from Ulster found themselves working in what was almost an urban replica of the domestic industry at home.

From 1860 onwards the census spasmodically lists the amount of personal and real estate. Table 3.3 shows the level of wealth for those heads of household for whom the information was recorded. The only group which displayed any significant level of wealth were those engaged in the retail sector. Skilled craftsmen are recorded with small amounts of personal income, around $200–400, but the two occupations which are associated with some means are grocer and liquor dealer. Clearly the most profitable line of business for an Irish immigrant was that of liquor dealer. John Lavens who arrived from Derry in 1861 and who was recorded on the Cooke register as a farmer was worth $20,000 in real estate and $15,000 in personal estate in 1870. His wife Eliza was worth another $1,000 in personal estate. Alexander Young, who sailed with his parents in 1852, is recorded as a distiller in 1860. By 1880 he owned a liquor store and other property amounting to $500,000.

For the unskilled workers and those with few financial means the pooling of families' resources was important. Children were an important economic resource. Amongst the Cooke migrants, as among the larger Irish population in the city, there was a large percentage of older children at home, many in their twenties. Among the migrants located in the 1860 and 1870 censuses one-third of the households contained one or more children over the age of 20. In addition to these households there were a few cases of what appeared to be siblings, ranging in age from late 'teens to early thirties, living together without the presence of parents or an older generation. In some cases these families with older children were composed of two generations of skilled workers, tailors, carpenters, and weavers probably operating small workshops from their homes. In the case of unskilled workers' families it was a strategy for survival.

The changing industrial face of Philadelphia was a two-edged sword for the Irish. For the weavers of Kensington where handloom weaving was replaced by machinery and factories, it meant deskilling and loss of wage. As a result there was a mass exodus from the trade by the Irish. By 1880 handloom weaving had all but disappeared and the hourly wage of weavers and carpet weavers was below $1.25 – on a par with unskilled occupations such as day labourer or porter. At mid-century some 12 per cent of the immigrant Irish had listed their occupation as weavers and thirty years later only 1.6 per cent did so. Figure 3.5 reflects this exodus. Those migrants living in the north east of the city in 1870 were predominantly in the Port Richmond area. Only ten individuals are recorded as weavers in the 1870 census and of these half were carpet weavers. The presence of three female weavers probably indicates that these jobs were in factories and not in home-based production.

For the second generation of the 1870s and 1880s industry and mechanization brought changes and opportunities. Cloth production remained an important area of employment for some in jobs such as machine operatives in the cotton mills. The cotton and carpet mills employed males and females but for most of the female children who were born or grew up in Philadelphia employment as dressmakers, seamstresses or working in a shop remained most common. A few families continued to operate from their homes such as the family of Anthony Lafferty, a tailor, who arrived in the city in 1864. The 1870 census records him as a merchant tailor, his son John (23) as a tailor and his two daughters, Mary (26) and Sallie (18) as vestmakers. Most, however, either worked as artisans outside the home or worked in factories. It is perhaps significant that only two are recorded as labourers. The children of other artisans found employment in a variety of trades. Henry Smith who came to the city as a shoemaker was practising that trade in 1870. His eldest son, also a shoemaker, is recorded as living in the same house with his wife and two young children. Henry Senior's other sons are recorded as blacksmith, baker and coach-trimmer respectively.

In many respects the Smith family typify the changing experience of the families who sailed from Derry. When Henry Smith Sen. arrived in Philadelphia he was 52. He brought with him his wife and two sons. The presence in the household of two older sons in 1870 and the fact that the family's fare had been pre-paid suggests that the two older sons had arrived some years earlier and later had sent for the remainder of their family (the fact that one of those sons had two children both born in Philadelphia, the elder of whom was aged 3, suggests that they had preceded their father by at least three or four years). Six years after arriving in Philadelphia Henry Smith Sen. owned the house he lived in in the south of the city (his real estate is recorded as being worth $1,500) and with Henry Smith Jun.'s children present it was a three-generation household. In 1880 Henry Jun. was in his own house in the north of the city with his wife and three children. The 1880 census records Henry Jun. as a watchman which indicates downward mobility. Meanwhile Henry Sen., now in his late sixties, was still a shoemaker. Sharing his house was his wife and youngest son who, a coach trimmer in 1870, was now an upholsterer. The son was married to a Pennsylvanian woman and they had a 1-year-old child. For the young couple, living with the parents was probably a comfortable arrangement at an early stage in their lives and the responsibility of looking after the elderly parents in the years to come was the reciprocal side of the arrangement.

For the Cooke migrants social mobility was unspectactularly upward as they availed themselves of the new jobs and opportunities in Philadelphia's increasingly industrial occupational structure. Physical mobility was high within and out of the city. It is not surprising that only 7 of the 43 households found in 1850 could be traced through to the 1860 census as the city was swamped with Famine migrants from all over Ireland not all of whom could find long-term work and a home in Philadelphia. Of those who arrived in later years about half could be located in the subsequent census. In almost all cases they had changed residence although they frequently stayed within the same neighbourhood.[28]

The fact that the majority of these families had had their passages paid for them helps explain the unusually high rate of successful links from one census to the next. With family or friend connections and possibly a place to live or a job to go to they had a better chance of surviving in the city than those who arrived on their own. The 1840s and 1850s were tough times. Heavy German and Irish emigration in the 1840s led to surplus labour. Exacerbating this labour competition was machine replacement of jobs. Periodic lay-offs, fluctuating prices, wages and hours at times made conditions bleak and fuelled nativist sentiments. The fact that, as families, they could pool their resources aided their survival during this difficult period. At least in some ways Philadelphia in the mid-nineteenth century was not as alien an environment as other American urban centres. With its well-established Irish neighbourhoods, unusually high rate of home-based cloth production and small craft shops Philadelphia's urban environment was not a complete contrast to life in Ireland. These factors must surely have helped in adapting to the many changes involved in moving from Irish countryside to American city.

NOTES

1 Hereafter Londonderry will be abbreviated to Derry.
2 The Laggan was a fertile agricultural region which ran either side of the boundary between Derry and Donegal.
3 R. J. Dickson, *Ulster Emigration to Colonial America, 1718–1785*, Belfast, Ulster Historical Foundation, 1976, p. 13.
4 Dickson notes that in 1729 some 1,155 of the 1,708 immigrants who landed at Philadelphia were Irish, most of them from the north. ibid., p. 33.
5 ibid., p. 225.
6 These numbers are obtained from the United States shipping manifests of ships entering the port of Philadelphia. An Act of Congress specified that from 1 January 1820 captains of ships arriving from any foreign port must deliver to the Collector of Customs a sworn manifest containing the name of each passenger, their age, sex, occupation, nationality, and country or city of destination. These 'manifests', as they were called, also gave the vessel's name, port of registration and departure date, and occasionally also identified the owners of the vessel. In the case of Philadelphia, such manifests date back to 1800. They are currently held at the Center for Immigration Studies, Temple University-Balch Institute, Philadelphia.
7 The use of agents to act on behalf of the emigrant vessels was an established practice as early as the eighteenth century. Dickson cites some 38 agents throughout the counties of Derry, Donegal, Tyrone, Fermanagh and Armagh who acted for the 127 vessels which left Derry during the period 1770–5. See R. J. Dickson (1976), op. cit.
8 The registers of J. & J. Cooke are held in the Public Record Office of Northern Ireland (ref. D2893/1). They consist of three volumes covering the periods 1847–9, 1850–7 and 1858–67.
9 The main item used to identify and link the two initially separate sources of information is the stated name of the individual emigrant, whence the term 'nominal'. The biases and omissions in the two sources (other than those common to both) can thus be determined with a high degree of accuracy. Not only does the linkage allow comparison of the data but it also casts light on the preparation of the documents themselves.
10 The barony was introduced to Ireland by the Anglo-Normans as a unit of landownership. There are a total of 273 baronies within Ireland and the number within each county varies. The barony is further sub-divided into parishes and townlands. Apart from an administrative role the barony was also used as a legal division. It was used as a census division up to 1901.
11 The statistical validity of this correlation was assessed by computing the Spearman correlation coefficient between the volume of emigration, as indicated by the Cooke data, and population density in each barony. The Spearman test was used to minimize problems of non-normality in the data, and the test was restricted to the period of greatest emigration,

1847–51. Additional explanatory variables tested were the area, absolute population size, and Poor Law valuation of each barony but the inverse correlation between volume of emigration and population density was the only one to prove significant. Migration volume and population density had a correlation coefficient of −0.494 which with a sample size of 27 is significant at the 0.05 level. The correlation coefficient for the Poor Law valuation was −0.023.

12 These results support the views of MacDonagh who argued that small farmers with 5 to 15 acres were most likely to possess the means to emigrate. See Oliver MacDonagh, 'The Irish famine emigration to the United States', *Perspectives in American History*, 10, 1976, pp. 418–30.

13 The two agents – A. C. Craig and A. J. Catherwood – handled bookwork for J. & J. Cooke. Both were merchants in the city, were from Ulster families, and were members of The Friendly Sons of St Patrick, a benevolent Irish society based in the city of Philadelphia.

14 As part of the large Philadelphia Project nominal and other information from the 1850–90 censuses was entered on to large computer databases. Part of the output from these databases was alphabetic listings of heads of households by ethnic groups for each of the censuses. It was possible therefore to work solely with the Irish population of the city. By sorting the Cooke migrants alphabetically and by time period nominal record linkage could be attempted. Entries in the ethnicity files gave the reference to the more detailed ward and district files which were used for the linkage proper. For details see Theodore Herschberg, 'The Philadelphia Social History Project: A methodological history', unpublished Ph.D. thesis, Stanford University, 1973.

15 See 'Reports of the Secretary of State', *United States Congress, Serial Set; House Documents*, Washington, DC, 1846–51.

16 Another 1,041 sailed as part of family groups which were headed by only one adult or parent. In some cases these 'single parents' were widows but more frequently they were women travelling with their children to join husbands who had emigrated earlier. Many travelled on pre-paid tickets indicating that the husbands had sent them their passage. Attempts to trace these groups into the census were made but, in the absence of the name of a head of household, the success rate was much lower.

17 The 'grid unit' is an areal measure used by the PSHP which overlays a map of Philadelphia County to which all information on individuals collected by the project was related. Using this measure it is possible to locate individuals, firms, etc. geographically and to study their relationship over time. For details see Theodore Herschberg (1973), op. cit.

18 These figures are taken from research using the Irish Customs Lists for the port of Derry and United States shipping manifests of Derry ships. See D. M. Mageean, 'Ulster emigration to Philadelphia, 1847–1865: a case study using passenger lists' in P. J. Drudy (ed.), *The Irish in America*, Cambridge, Cambridge University Press, 1985.

19 S. Cooke, *The Maiden City and the Western Ocean*, Dublin, Morris & Co., 1961, pp. 132–3.

20 Sam Bass Warner, *The Private City – Philadelphia in Three Periods of Growth*, Philadelphia, University of Pennsylvania Press, 1968.

21 Dale Light, 'Class, ethnicity and the urban ecology in a nineteenth-century

city: Philadelphia's Irish, 1840–1890,' unpublished Ph.D. thesis, University of Pennsylvania, 1979, p. viii.

22 Philadelphia's grid originated in the 1682 plan of William Penn and his surveyor.

23 Sam Bass Warner (1968), op. cit., p. 52.

24 The figures plot the residence of those who arrived in Philadelphia in the years immediately preceding each census. They do not show the location of households of those who were traced from one census into the next, nor do they show the location of those who lived outside the city boundaries.

25 Dale Light (1979), op. cit., p. 43.

26 Sam Bass Warner (1968), op. cit., p. 75–8.

27 Dennis Clark, *The Irish in Philadelphia – Ten Generations of Urban Experience*, Philadelphia, Temple University Press, 1973, p. 69.

28 Of the 43 families who arrived in Philadelphia during the years 1847–9 and who were found in the 1850 census only 7 could be located in the 1860 census. Of the 53 families arriving in the 1850s and found in the 1860 census 22 were located in the 1870 census. Twenty-one families who arrived in the years 1860–5 were found in the 1870 census and of these 12 were located in the 1880 census.

4 Empire migration and social reform 1880–1950

Stephen Constantine

This chapter is based on two propositions. The first is that in the period from c.1880 to c.1950 the British Empire overseas mattered. In the world perspective of many politicians, businessmen, opinion-makers and philanthropists the Empire appeared an economic and political asset which was or should be made supportive of the United Kingdom in tackling her internal and external problems. Empire was opportunity.[1] The second proposition relates to the history of welfare policy. We must avoid the assumption that there developed in Britain from the late nineteenth century a single social reform movement which had as its sole purpose the establishment of the Welfare State, that is, predominantly state-run social services offering domestic-based solutions to perceived social needs.[2] More attention must be paid to charities and voluntary services which worked either in place of or in conjunction with the state. We must also consider the programmes of those who proposed overseas or Empire solutions, and not simply domestic ones, to social problems. The argument of this chapter may thus be clarified by putting the two propositions together and retitling it: not Empire migration *and* social reform, but Empire migration *as* social reform.

We need to begin as contemporaries did with a recognition of the major social problems from which they believed British society suffered. Particular decades of crisis drew attention to such matters, especially the 1880s, the early 1910s, the years of the First World War and immediate postwar, and during the prolonged agony of the slump in the 1920s and 1930s. Investigations and popular agitation focused concern generally on industrial and social conditions and specifically on towns. The town appeared both the centre and the cause of problems. Excessive urbanization and the decline in the rural population, it seemed, had led to an over-concentration of labour, subjecting people to debilitating economic and social experiences and under-

DOI: 10.4324/9781003172918-5

mining their health, their morals and their political reliability.[3] Responses to these damaging and alarming circumstances certainly included the promotion of domestic state social reform, beginning effectively with the Liberal welfare measures before 1914, but they also involved the expansion of such charity operations as the Salvation Army.[4] They also frequently introduced a 'back to the land' element which sought to repair the damage wrought by harsh urban environments by introducing some of the perceived qualities of rural life into urban existence, encouraging, for example, Garden Cities, allotments and the incorporation of gardens in the design of council housing.[5]

However, this chapter concentrates on a response least of all recognized in the secondary literature. It places alongside domestic reforms a parallel but connected imperial programme. They shared the same aims – economic and social improvements and political security at home and overseas – but they embraced markedly different methods. The imperial strategy was attracted to tariffs for the protection of employment and to capital investment in the Empire to generate prosperity.[6] More pertinent here were attempts to encourage a greater flow of British emigrants to new homes within the settler societies of the British Empire. Such measures have long historical roots, but campaigns became more conspicuous from the 1880s and culminated in a major state commitment, the Empire Settlement Act of 1922. This measure was revised and renewed in 1937 for a further fifteen years and was again extended several times in the 1950s and 1960s.[7]

THE IDEOLOGY OF EMPIRE SETTLEMENT

Leo Amery, Secretary of State for the Colonies 1924–9 and a key political supporter of the movement, described Empire settlement in 1924 as 'simply social reform writ large'.[8] It is indeed crucial to see Empire migration and domestic social reform in the same context, as responses to a commonly perceived economic, social and political crisis. Some activists, for example, could switch easily from domestic to imperial campaigns. Henry Rider Haggard's anxieties on the home front about rural depopulation were expressed in *Rural England*, 1902, but he was also an enthusiastic advocate of the Empire solution to urban problems and the author of an important report on *The After-War Settlement and Employment of Ex-Service Men in the Oversea Dominions* in 1916. Similarly Christopher Turnor considered *Land Problems and National Welfare* in 1911 and *Land Settlement for Ex-Servicemen in the Dominions* in 1920.

Balanced alternatives appeared to open up for individuals too. A resident of Letchworth Garden City recorded in 1930:

> Thirty years ago I was in a London factory, artificial light most of the time, and wife in rooms with children. It worried me what would happen if I got out of work. We determined to emigrate; went on the *Ruapehu*, a New Zealand ship, saw the accommodation and were preparing to go. Got stock of clothes, needles and cottons, tools, wood-man's axe, and what we thought might be wanted. Then came the Garden City movement, and instead of leaving all friends and relatives, we built a cottage here for £300 and rented 2½ acres of ground.[9]

Some operators saw the domestic and imperial social reform campaigns as directly linked. General Booth planned for the Salvation Army first to rescue the fallen from the inner cities via a City Colony from which the redeemed would then be settled on a Farm Colony in rural Britain: thereafter some would be sent abroad to the Colony Across the Sea.[10] Likewise Dr Barnardo despatched his rescued children from the sanctuaries of his children's homes to either foster parents in Britain or to new lives overseas in the Empire.[11] But some saw Empire settlement as the better or only truly effective long-term programme:

> Migrate or, in many cases, starve! Which is it to be? The gradual impoverishment of the country, the exhaustion of the funds available for doles, perhaps to be followed by insurrections . . . or shall it be the ordered march of a migrant army . . . moving towards a new life full of fresh hopes and possibilities, taking up fresh land in the empty spaces of the British dominions . . .?[12]

The appeal of Empire migration to its sponsors in this country was enhanced because it seemed self-evidently to meet British and also dominions' needs. There was an assumed natural harmony between them. Emigration would remove the perceived excess supply of labour from Britain which was causing low wages, unemployment and overcrowding. Critics argued that it would deprive industry of cheap labour, increase migration to the towns and encourage a rise in the birth rate, thus cancelling its claimed benefits. But sponsors either implied that it was a way of getting rid of the least valued social strata, the most depraved or deprived, or, more constructively, that the shifting of labour of marginal utility to the British economy would bring considerable benefits not least to Britain when relocated in the dominions where a labour shortage was perceived. As General Booth put it, 'the transfer of the entire surplus population of this country is not only possible, but would . . . be effected with enormous advantage.'[13]

Emigration enthusiasts regularly contrasted population densities in Britain with those in the dominions. For example, an essay of 1922, pertinently entitled 'Unemployment and the Empire', claimed that the figure for England was 650 people per square mile but in New Zealand it was only 11.7, in Canada 2.5, in Australia 1.8 and in South Africa 1.8 (conceding that these last represented whites only).[14] This seemed unequivocal evidence of underpopulation in the dominions and therefore of undeveloped resources. The House of Commons Empire Development and Settlement Research Committee reported in 1933 that 'this astonishing paradox exists – that whilst there are millions of idle Britons in the homeland, there are hundreds of millions of acres of unoccupied territory in healthy areas of the Empire overseas capable of development'.[15] The transfer of British manpower to the dominions would therefore increase the output of those dominions' economies, bringing benefits to Britain since the bulk of their products flowed back to the mother country, and this would increase their prospects and consequently purchasing power, enabling them to swell as markets for British manufactured goods. Empire migration was evidently part of a long-term development strategy bringing economic and consequent social benefits to Britain.[16]

A second appeal specifically concerned women and another perceived need for Empire migration as social reform. It is true that for some women emigration and life in the dominions represented liberation and opportunity, a way of escaping the constrictions of domestic British society which limited so severely their occupational and sexual roles.[17] But most commentators, philanthropists and politicians did not see women's emigration as a route to emancipation. The ethic of Empire was masculine, and women's roles were defined to comply. Emigration was still social reform, but to enable women to fulfil in the dominions the 'natural destinies' which the peculiar imbalances of British society were apparently denying them. Women were surplus to Britain, because they outnumbered men. In the crucial age group of 20 to 39 in England and Wales in 1901 there were 1,105 women for every 1,000 men.[18] It appeared evidently necessary to find the 'spare' women either employment or husbands. The solution lay readily to hand in the dominions where men outnumbered women. In New Zealand, for example, in the same age range in 1901 there were only 948 females for every 1,000 males.[19] Here were proper openings for women, in the labour force, as farm labourers or domestic servants, and as wives, bringing additional advantages since an increase in marriage ratios ought to increase the birth rate and therefore the population of each dominion. This was valued for economic and for military reasons. Lord Milner, writing as Secretary of State for the Colonies in 1919, noted that:

> there is at present a large surplus of women in this country of the age suitable for active work, marriage and migration. We believe that it is in the interests of the Empire as a whole that such of these women as are fitted for the life . . . should settle overseas.[20]

A later advocate declared in 1934: 'At this moment, in Queensland, there is a shortage of 40,000 women to care for our men and to keep them straight.'[21]

A third advantage, asserted as a triumphant vindication of the virtue of Empire migration as social reform, was that it could be used to transform residents of *urban* Britain into *rural* producers in the dominions. There was of course an economic aspect to this. The dominions were thought of as producers of primary products supplying British markets and mouths with raw materials and food, and they were assumed to need labour for farms and to some extent farmers with capital. In return, as part of the natural harmony, the dominions should be passive recipients of British manufactured goods, thus bringing economic and social benefits to the British labour which remained at home, and rewards to British capital. But there were also physical, military and moral aspects: it was believed that the rural society of the dominions would nurture and retain the qualities of life sadly ebbing from Britain's urbanizing society. Here in the dominions would be reared a healthier stock, a reliable, upright and moral people, an imperial yeomanry, as J. A. Froude perceived them, constituting the racial defences of the British Empire in an unstable and threatening world.[22] Sir John Marriott expressed it unambiguously: 'Such a land of promise as New Zealand is surely capable of healing, cleansing, and moulding to its own splendid traditions even rather unclean, uncouth, and unpromising material.'[23] Emigrating, crossing the water, would be a new baptism, washing away the sins of urban Britain, purifying, making good.

EMIGRATION AND VOLUNTARY SOCIETIES

Advocates of Empire migration as social reform were reasonably confident of the potential of their proposals because for much of the period, certainly up to the end of the 1920s, they seemed to be working with the grain. British society was already mobile, with ample evidence not only of internal migration but of a continuing tradition of external migration. There was no question of having to create an interest in emigration, but rather of further encouraging and especially of channelling that flood to acceptable Empire destinations. Altogether between 1815 and 1912 over 21 million people had emigrated from the United Kingdom.[24] It is said that European emigration in the nineteenth and twentieth centuries was essentially voluntary. Emigrants certainly made what they believed to be independent decisions to emigrate, and apparently appeared to have a free choice of destinations. However, in practice their decisions were determined by some tight economic, political and ideological structures, and they were affected by narrow channels of information, from family or friends overseas or from official and unofficial agents at home. These constricted certain options and opened up others. The decision to migrate has been likened to the decision to marry: it is an individual decision, but there are predisposing circumstances bringing particular couples together.[25]

Those who publicly advocated emigration performed several functions shaping those predisposing circumstances. They publicized and legitimized the idea of Empire migration, particularly as a vehicle for social reform, and they encouraged individuals to finance such operations or to follow that route to individual self-advancement. Others provided the agencies which enabled people to emigrate: these could be philanthropic organizations, shipping companies or trade unions. In addition some invited, urged, even demanded Imperial government intervention to assist their programmes.

Quite a lot is known, for example, about trade union support for the emigration of out-of-work or discontented members. Over 40,000 members of the National Agricultural Labourers' Union and their families were helped overseas between 1872 and 1881. This was a form of collective self-help which lost favour after 1880, though a few unions thereafter still continued to operate emigration funds and helped members to 'escape'.[26] Not enough is yet known about the publicity, recruiting and lobbying roles of shipping companies, passage brokers and their agents after 1880. Transporting emigrants overseas could be immensely profitable, and on certain shipping routes to the dominions, British and dominion shipping companies enjoyed a virtual monopoly.[27]

Much more public, consistent and vociferous were the philanthropic organizations. Charities involved in the emigration of the poor go back right through the nineteenth century and indeed into earlier periods. But several were revitalized and many new operations were started in response to the perceived urban crisis after 1880. There were those groups concerned to support the general emigration of families or individuals usually to Empire destinations, for example, the Church Emigration Society formed in 1886, the Self-Help Emigration Society operating in London and Liverpool from the 1880s, the YMCA also active from 1882, the East End Emigration Fund set up in 1881 (and still producing annual reports in the 1950s), the Church Army Emigration Department established in 1906 and perhaps especially the Salvation Army which formed its Migration and Settlement Department to fulfil General Booth's programme in 1903 and which claimed to have assisted 80,000 emigrants by 1914 and some 250,000 by 1938. Such organizations provided advice, information, sometimes supervision on board ship, often reception services in the dominions and frequently cash help for the purchase of tickets.[28]

Supervision on board and reception overseas were deemed particularly important by those voluntary bodies specifically concerned with the emigration of single women. The majority of independent emigrants were men, and women's emigration societies aimed to remove those physical and moral dangers facing single women emigrants which were thought to deter women from emigrating. The Female Middle Class Emigration Society had been in business since 1862. As its name announced, it aimed to find legitimate occupations overseas for educated middle-class women, mainly as governesses. But it was to merge with other women's groups formed in the early 1880s and to reappear as the British Women's Emigration Association in 1884 with interests widened to include the recruiting and dispatch overseas of domestic servants, often on behalf of dominions' governments and employers. The BWEA and similar bodies assisted over 20,000 women to emigrate between 1884 and 1914.[29] An additional campaign by an offshoot of the BWEA was designed to recruit single women to settle in South Africa as part of Lord Milner's programme to consolidate British control after the military conquests in the Boer War. Nearly 6,000 young women were sent out, ostensibly to join the labour force as domestic servants but also consciously as marriage partners for British male settlers, to increase Anglo-Saxon stock and out-breed the Boers.[30] Pregnancy was the continuation of war by other means.

There were also the children's emigration societies and the movements to assist juvenile settlers in the Empire. Sending out youngsters was thought to be particularly valuable. First, by emigration, they escaped the corrupting influence of an evil urban environment. Second, being young they were thought to be more adaptable to the novel conditions they would find in the dominions, and were therefore easier to assimilate. The honest observer might also admit that they were a cheaper form of labour than adults and therefore often more employable (and indeed they were often treated as paid- or semi-paid employees in the dominions at ages when this would have been illegal in Britain). Altogether, children and juveniles were thought highly suitable for transfer from urban Britain to the rural dominions.[31]

Thomas Sedgwick was one enthusiast. He had been involved in the Boys Club movement in London and had attempted to rescue lads from what he saw as dead-end jobs, even launching a campaign to find better careers for redundant young golf caddies. But then in 1910 he organized the emigration of his first party of fifty boys from London and Liverpool to take up jobs as young farm labourers in New Zealand. The ethos of many such movements was summed up in the title of his 1913 report: *Town Lads on Imperial Farms*. 'Imperial Migration', he declared, 'weakens the vicious home circle of Poverty, Unemployment and Drink, and paves the way for Wages Reform, Social Reform and the improvement of the British race.'[32] A similar purpose inspired Rhodesian-born Kingsley Fairbridge. As a young man on a visit to London he saw the urban conditions which led him to found in Oxford in 1909 the Child Emigration Society and to establish Fairbridge Farm Schools in the dominions, the first in Australia in 1912. He recorded in his autobiography what he claimed was the vision which flashed upon his inward eye one day back home in Africa and which was to motivate him for his life's work:

> When you close your eyes on a hot day you may see things that have remained half hidden at the back of your brain. That day I saw a street in the east end of London. It was a street crowded with children – dirty children, yet lovable. . . . No decent air, not enough food. The waste of it all! Children's lives wasting while the Empire cried aloud for men. There were workhouses full, orphanages full – and no farmers. . . . And then I saw it quite clearly: *Train the children to be farmers*! . . . Shift the orphanages of Britain . . . to the shores of Greater Britain, where farmers and farmers' wives are *wanted*. . . . I saw little children shedding the bondage of bitter circumstances, and stretching their legs and minds amid the thousand interests of the farm. I saw waste turned to providence, the waste of unneeded humanity converted to the husbandry of unpeopled acres.[33]

Fairbridge's vision was not unlike that which drove Dr Barnardo. In the case of the Barnardo Homes, as with other refuges for children, there was a practical need too. The principle of the ever-open-door had been adopted to guide policy: no child would be turned away. Orphans, waifs and strays, children whose parents could no longer support them, all were taken in. But the open entrance at the front needed a back exit, to dispose of the children who could no longer be accommodated in the homes or fostered outside with British families. It should be said that in some cases the aim was to put the children beyond the reach of certain parents Dr Barnardo thought unsuitable. From 1882 he was busy arranging the emigration of children, usually with, sometimes without, parental consent. His commitment to the imperial social reform programme was explicit:

> We in England with our 470 inhabitants to the square mile are choking, elbowing, starving each other in the struggle for existence. Yet the British Colonies over the seas are crying out for men to till their acres. . . . Canada alone, with an acreage nearly equal to the whole of Europe, possesses only the population of London. Here is a boundless field for settlers, and for just such settlers as can be selected from my family – boys and girls of good physique, of tested moral character, of upright habits, able to make trained use of their hands, with few ties to bind them to the mother country, and at an age when they are easily adaptable to almost any climatic extremes.

Altogether about 80,000 children mainly under the age of 14 were sent to Canada alone between 1868 and 1925 by Dr Barnardo's Homes, the Macpherson Homes, Middlemore Homes and other children's charities. Only one-third were orphans.[34] This practice continued until long after the Second World War; the last Barnardo's children to be sent overseas were shipped out to Australia in 1967.[35]

THE STATE AND EMPIRE MIGRATION

The achievements of voluntary agencies are not to be measured solely by the number of emigrants they shipped to the Empire: in a peak period 1910–13 they accounted at best for perhaps 10 per cent of the total number of Empire migrants.[36] More important was their success in forcing their social reform programme upon the attention of the public, to achieve a partnership with the public authorities, and ultimately to draw the Imperial government into substantial financial commitments after the First World War. Of course, it has to be acknowledged that earlier in the eighteenth and nineteenth centuries central and local authorities had employed forced or assisted emigration as a welfare strategy, largely by regarding colonies as receptacles in which to dump the undesirable and disreputable, for the better purification of the remaining British society at home. Transportation as a penal policy had been designed to deter crime in Britain, to dispose of the corrupting presence of known criminals, and only lastly as a way of increasing the labour supplies needed by the colonists. About 50,000 convicts were transported to the American colonies in the eighteenth century and some 160,000 to Australia between 1788 and 1868.[37] There were also state experiments after the Napoleonic wars to assist paupers (among others) to settle in South Africa and Canada, and a clause in the New Poor Law, now rarely noticed in the standard histories of welfare policy, allowed Boards of Guardians to assist the emigration of those in need: nearly 26,000, mainly agricultural labourers, consequently departed these shores between 1834 and 1860. This policy, roundly condemned by many in this country at the time as 'shovelling out paupers', hardly met with the approval of the colonial authorities either, who preferred their immigrants to be respectable and independent. Their needs were met more acceptably by the Imperial government's Colonial Land and Emigration Commissioners who sold estates in the colonies to speculators and farmers and used the proceeds to subsidize passages for emigrating labourers, over 370,000 between 1840 and 1869. But this was a responsibility which self-governing colonies preferred to undertake themselves, and when as a result CLEC's operations declined and then ceased, the Imperial government withdrew almost entirely from positive involvement in emigration matters.[38]

However, from the 1880s the external and internal implications of urban crises drove observers to press government to resume responsibility for an enhanced emigration and social welfare programme. 1883 saw the formation of Lord Brabazon's National Association for Promoting State-Directed Colonization,[39] followed by other philanthropic emigration bodies. They acted partly as a substitute for state action, but increasingly as lobbyists seeking a partnership with the state, and a share of its funds. In 1910 the Royal Colonial Institute gathered together at a conference representatives of fifty organizations, mainly voluntary emigration societies, who concluded by establishing a standing committee to lobby for closer state involvement with their campaigns. Later, during the war and post-war years, this body and other interested parties repeatedly reminded the government of its duty to offer, sustain, or enlarge its support for Empire migration in general and for the voluntary emigration societies in particular.[40] Meanwhile, further pressure was building up on the

Imperial government, this time from the dominions themselves, especially from Australia, eager to get the Imperial authorities to improve the rate of emigration to their territories, preferably at some expense to the British taxpayer.[41]

The state's response to all this was initially highly reluctant. Most ministers, and virtually all involved civil servants, shared a widespread belief that emigration if desirable was best left to the individual emigrant or to undiluted philanthropic enterprise. Doubts were even expressed about the existence of surplus labour in Britain. But there were, gradually, concessions. Most importantly we can see from the 1880s onwards a hesitant adoption by the state of parallel programmes of domestic *and* of imperial social reform and the gradual extension of these parallel lines. The establishment in 1886 of the Emigrants' Information Office was one sign, although this merely issued publicity and information on opportunities for intending emigrants overseas, particularly in the dominions. More practical welfare measures included a revived use by the Local Government Board of the Poor Law's emigration clause, especially to assist child emigration. Altogether 16,108 individuals were thus dealt with between 1880 and 1913, mainly children sent to Canada after 1905. Similarly the Reformatory and Industrial Schools Act of 1891, supplanted by the Children's Act of 1908, allowed for assisted emigration under Home Office auspices, and there were 3,097 cases between 1900 and 1914. Likewise the Unemployed Workmen's Act of 1905 also allowed for assisted emigration, and 27,465 emigrants were dispatched between 1906 and 1914: the Central Unemployed Board for London emigrated about half the people referred to it.[42]

However, the combination of pressures from home and overseas only began to lead the government towards substantial new commitments in the flush of imperial co-operation and heightened imperial sentiment which distinguished the period during and immediately after the First World War. The arrival at the Colonial Office in January 1919 of Milner and Amery, imperial enthusiasts with a concern for social reform, had a profound impact, but even so the full-blown acceptance by government of a state-assisted Empire migration programme only came when economic depression after the war dramatically intensified concern about unemployment and its baleful social and potentially political consequences. At last even the sceptics were persuaded that Britain had surplus labour and that long-term interests as well as short-term obligations required the adoption of a comparatively expensive state-run strategy of redeploying labour overseas in the dominions.

What then becomes apparent after the First World War is a further extension of those parallel lines, the programmes of domestic and imperial social reform. On the one hand, in 1919 to meet the immediate needs of demobbed troops and to buy social peace the government granted a non-contributory out-of-work donation. This was the first step towards the unemployment insurance legislation of 1920 and all the subsequent extensions passed in the 1920s and 1930s during the depression.[43] On the other hand, 1919 also witnessed the inauguration of a programme to settle in the dominions, entirely at British taxpayers' expense, such ex-servicemen and women and their dependants who wished to go and were acceptable to the dominions' authorities. Between 1919 and 1924 over 86,000 took their chances at a cost to the British taxpayer of £2,418,263.[44] And this, too, was a first step, to the legislation passed under the stress of depression, the Empire Settlement Act of 1922. It was a major commitment, up to £3 million per year for fifteen years, open to all, and it was renewed in 1937 albeit with a lower financial ceiling. Between 1922 and 1935 the act provided assisted passages for 405,242 British emigrants.[45]

The parallels and connections between domestic and imperial policies were made explicit. Throughout the 1920s, cabinet unemployment committees, whether Coalition, Conservative or Labour, listed as compatible options domestic relief works on the one hand and overseas settlement and other forms of Empire development on the other. Milner argued to cabinet in 1920 that 'all money expended on the oversea settlement of suitable settlers from this country relieves to that extent the housing problem here and also tends to relieve in still greater proportion the problem of unemployment.' Similarly, Sir Alfred Mond, Minister of Health, aimed to persuade the cabinet in 1921 that 'one most important element in any comprehensive policy for dealing with unemployment now and hereafter must be the encouragement of emigration from the country on a large scale, with the object of relieving congestion of population in the main centres.'[46] We may note in addition the report of the government-appointed Industrial Transference Board in 1928, which acknowledged the existence in this country of structural unemployment and the unlikelihood of a revival of employment opportunities particularly for 200,000 miners in the depressed areas: the Board urged improved facilities to enable these surplus workers either to migrate to the more buoyant regional economies of the south and south east of England, or to emigrate to what were perceived as the underdeveloped and welcoming economies of Australia, Canada and New Zealand. The unemployed, signing on at Labour Exchanges in the 1920s, were greeted by Oversea Settlement Committee posters on the walls, urging them to consider emigration as a solution to their difficulties.[47]

Three characteristics of the Empire Settlement Act deserve emphasis. First, the £3 million a year made available by the act was to be spent mainly on either assisted passages for emigrants, making the price of a ticket much cheaper, or on land settlement schemes, putting farmers and farm workers on to largely virgin territory in the dominions and meeting some development costs. Evidently the idea was still strongly endorsed that the emigrants should leave urban Britain and become farmers or farm labourers (or their wives) in the rural dominions. This, of course, might involve training schemes, and an inadequate number of these was run by the Ministry of Labour, local education committees and voluntary societies, providing agricultural training, and indeed courses on domestic service.[48] Second, it was accepted that schemes under the act required the full co-operation of the dominions' authorities, partly to share the expenses on a 50:50 basis, partly because it was accepted that the dominions would in any case insist on screening immigrants and rejecting those they deemed unsuitable for state support. The Imperial government's authority was clearly limited. The result was the signature of assisted passage agreements with most dominion governments plus Southern Rhodesia, and ambitious land settlement plans were agreed with Australia, Canada, and Southern Rhodesia during the 1920s.[49] Third, the act also allowed the government's Oversea Settlement Committee to work with the voluntary emigration societies on the basis of shared costs. Evidently the societies were recognized as valued partners, worthy of state subsidy, able to use their experience of philanthropic work in the tricky business of selecting, sometimes training, and often caring for emigrants on their journeys and on their arrivals overseas. For example, the various women's emigration societies had been amalgamated in 1919 with state encouragement into the Society for the Oversea Settlement of British Women, and this subsequently was recognized as the Women's Branch of the Oversea Settlement Department of the Colonial Office. Similarly, child and juvenile emigration societies like Dr Barnardo's and the Church of England Waifs and Strays Society were henceforth part funded by the state. The new system supported old activities and encouraged new initiatives, for example, the formation of local migration committees in various towns and the creation of a Migration Department by the Boy Scouts Association which issued posters to all troops in the country and arranged for the emigration of some 5,000 scouts between 1922 and 1932. The Boy Scouts' migration operations concluded only in the

1960s. Clearly the Empire Settlement Act was not intended to replace the activities of the voluntary bodies but to harness and stimulate their energies.[50]

ASSESSMENT

But how effective were all these efforts? In retrospect, protagonists of the Empire migration movement looked back with divided feelings. There are problems with the statistics, but the records appear to show, first, an unsteady rise in the total volume of emigration from the United Kingdom, from 1,073,374 in 1871–80 to 1,816,618 in 1901–10 and 1,811,553 in 1920–9, followed by a dramatic fall to a mere 334,467 in 1930–8. Indeed, there was net immigration to Britain in the 1930s.[51] The figures do, however, show that only about one-third of passengers left for Empire destinations 1871–80 and about one-half 1901–10, yet nearly three-quarters of emigrants 1920–9.[52] There is some evidence in these figures of the possible impact of providing assisted emigration to the Empire: it accounted for over 31 per cent of total emigration to all destinations in the peak period between 1923–9.[53] It also probably increased the ratio of female to male emigrants and the number of children under 12.[54] But there is little clear evidence that a significant number of assisted emigrants actually changed jobs from urban industrial to rural agricultural, as Empire migration enthusiasts desired.[55] Finally, it should be noted that expenditure under the Empire Settlement Act was always much less than the annual £3 million allocation, reaching peak figures of £1.1 million to £1.2 million only from 1926–7 to 1928–9 and in total amounting to only £6,708,257 in all the years from 1922–3 to 1934–5.[56]

There are many reasons for the disappointing aspects of these figures. First, it became evident by the 1930s that the principal obstacles to mass migration to the dominions lay in the dominions themselves. Most obviously much depended on the actual capacity of the dominions to absorb labour from overseas. In fact, the absorptive capacity of the dominions had been grossly exaggerated by enthusiasts. In truth the low population densities of the dominions owed much to the hostility of Arctic Canada, the Australian deserts, the Southern Alps of New Zealand. . . . Dreams of a nation of 200 million Australians or even 10 million Kiwis foundered on geography and climatic realities.[57] Moreover, the further development of much dominion territory was probably limited by a diversion of essential fructifying British capital in the 1920s and 1930s away from overseas to domestic investments.[58] This obviously reflected contemporary assessments of the buoyancy of markets for the primary products which further development in the dominions was likely to generate. The 1930s especially, with a collapse globally in prices for primary products, were hardly the opportune time to put more primary products on the market. Many of the land settlement schemes in Australia and Canada set up in the 1920s collapsed in great distress in the 1930s. Hence much of the net immigration to Britain in that decade. It was bad enough being out of a job in Jarrow, but it felt worse in Wagga Wagga.

There was too a political factor, potentially obstructive of mass emigration to the dominions even in the best years. The dominions were nation states, not as General Booth described them: 'simply pieces of Britain distributed about the world, enabling the Britisher to have access to the richest parts of the earth.'[59] By the time philanthropic societies and the Imperial government got round to urging increased immigration upon them, these nations had already established not only their own mechanisms for keeping out undesirables – in brief, if crudely, blacks, yellows, reds and the sick[60] – but also priorities for the kind of immigrants they did want. Dominions' politicians and lobby groups were conscious that immigration controls were techniques of social engineering. Theirs were still plastic societies, which they believed could be moulded to desirable shapes. Desirable futures differed, of course, according to the class and interest of the lobby concerned, but on balance the dominant groups sought, first, to ensure a ready supply of agricultural labour for their mainly agrarian destinies, and, second, to regulate the inflows to a volume which could be assimilated easily enough not to antagonize too seriously the well-organized, articulate, politically significant labour movements in these countries, all highly suspicious of new immigrants. Hence the tendency to restrict inflows of labour when the local economy hiccuped. Hence also the reluctance to take unseen the former industrial workers of Britain who, inevitably, must have formed the bulk of the men applying in industrial Britain for assisted passages. The number of applicants was always much greater than the number of accepted immigrants.[61]

But in addition, as the inter-war period proceeded, doubts began to grow in Britain about the prospects and even desirability of high levels of sustained emigration from Britain. By the 1930s, even in the depression, observers were concerned by the fall in the birth rate. Would further emigration, inevitably of the young, not leave the country with a dangerously ageing population? And did Britain not risk losing abroad labour needed at home? Already there was reported a shocking shortage of domestic servants; the number of agricultural labourers was too few for British farms; and the prospect of some skilled workers slipping into the dominions to nurse along their growing secondary industries was alarming to British industrialists struggling to keep their overseas markets. The claimed complementarity of interests between Britain and the dominions seemed to be breaking down.[62]

Finally, not among the most important explanations for the limited scale of Empire migration in the twentieth century, but central to the theme of this chapter, is the subject of a complaint frequently aired from the 1920s. There were suspicions that the evolution of the domestic social reform programme was in fact inhibiting the imperial strategy. It was argued that the hugely expensive new welfare provisions operating from the 1920s, such as unemployment benefits, widows', orphans' and old age pensions, health insurance and council housing, induced in the socially disabled in Britain a dependence on domestic welfare. This dissuaded them from taking the more invigorating, rewarding and permanent road to social reform, emigration. Complaints and worries were sufficient to persuade Amery to appoint an inter-departmental committee. It reported in 1926 that while social insurance schemes were not the major cause of the disappointing volume of Empire migration, they did play their part:

> These schemes have an effect in discouraging migration, both directly as a result of the sense of security they induce, and indirectly in that they raise the standards of living in this country, and so counteract to an appreciable extent the attraction of the life of independence offered in the Dominions.

The Oversea Settlement Board agreed in 1938: 'Unemployment and health insurance, improved public assistance, contributory old age, widows' and orphans' pensions, improved educational and medical facilities, have all served to create a sense of social security and stability which in itself militates against the inclination to migrate.' Similarly the Royal Commission on Population in 1949 more generally concluded that 'There is less inducement . . . to emigrate when . . . it is possible to provide through social services and measures of social security a higher standard of life at home.'[63]

To conclude: it can be reasonably argued that the evolution of state welfare in Britain, in partnership with voluntary services, followed two related and rival routes. One, which came to dominate, emphasized domestic welfare programmes of income maintenance, health care and housing provision. The other placed its faith in imperial economic growth and in Empire migration as more rewarding, constructive and above all permanent solutions to the welfare needs of the British people. There were, it is clear, particular difficulties at home and in the dominions which ensured that the imperial programme was never implemented to the degree that would have satisfied its exponents. But for a while the two programmes of reform lay side by side as alternative roads to social welfare.

ACKNOWLEDGEMENTS

The research upon which this chapter draws was supported financially by the University of Lancaster Humanities Research Committee and by the British Academy Small Grants Research Fund in the Humanities: I record this assistance with gratitude.

NOTES

1 J. M. MacKenzie, *Propaganda and Empire: the Manipulation of British Public Opinion, 1880–1960*, Manchester, Manchester University Press, 1984; J. M. MacKenzie (ed.), *Imperialism and Popular Culture*, Manchester, Manchester University Press, 1986; Stephen Constantine, *The Making of British Colonial Development Policy 1914–1940*, London, Cass, 1984; I. M. Drummond, *British Economic Policy and the Empire 1919–1939*, London, Allen & Unwin, 1972; John Darwin, 'Imperialism in decline? Tendencies in British imperial policy between the wars', *Historical Journal*, vol. 23, 1980, pp. 657–79.

2 For an example of the older approach see M. Bruce, *The Coming of the Welfare State*, London, Batsford, 1961.

3 J. H. Treble, *Urban Poverty in Britain 1830–1914*, London, Batsford, 1979; Stephen Constantine, *Unemployment in Britain between the Wars*, London, Longman, 1980; J. Saville, *Rural Depopulation in England and Wales 1851–1951*, London, Routledge & Kegan Paul, 1957; General Booth, *In Darkest England and the Way Out*, London, Salvation Army, 1890.

4 P. Thane, *The Foundations of the Welfare State*, London, Longman, 1982; D. Owen, *English Philanthropy 1660–1960*, London, Oxford University Press, 1964; O. Checkland, *Philanthropy in Victorian Scotland*, Edinburgh, John Donald, 1980; H. A. Mess, *Voluntary Social Services since 1918*, London, Kegan Paul, 1948.

5 J. Marsh, *Back to the Land: the Pastoral Impulse in England from 1880 to 1914*, London, Quartet, 1982; W. Ashworth, *The Genesis of Modern British Town Planning*, London, Routledge & Kegan Paul, 1954; C. S. Orwin and W. F. Darke, *Back to the Land*, London, King, 1935; C. R. and H. C. Fay, 'The Allotment Movement in England and Wales', *Year Book of Agricultural Co-operation*, Cambridge, Heffer, 1942, pp. 82–130; Stephen Constantine, 'Amateur gardening and popular recreation in the nineteenth and twentieth centuries', *Journal of Social History*, vol. 14, 1981, pp. 387–406.

6 B. H. Brown, *The Tariff Reform Movement in Great Britain 1881–95*, New York, Columbia University Press, 1943; A. Sykes, *Tariff Reform in British Politics 1903–1913*, Oxford, Clarendon Press, 1979; I. M. Drummond, *Imperial Economic Policy 1917–1939*, London, Allen & Unwin, 1974; Constantine, *The Making of British Colonial Development Policy*.

7 The standard short history is G. F. Plant, *Oversea Settlement: Migration from the United Kingdom to the Dominions*, London, Oxford University Press, 1951. See also S. Wertimer, 'Migration from the United Kingdom to the Dominions in the inter-war years, with special reference to the Empire Settlement Act of 1922', Ph.D. Thesis, University of London, 1952, and Drummond, *Imperial Economic Policy*, chapters 2 and 3. I also readily acknowledge my debt to Keith I. Williams, 'The British State, social imperialism and emigration 1900–22: the ideology and antecedents of the Empire Settlement Act of 1922', Ph.D. Thesis, University of London, 1985, and 'A way out of our troubles: the politics of Empire settlement 1900–22' in Stephen Constantine (ed.), *Emigrants and Empire: British Settlement in the Dominions between the Wars*, Manchester, Manchester University Press, 1990. The last phase is described briefly in G. F. McCleary, *Peopling the British Commonwealth*, London, Faber & Faber, 1965, pp. 128–45.

8 Hansard, *Parliamentary Debates*, House of Commons, vol. 174, col. 570, 28 May 1924.

9 Marsh, *Back to the Land*, p. 231.

10 Booth, *Darkest England*, pp. 90–155 and especially the vivid coloured frontispiece. See also General Booth, 'Our emigration plans', *Proceedings of the Royal Colonial Institute*, vol. 37, 1905–6, pp. 137–54.

11 Gillian Wagner, *Children of the Empire*, London, Weidenfeld & Nicolson, 1982.

12 G. E. Mappin, 'Migration as a paying proposition', *United Empire*, vol. 13, May 1922, p. 326.

13 Booth, *Darkest England*, p. 148.

14 J. Saxon Mills, 'Unemployment and the Empire', *Contemporary Review*, March 1922, p. 317.

15 'The Redistribution of the Population of the British Empire', report of the Empire Development and Settlement Research Committee, November 1933, reprinted by Dominion Settlement Association and New Zealand Land Settlement and Development League, November 1934, copy in Malcolm MacDonald papers, Department of Palaeography, University of Durham. I am grateful to the Trustees of the Malcolm MacDonald papers and to the University of Durham for permission to consult these records.

16 See, for example, memo by Government Emigration Committee, February 1919, with CAB24/75/GT6846, Public Record Office; also L. S. Amery, 'Migration within the Empire', *United Empire*, vol. 13, April 1922, pp. 206–18.

17 A. J. Hammerton, *Emigrant Gentlewomen: Genteel Poverty and Female Emigration, 1830–1914*, London, Croom Helm, 1979; F. Musgrove, *The Migratory Elite*, London, Heinemann, 1963, p. 31; P. Clarke, *The Governess: Letters from the Colonies, 1862–1882*, London, Hutchinson, 1985; J. Trollope, *Britannia's Daughters: Women of the British Empire*, London, Cresset, 1988, chapters 2, 7, 9.

18 D. C. Marsh, *The Changing Social Structure of England and Wales 1871–1961*, London, Routledge & Kegan Paul, 1965, p. 20.
19 Calculated from G. T. Bloomfield, *New Zealand: a Handbook of Historical Statistics*, Boston, Hall, 1984, p. 50.
20 Milner to Devonshire, Governor-General of Canada, 11 April 1919, Milner Papers, Box 383, ff. 20–2, Bodleian Library, Oxford.
21 A. G. B. West, 'Empire settlement and unemployment', Georgian Pamphlet 1, sold for the benefit of the St George's Day Fund for Child Migration, 1934.
22 J. A. Froude, *Oceana*, London, Longmans Green, 1886, p. 212.
23 Sir John A. R. Marriott, *Empire Settlement*, London, Oxford University Press, Humphrey Milford, 1927, p. 90.
24 Gross figures not net; W. A. Carrothers, *Emigration from the British Isles*, London, King, 1929, pp. 305–6.
25 J. A. Jackson, *Migration*, London, Longman, 1986, p. 38.
26 C. Erickson, 'The encouragement of emigration by British trade unions, 1850–1900', *Population Studies*, vol. 3, 1949–50, pp. 248–73; R. V. Clements, 'Trade unions and emigration, 1840–80', *Population Studies*, vol. 9, 1955–6, pp. 167–80; P. Horn, 'Agricultural trade unionism and emigration, 1872–1881', *Historical Journal*, vol. 15, 1972, pp. 87–102; H. L. Malchow, 'Trade unions and emigration in late Victorian England: a national lobby for State Aid', *Journal of British Studies*, vol. 15, 1976, pp. 92–116; for a list of trade unions still providing an emigration benefit in 1913 see *Emigrants' Information Office Handbook No. 11*, June 1913, p. 94.
27 C. Newbury, 'Labour migration in the imperial phase: an essay in interpretation', *Journal of Imperial and Commonwealth History*, vol. 3, 1975, pp. 240–1.
28 Carrothers lists societies promoting emigration in 1886, *Emigration*, pp. 319–20; also Williams, 'The British State, social imperialism and emigration', pp. 286–8, 296–8; and Brig. M. Owen Culshaw, 'Empire migration and settlement: Salvation Army methods and aims', in H. E. Harper (ed.), *Empire Problems*, London, Muller, 1939, pp. 166–7.
29 G. F. Plant, *A Survey of Voluntary Effort in Women's Empire Migration*, London, Society for the Oversea Settlement of British Women, 1950; U. Monk, *New Horizons: a hundred years of women's migration*, London, HMSO, 1963; Hammerton, *Emigrant Gentlewomen*, chapters 5, 6; S. Buckley, 'British female emigration and imperial development: experiments in Canada 1885–1931', *Hecate*, vol. 3, 1977, pp. 26–40; B. Roberts, 'A work of Empire: Canadian reformers and British female immigration', in L. Kealey (ed.), *A Not Unreasonable Claim: Women and Reform in Canada 1880–1920*, Toronto, Women's Educational Press, 1979, pp. 185–233. For surviving records see especially P. Hamilton and J. Gothard, 'The other half? Sources on British female emigration at the Fawcett Library, with Special Reference to Australia', *Women's Studies International Forum*, vol. 10, 1987, pp. 305–9.
30 B. L. Blakeley, 'Women and imperialism: the colonial office and female emigration to South Africa, 1901–10', *Albion*, vol. 13, 1981, pp. 131–49; J. J. van Helten and K. Williams, 'The crying need of South Africa: the

emigration of single British women to the Transvaal, 1901–10', *Journal of Southern African Studies*, vol. 10, 1983, pp. 17–38.

31 Wagner, *Children of the Empire:* J. Parr, *Labouring Children: British Immigrant Apprentices to Canada, 1869–1924*, London, Croom Helm, 1980; A. G. Scholes, *Education for Empire Settlement: a Study of Juvenile Migration*, London, Longmans Green, 1932; R. A. Parker, 'The emigration of unaccompanied British children to Canada 1867–1917', ESRC End of Grant Report, 1982.

32 T. E. Sedgwick, *Town Lads on Imperial Farms*, London, King, 1913, p. 5; 'Thomas Sedgwick and juvenile migration', *Royal Commonwealth Society Library Notes*, no. 71, 1962; the Sedgwick Papers are in the RCS Library.

33 Kingsley Fairbridge, *The Story of Kingsley Fairbridge by Himself*, London, Oxford University Press, 1927, pp. 142–3; Ruby Fairbridge, *Pinjarra: the Building of a Farm School*, London, Oxford University Press, 1937.

34 Quotation from K. Bagnell, *The Little Immigrants: the Orphans who Came to Canada*, Toronto, Macmillan, 1980, pp. 140–1; figures from Parr, *Labouring Children*, p. 11; but see also Wagner, *Children of the Empire*, p. 259. For some of the children's experiences see P. Harrison, *The Home Children: Their Personal Stories*, Winnipeg, Watson and Dwyer, 1979.

35 P. Bean and J. Melville, *Lost Children of the Empire*, London, Unwin Hyman, 1989.

36 Williams, 'The British State, social imperialism and emigration', p. 104.

37 B. Bailyn, *The Peopling of British North America: An Introduction*, London, Tauris, 1987, especially p. 61; A. R. Ekirch, *Bound for America: the Transportation of British Convicts to the Colonies, 1718–1775*, Oxford, Clarendon Press, 1987; A. G. L. Shaw, *Convicts and the Colonies*, London, Faber & Faber, 1966; R. Hughes, *The Fatal Shore*, London, Collins Harvill, 1987, especially p. 2.

38 H. J. M. Johnston, *British Emigration Policy 1815–1830: Shovelling Out Paupers*, Oxford, Clarendon Press, 1972; W. S. Shepperson, *British Emigration to North America*, Oxford, Blackwell, 1957, p. 48; F. H. Hitchins, *The Colonial Land and Emigration Commission*, Philadelphia, University of Pennsylvania Press, 1931, especially p. 211.

39 Lord Brabazon, *State-Directed Colonization – Its Necessity*, London, Stanford, 1886; H. L. Malchow, *Population Pressures: Emigration and Government in Late Nineteenth-Century Britain*, Palo Alto, California, SPOSS Inc., 1979, chapters 4–8.

40 'The Emigration Conference', *United Empire*, vol. 1, July 1910, pp. 510–21, and 'The Empire Migration Conference', ibid., vol. 18, November 1927, pp. 606–18. The papers of the Emigration Committee are in the RCS Library. See also T. R. Reese, *The History of the Royal Commonwealth Society 1868–1968*, London, Oxford University Press, 1968, pp. 161–8.

41 *Proceedings of the Colonial Conference, 1907*, Cd. 3523, 1907, pp. 153–78; *Proceedings of the Imperial Conference, 1911*, Cd. 5745, pp. 198–205.

42 Williams, 'The British State, social imperialism and emigration', pp. 87–94, 282–5; Scholes, *Education for Empire Settlement*, p. 28; J. Harris, *Unemployment and Politics*, Oxford, Clarendon Press, 1972, pp. 184–7.

43 B. B. Gilbert, *British Social Policy 1914–1939*, London, Batsford, 1970, pp. 51–97. See also the Addison Housing Act of 1919, the first, but not the

last, major state commitment to the building of council housing, ibid., pp. 137–61, 197–203.

44 J. A. Schultz, 'Finding homes fit for heroes: the Great War and Empire Settlement', *Canadian Journal of History*, vol. 18, 1983, pp. 99–110; K. Fedorowich, 'The assisted emigration of British ex-servicemen to the Dominions, 1914–1922', in Constantine (ed.), *Emigrants and Empire*; Plant, *Oversea Settlement*, especially p. 74.

45 Williams, 'The British State, social imperialism and emigration', pp. 200–70, 293; D. Kennedy, 'Empire migration in post-war reconstruction: the role of the Oversea Settlement Committee, 1919–22', *Albion*, vol. 20, 1988, pp. 403–19; Drummond, *Imperial Economic Policy*, pp. 23–144; Plant, *Oversea Settlement*, pp. 61–156; Wertimer, 'Migration', pp. 51–211, 272–395.

46 CAB24/112/CP1984, Public Record Office; Williams, 'The British State, social imperialism and emigration', pp. 244–5.

47 *Report of the Industrial Transference Board*, Cmd. 3156, 1928; Walter Greenwood, *There Was A Time*, London, Cape, p. 219.

48 Plant, *Oversea Settlement*, pp. 85–6, 140–7; *Report of the Ministry of Labour for the Year 1927*, Cmd. 3090, 1928, pp. 92–5; *Liverpool Education Committee Minutes 1931–2*, p. 14.

49 Plant, *Oversea Settlement*, pp. 87–111; Wertimer, 'Migration', tables XII–XVI.

50 Plant, *Oversea Settlement*, pp. 135–40; Wertimer, 'Migration', table XVII; B. L. Blakeley, 'The Society for the Oversea Settlement of British Women and the problems of Empire Settlement, 1917–1936', *Albion*, vol. 20, 1988, pp. 421–44; J. Gothard, 'The healthy, wholesome British domestic girl: single female migration and the Empire Settlement Act, 1922–1930', in Constantine (ed.), *Emigrants and Empire*; A. Warren, 'Citizens of the Empire: Baden-Powell, scouts and guides and an imperial ideal, 1900–40', in MacKenzie (ed.), *Imperialism and Popular Culture*, pp. 246–7; Scout Association Archives, Founder's Papers, Migration TC/27, Migration Scheme TC/215, Policy: Migration: Oversea Settlement 221/108; 'Scouts will be keen to hear all about the chances of settlement oversea and will refuse to dawdle about in smoky streets, looking for scanty and poorly paid jobs': *The Call of Empire*, 1929, p. 1.

51 Based on Carrothers, *Emigration*, pp. 308–9 and Plant, *Oversea Settlement*, pp. 174–5, deflating the earlier gross outward passenger figures (of 1,678,919 and 2,841,464), which are all that are available before 1912, by the same ratio as existed between passengers and emigrants for 1920–9 (passenger totals 2,833,541).

52 Based on Carrothers, *Emigration*, pp. 308–9 and Plant, *Oversea Settlement*, pp. 174–6. Compare to Wertimer, 'Migration', table VII.

53 Based on Williams, 'The British State, social imperialism and emigration', p. 293, and Plant, *Oversea Settlement*, pp. 174–5.

54 Wertimer, 'Migration', based on tables XL and LIV.

55 Drummond, *Imperial Economic Policy*, pp. 140–1.

56 Hansard, *Parliamentary Debates*, House of Commons, vol. 304, col. 1244, 18 July 1935.

57 The demolition was effectively completed by W. D. Forsyth, *The Myth of Open Spaces*, Melbourne, Melbourne University Press, 1942, especially

pp. 54–97; but see also I. Bowman (ed.), *Limits of Land Settlement: a Report on Present-Day Possibilities*, New York, Council on Foreign Relations, 1937.

58 D. H. Aldcroft, *The Inter-War Economy: Britain 1919–1939*, London, Batsford, 1970, p. 58.

59 Booth, *Darkest England*, p. 144.

60 Racial discrimination against coloured immigrants is well-attested in R. A. Huttenback, *Racism and Empire: White Settlers and Colored Immigrants in the British Self-Governing Colonies 1830–1910*, Ithaca and London, Cornell University Press, 1976. The use of medical inspection to exclude the sick and of Undesirable Immigrants laws to exclude socialists and others was commonplace: see, for example, the list of prohibited immigrants in *Handbook of the Dominion of New Zealand*, Oversea Settlement Department, 1926, p. 18.

61 See essays by John Schultz, Michael Roe, Stephen Constantine and Edna Bradlow in Constantine (ed.), *Emigrants and Empire*, also J. A. Schultz, 'Canadian attitudes towards Empire Settlement, 1919-1930', *Journal of Imperial and Commonwealth History*, vol. 1, 1973, pp. 237–51.

62 See, for example, 'Empire Migration', *Round Table*, vol. 25, December 1934, pp. 60–78, and minutes of 54th meeting of Oversea Settlement Board, 4 May 1939, DO 114/90 Confidential Print Doms. No. 182, Public Record Office.

63 *Report of the Inter-Departmental Committee appointed to consider the Effect on Migration of Schemes of Social Insurance*, Cmd. 2608, 1926, p. 25; *Report of the Oversea Settlement Board 1936–38*, Cmd. 5766, 1938, p. 11; *Report of the Royal Commission on Population*, Cmd. 7695, 1949, p. 123. See also Marriott, *Empire Settlement*, pp. 108–11.

Part II
Internal migration in Britain

5 Migration in early-modern Scotland and England

A comparative perspective

Ian D. Whyte

INTRODUCTION

Patterns of migration and population mobility in the past have been studied at a variety of scales; local, regional and sometimes national, but only rarely have comparisons been made between countries with different social and economic characteristics. This approach can highlight differences in the scale, pattern, causes and effects of migration, and in the underlying structures which influenced them.

Comparisons of this sort are especially valuable between adjacent countries. For England a good deal of research has been undertaken into the nature and role of migration in early-modern society.[1] The old myth of an immobile society in the pre-industrial period has long been demolished. English society at this period is now seen as highly mobile, particularly when compared with other European countries. Macfarlane has stressed this as one of the key elements in his definition of English 'individualism', contrasting it with the immobility of continental peasant societies. 'There was something distinctive about England', he claims in relation to migration and mobility as with other aspects of English society.[2]

But where does Scotland lie in relation to such a contrast? The Scots were notably mobile in the nineteenth and twentieth centuries both within Britain and as emigrants. There is less evidence of their mobility, internally or externally, in earlier times. Certainly Scots traders, mercenaries and scholars were active abroad in late-medieval and early-modern times[3] but how characteristic were these specialist groups of the population as a whole? The aims of this chapter are to consider in what ways and to what degree the processes and patterns of migration in Scotland differed from those of England during the sixteenth, seventeenth and eighteenth centuries and to examine the background influences that produced such differences. This can best

DOI: 10.4324/9781003172918-7

be done by using England, whose patterns of migration and mobility have been the subject of considerable research, as a yardstick against which our more incomplete knowledge of Scotland can be assessed.

CONTROLS ON MIGRATION: GEOGRAPHICAL AND ECONOMIC

In studying controls on mobility in any early-modern society it is difficult to distinguish between the theoretical effects of national legislation and local power structures that may have controlled population movements, and the ways in which these frameworks actually operated at local and regional levels. In Scotland a number of institutional features might, in theory, have discouraged mobility and reduced migration compared with England. These included strong landlord control at a local level and, during the seventeenth century at least, restrictions on movement caused by the moral conformity imposed by the kirk sessions. Recent work has demonstrated that these controls did not, in practice, inhibit movement.[4] While actual levels of migration and population turnover are hard to calculate, the Scottish pattern of migration seems to have been closer to that of England with its high rates of turnover than the lower levels of movement which were more characteristic of peasant societies on the European mainland.[5]

A major barrier to migration existed in sixteenth- and seventeenth-century Scotland which had no counterpart in England. This was the divide between Highland and Lowland based on differences of language as well as culture and society. The Highland–Lowland contrast was probably at its sharpest during the early seventeenth century[6] and although it was only an example of the mutual distrust between mountain dweller and lowlander which can be found throughout early-modern Europe, it was an extreme one.[7] Contact between the Highlands and Lowlands did occur through two-way trade across the Highland line,[8] but Highlanders who ventured to the Lowlands were viewed with distrust and suspicion while Highland society was largely closed to Lowlanders even in the early eighteenth century.[9] There was no dichotomy on this scale in England. Probably the most important single change in Scottish migration patterns during the eighteenth century was the increasing permeability of the Highland–Lowland boundary, particularly the development of seasonal and permanent out-migration from the Highlands to the Lowlands.[10]

In early-modern England there were marked contrasts between the economic and social structures of adjacent regions leading to migratory flows between them, and much emphasis has been laid on the contrast between arable and wood-pasture areas.[11] Surplus population tended to move from champion areas to wood-pasture or upland regions in search of opportunities and land, although this flow could be reversed in years of dearth when starvation forced the inhabitants of more marginal areas on to the roads towards the cereal-growing lowlands.

In Scotland there was no counterpart of England's wood-pasture regions as areas of in-migration and squatter settlement. Certainly there were regional variations in the farming economy and in the structure of rural society. For instance there was an emphasis on cereal cultivation in the lowlands and livestock rearing in the uplands[12] and by the later seventeenth century average holding size appears to have been greater in south east Scotland than north of the Tay or in the western Lowlands.[13] However, these were minor variations on a fairly uniform theme. All indications suggest that the balance between population and resources generated less pressure than in Tudor and early Stuart England.

The tenurial status of much rough pasture in Scotland also prevented the development of fringes of squatter settlement which could absorb surplus labour from the more populous lowlands as occurred in many parts of the Pennines.[14] Extensive areas of uplands were held as commonty, in joint ownership between a number of proprietors.[15] Under this system the shared rights of all proprietors could only be maintained by keeping the land in stinted pasture. Encroachment for cultivation infringed the landowners' collective rights and was vigorously resisted. This helps to explain why upland regions with concentrations of rural industry tied to smallholding agriculture did not develop in Scotland as they did in the Pennines or many lowland wood-pasture areas in England.[16] Moreover, regional contrasts in holding sizes were not sufficiently great to generate migratory movements in search of land as did the contrast between champion and wood-pasture areas in England. In Scotland, holding structures were carefully controlled by landlords who did not encourage excessive subdivision, in the way that sometimes occurred in Ireland, until the advent of crofting in the north west Highlands at the end of the eighteenth century. Nowhere does one find the areas of immigrant, squatter settlement that characterized many parts of England.

CONTROLS ON MIGRATION: DEMOGRAPHIC, SOCIAL AND INSTITUTIONAL

The relationship between population levels and resources was an important influence on migration in both England and Scotland. In England, population growth in the later sixteenth and early seventeenth centuries led to poverty and increasing vagrancy.[17] By contrast, during the later seventeenth and early eighteenth centuries the slackening of population growth was accompanied by a drop in the kind of long-distance movement which Clark has termed 'subsistence migration'.[18] We know far less about demographic trends in Scotland but there are indications that here too a substantial rise in population occurred during the later sixteenth and early seventeenth centuries.[19] This rise in population was checked by severe famine in 1623 and outbreaks of plague during the 1640s.[20] Between 1660 and the 1690s there may have been some recovery but the famines in the later 1690s cut Scotland's population by up to one-fifth due to increased mortality and a wave of emigration.[21] By the time of Webster's census in 1755 Scotland's population had probably only recovered to around its 1690 level. Overall, indications are that population growth in Scotland did not press so hard on resources as in Tudor and early Stuart England. Growth was checked by periodic severe subsistence crises which affected the entire country until the end of the seventeenth century and by levels of emigration that were probably greater proportionally than in England. However, as will be discussed below, these crises continued to generate waves of vagrant subsistence migration which had no counterpart in later seventeenth-century England.

As regards institutional controls on migration, Scotland was, until the mid-eighteenth century, characterized by a devolved, *laissez-faire* system of government and administration in which extensive powers were granted to local magnates through a system of franchises, or legal jurisdictions.[22] These, rather than administration at a shire level on the English pattern, were the effective agents of law and order in the localities.[23] The Scottish Parliament and Privy Council, even in the later seventeenth century, had little hope of making unpopular legislation stick. A system of Justices of the Peace, modelled on English lines, had been authorized by James VI early in the seventeenth century but was largely ineffectual until the eighteenth century.[24] James VI also instituted legislation on vagrancy and poor relief which was clearly borrowed from Elizabethan England.[25] This could be interpreted as indicating that Scotland had similar problems to England in these areas and was adopting similar measures to tackle them. More probably, however, it was merely slavish imitation. In England, the operation of the Poor Laws and controls on movement culminating in the Settlement Act of 1662 provided a general framework for controlling mobility which could be applied differentially at local levels to suit local circumstances.[26] In Scotland responsibility for poor relief lay not in the hands of secular officials but with the ministers and kirk sessions, groups of church elders elected from among the more godly and worthy inhabitants of each parish. Poor relief was raised by voluntary contributions not by a standardized levy and the ways in which these funds were managed and the monies disbursed depended on the whim of individual kirk sessions.[27]

The existence of open and closed parishes in eighteenth-century England shows that landlord control over population movement was patchy.[28] So far insufficient work has been done on Scottish kirk session records to see to what extent they varied in their management of poor relief and their handling of the vagrant poor[29] but at a parish level Scottish society had one control on migration that did not exist in England. These were the testimonials of good moral conduct issued by kirk sessions.[30] Anyone wanting to settle in a different parish needed to obtain one of these certificates from the parish in which they currently lived. Failure to obtain an acceptable testimonial might mean banishment from the parish. In practice, the fact that testimonials survive differentially among kirk session records, abundant for some parishes, absent for others, probably indicates that the system varied in the rigorousness of its operation between parishes and within parishes through time. Although the system operated in many smaller burghs, in the larger towns it was probably harder, even in the seventeenth century, to keep track of newcomers and easier to evade kirk discipline. The ability of the kirk sessions to enforce moral conformity and to control mobility in this way declined during the eighteenth century and by the 1790s many ministers were complaining that it was impossible to keep track of immigrants into rapidly growing urban and industrial areas.[31]

Landowners and estate officers could also influence migration by controlling tenancy and subtenancy. In Scotland large estates were common and most of the land was worked by leasehold tenants or tenants at will.[32] Although many farms were held in multiple tenancy during the sixteenth and seventeenth centuries the long-term trend was towards holding amalgamation and a reduction in the number of tenancies.[33] Holdings were worked by the families of the tenants themselves, assisted by farm servants and by cottars, who sublet small portions of the arable land in return for providing labour on the tenants' holdings. Cottars and their families formed the bulk of the population in many Lowland parishes and their numbers were often carefully controlled by estate administrations.[34]

RURAL SOCIETY

Although migration into the towns was increasingly important in early-modern Scotland, movements within the countryside were more significant in total. Studies of mobility based on testimonials and other sources have shown a pattern very similar to England with high levels of movement, operating mostly over short distances.[35] Around three-quarters of migrants travelled less than 10 km and women appear to have been more mobile then men. So far detailed studies have not been carried out in order to establish whether turnover rates of population were as high as in some English communities.[36] To understand the nature of migration and mobility within the countryside it is necessary to look in more detail at the structure of Scottish rural society and at the ways in which it resembled and differed from that of England.

A feature of mobility in English rural society was the high level of turnover of young single people, men and women, caused by the prevalence of what Kussmaul has called 'servants in husbandry'.[37] Similar systems of service existed in Scotland. The origins of this social group in Scotland are not clear but it was widespread by the sixteenth century. In the seventeenth century the proportion of the population which spent some time as servants was probably comparable to the one-quarter to one-third estimated for England. A period in service in another household was probably the normal expectation of children from cottar families and from many tenant families too. Farm servants were most numerous in those parts of the Lowlands where larger single-tenant farms had begun to emerge by the end of the seventeenth century.[38] However, servants formed a significant element in the rural population throughout the Lowlands and also existed in the Highlands.[39] Farm service persisted much later in Scotland than in England. In Scotland the system was adapted to the new commercialized farming systems of the nineteenth century while in England farm service declined.[40] The Scottish rural population in the later eighteenth century may thus have been more mobile than in many parts of England where much farm work was done by day labourers.[41] The mobility of servants was comparable with England and was characterized by frequent moves at the end of annual contracts, but usually over fairly limited distances.[42]

It has been mentioned that a high proportion of farmers in Scotland were tenants, holding from year to year at the will of the proprietor or with short written leases. Later writers on agricultural improvement frequently blamed insecurity of tenure for the reluctance of tenants to invest time and labour in agricultural improvements.[43] Such insecurity might have been expected to cause high levels of turnover among the tenantry. Detailed studies of tenancy indicate that in practice considerable security did exist with sons frequently succeeding fathers.[44] This was obviously a force for stability. However, given that proprietors did not permit unlimited subdivision of holdings, as occurred in Ireland, younger sons of tenants were probably a more mobile group. They had the option of remaining on the family holding in a subordinate position but all the population listings that we have suggest that this was uncommon.[45] They might have moved downwards socially into the cottar class and stayed within the same community or they might have moved in search of holdings or other opportunities elsewhere. So far little work has been done on the inheritance strategies of tenant farmers but indications are that, after provision had been made for widows, most of the resources normally went to the eldest son. Younger sons and daughters might have received small portions but these were rarely sufficient to afford them a living. Mobility among the sons and daughters of tenants must then have been commonplace.

In Scotland established tenants were also mobile both within and between estates, sometimes from smaller to larger holdings and generally over limited distances.[46] However, within a multiple tenant framework several options were available for adjusting holding size without a migratory move being necessary, and this may have reduced tenant mobility.[47] Leases for longer periods became more common during the later seventeenth century but their introduction does not appear to have had a significant effect on levels of tenant mobility.[48]

The occurrence of major subsistence crises in Scotland down to the late seventeenth century might lead one to expect significant numbers of failed or broken tenants but detailed studies of payments made to paupers and vagrants by kirk sessions indicate that a high proportion of the resident poor were cottars rather than bankrupt and broken tenants, who did not form as large a group as sometimes has been suspected.[49] Proprietors and estate officers usually made great efforts to retain tenants when times were difficult – partly out of paternalism but also, one suspects, because they did not want tenants to remove leaving unpaid arrears of rent. On the estates of the Earls of Panmure, for example, turnover of tenants during the crisis of the late 1690s was actually lower than in previous good years.[50] There was nowhere for them to go with conditions generally being so severe.

There are indications that cottars formed a more mobile group in rural society than did tenants and there are clear parallels here between the relative mobility of English yeomen and husbandmen on one hand and labourers on the other.[51] The degree to which cottars were attached to the land must have been less than tenants. Their possession of trades and crafts and their lack of material possessions, particularly agricultural equipment and livestock, compared with tenants, may have made it easier for them to move. They sometimes changed holdings with particular tenants but must also have moved more frequently.[52]

Patterns of mobility at marriage have only received limited attention in Scotland. The larger size of Scottish parishes makes calculations of levels of endogamy and exogamy difficult to compare with England. However, there is clear evidence that marriage patterns between the two countries were comparable with substantial proportions of marriages taking place between rather than within communities, albeit generally over limited distances.[53] The dispersed nature of Scottish rural settlement and the lower overall population densities tended to encourage wider contacts.

MIGRATION TO THE TOWNS

In England movement into the larger towns was an important aspect of migration, one which was essential for urban growth and which also acted as a demographic safety valve, reducing population pressure in the countryside.[54] In considering whether this was the case in Scotland we must first examine urbanization north of the Border and some of the characteristic features of the Scottish urban hierarchy.

In the late sixteenth century Scotland had a low level of urbanization, but during the seventeenth and eighteenth centuries the growth rate of the urban population was rapid, proceeding at times at a faster rate than England, albeit from a much lower base.[55] By the later eighteenth century Scotland was not far behind England in terms of the proportion of the population living in larger towns, making it one of the most urbanized countries in Europe.[56] However, there were some major contrasts with England in the ways in which the urban population was distributed: throughout the period Edinburgh contained a far smaller proportion of the Scottish population than London did for England. By the early eighteenth century Edinburgh with its suburbs and satellite port of Leith may have held up to 50,000 inhabitants, making it a medium-rank city by European standards. But this was only 4.5 per cent of the Scottish population. Unlike England the other main Scottish regional centres, Glasgow, Aberdeen, Dundee and Perth, had an aggregate population as large as that of the capital. Thus one might expect that patterns of migration into the major Scottish towns would have been markedly regional in character, with Edinburgh having less of a national recruitment pattern than London.

Little work has been done on migration into Scottish towns at this period. Some of the sources which are available for studying this are comparable with English ones but there is no Scottish equivalent of the ecclesiastical court depositions which have proved so useful in studying migration into English towns.[57] Preliminary analysis of migration into Edinburgh and some other Scottish towns suggests that the basic features of urban in-migration were similar to those of England. Edinburgh did attract migrants from throughout Scotland. However, while the migration field for apprentices was contracting during the eighteenth century as the apprenticeship system began to decline, the general field of migration for the city continued to increase until the 1780s.[58] This contrasts with London whose migration field began to contract at a much earlier date.[59] This suggests that there was a time lag in the evolution of Scottish migration fields which fits in with the known pattern of urbanization.

The geographical origins of migrants to Edinburgh changed markedly during the eighteenth century. A decline in the proportion of migrants originating from the Scottish Borders may have been due to the rise of Tyneside as a source of employment. There was a comparable decline in migrants from west-central Scotland with the rise of Glasgow and other expanding industrial and commercial centres. On the other hand there was a great increase in the proportion of migrants originating from England, reflecting increasing contacts between the two countries in the decades following the Union of 1707. There was also a comparable increase, in the later eighteenth century, in migration from the Highlands.[60] The known pattern of migration into Glasgow and smaller industrial centres like Kilmarnock complements that of Edinburgh with substantial increases in recruitment from within west-central Scotland, and a growth of long-distance migration, particularly from the Highlands.[61] Towns like Aberdeen and Inverness, which lay outside the rapidly industrializing central belt, showed a more stable pattern of migration in the eighteenth century reflecting the dominance of these centres over particular regions.[62]

VAGRANCY

A major contrast between the economy and society of Scotland and England was the late continuance of subsistence crises north of the Border. Southern England was free of such crises from the end of the sixteenth century and northern England from the 1620s.[63] The last subsistence crisis of national proportions occurred in Scotland during the 1690s and the Highlands continued to suffer periodic, if increasingly attenuated, famine throughout the eighteenth century, notably in 1782.[64] In Scotland the problem was caused by a combination of small holdings, inefficient agriculture, poor transport, lack of an integrated national market, a climate which was often marginal for cereals on which the diet of most people was based, and the inadequacy of local poor relief. There was a clear time lag between the two countries; in England large-scale subsistence migration had died out by the later seventeenth century but in Scotland it continued in a modified form into the eighteenth century.

Unlike England, funds for parish poor relief in Scotland came mostly from voluntary contributions and were designed as a supplement to assistance from family and neighbours rather than as a full support.[65] Mitchison's study of East Lothian parishes during the famines of the 1690s shows that while some kirk sessions distributed their resources to maximum effect others hoarded them and let their resident poor starve or take to the roads.[66] Each crisis set waves of starving vagrants on the move, through the countryside and into the towns.[67] During the crisis of the 1690s the authorities in Edinburgh had to set up temporary relief camps for starving vagrants and there are hints of similar measures in the earlier crisis of 1623.[68] Smaller towns experienced similar problems. One contemporary commentator estimated that the numbers of begging poor in Scotland doubled to 200,000 during the 1690s.[69] The figures are dubious but the scale of increase may be realistic.

These crises were superimposed on a pattern of endemic vagrancy. Vagrancy was most evident during periods of population pressure such as the later sixteenth and early seventeenth centuries. Levels of vagrancy also seem to have been building up again in the later seventeenth century when foreign wars caused trade slumps which may have forced many industrial workers on to the roads.[70] Overall the general level of vagrancy in Scotland during the seventeenth and eighteenth centuries, outside particular crisis years, appears to have been greater than in England. This was largely due to the same background causes which made periodic subsistence crises so severe.

During the eighteenth century the problem receded in the Lowlands as greater agricultural productivity, more effective poor relief, and better co-ordinated emergency measures during particularly hard years kept the poor within their own parishes.[71] However, when the *Old Statistical Account* was written in the 1790s, the scale of vagrancy was still being commented on in parish after parish, though the people on the move may have included a much greater proportion of Highlanders and Irish than a century earlier.[72]

As in Tudor and early Stuart England, the Scottish legislature seemed to be obsessed with the potential social impact of vagrancy and poverty, the former being viewed rather more seriously.[73] Scottish legislation echoed that of England in considering that the able-bodied poor who were capable of work yet were unemployed were a threat to social order, and that charity should be reserved for the old and infirm. Some of the underlying causes of poverty and vagrancy in England, such as depopulation due to enclosure and engrossing of holdings in some regions, did not apply in Scotland. Other causes, such as the effects of industrial slumps, may have existed in Scotland but have yet to be identified. In England poverty diminished as agricultural productivity rose and population growth slackened in the later seventeenth century while more effective poor relief and controls on settlement helped reduce vagrancy.[74] To some degree this also happened in Lowland Scotland. The famine of 1623, the epidemics of the 1640s and substantial emigration, including the Ulster Plantations, may have altered the balance between population and resources after sustained population growth during the later sixteenth and early seventeenth centuries.[75] The crisis of the 1690s came after several decades of generally favourable harvests and was never repeated outside the Highlands.[76]

Beier has shown that in England there was a considerable difference between the official view of vagrants as a major threat to the state, and reality.[77] This was also true in Scotland but there may have been more reason for the authorities, and the population in general, to be concerned about vagrants in Scotland. In a country where population was dispersed in small clusters and single dwellings sorning, or begging with menaces, could threaten small outlying communities. There were extensive sparsely settled uplands and moors where beggars could congregate and readily move around. The carrying of arms also seems to have been more frequent in late seventeenth-century Scotland than south of the Border.[78] Despite the popular image it was unusual for English vagrants to travel in large groups but in Scotland bands of beggars are recorded more frequently.[79] Sometimes they could terrorize a whole district like the group led by the celebrated gypsy leader James MacPherson who was hanged at Banff in 1700.[80]

It has been shown that on a broad scale patterns of movement of vagrants in England were not random but incorporated distinct directional flows from upland to lowland and from west to east.[81] So far insufficient data are available for Scottish parishes to make direct comparison but some vagrants had clearly travelled over long distances; some had even come north from England, perhaps because casual relief to strangers was more readily available in Scotland.[82] There was certainly a drift from the Highlands to the Lowlands in the eighteenth century and probably earlier.[83] By the late eighteenth century the movement of vagrants from Highlands to Lowlands is comparable in many respects to the movement of Irish to England at the same period.[84] It has been noted, however, that many vagrants operated within a more limited radius. This can be demonstrated in some Scottish parishes where particular vagrants sometimes turn up at the same season for several consecutive years. They seem to have been moving through a regular circuit of parishes, their travels perhaps linked to seasonal variations in the market for casual labour.[85]

THE HIGHLANDS

Much of the discussion so far has focused on the Scottish Lowlands which were geographically and economically similar in many respects to parts of northern England. The Scottish Highlands, however, had a physical environment which was harsher and more severe than the upland areas of England and a social structure which had no parallels south of the Border or indeed elsewhere in western Europe. The Highlands preserved a kinship-based society which, although starting to change under the impact of growing commercial influences by the later seventeenth century, still preserved many archaic social characteristics which contrasted markedly with Lowland and English society. Great stress has been placed on the strong kinship and territorial bonds which operated within the Highland system of clanship and the widespread occurrence of inter-clan feuding.[86] Such conditions do not appear conducive to high levels of mobility and might lead one to suppose that the amount of migration within the Highlands was limited compared with the Lowlands or England until the often traumatic social and economic changes of the later eighteenth and early nineteenth centuries. On this basis the rise of large-scale temporary and permanent migration from the Highlands can be interpreted as a late eighteenth-century phenomenon caused by the belated integration of this region into the capitalist economy of the rest of Britain.[87] However, the structure and operation of the lower levels of clan society in the Highlands before the mid-eighteenth century have received remarkably little attention. Low levels of migration have been assumed rather than proved. Just as Macfarlane looked to northern England for the survival of an immobile peasantry with a residual element of clanship and failed to find it,[88] so too when we look more closely at the Highlands does the traditional picture of a static society start to become blurred.

For the Highlands the poor quality or total lack of many of the sources which shed light on migration in the Lowlands makes research difficult. Nevertheless, there are indications that even within the apparently more static and restrictive framework of clanship, levels of mobility may have been higher than has been believed. Regular contacts between the west Highlands and Ulster, as well as trade with the Lowlands, are important features of the Highlands in the seventeenth century.[89] Inter-clan violence diminished markedly during the late seventeenth and early eighteenth centuries. There was far less homogeneity of surnames among the lower levels of clan society than has often been supposed, suggesting that a good deal of inter-clan mobility did occur.[90] MacPherson's study of marriages in the parish of Laggan from late medieval times has shown that persistent directional patterns of contact existed.[91] Although documents relating to tenancy are far poorer than for the Lowlands it is clear that in some areas, where successive late seventeenth-century rentals are available, that the turnover of population between successive rentals only a few years apart was considerable. This is notable in the case of Rannoch, admittedly a particularly turbulent area, but it has also been demonstrated for parts of the estates of the Dukes of Argyll.[92]

The fact that a class of servants, analogous to Lowland farm servants, existed in the Highlands has also escaped attention or comment. Shaw's study of the inventories of the goods, gear and debts of farmers in the Western Isles indicated that most of them were paying fees to farm servants.[93] Whether this group was as mobile as servants in the Lowlands or England and whether the same pattern of annual contracts and established hiring fairs existed remains to be discovered.

Elements of long-distance mobility did exist in the Highlands during the seventeenth century, notably the cattle droving trade which brought drovers from the west Highlands and even the Islands to the Lowlands and even south of the Border. However, a study of apprenticeship migration into Glasgow and Edinburgh, and of women moving into Edinburgh before marriage, does suggest that permanent movement from the Highlands to the Lowlands was comparatively limited in the early decades of the eighteenth century but increased dramatically in the second half of the century.[94] The numbers of women with Highland origins who had moved to Edinburgh before marriage in any particular decade increased by around eleven times between the first decades of the eighteenth century and the 1780s. This is paralleled by a large increase in the proportion of migrant apprentices moving to Glasgow who were drawn from the Highlands, and also a trend as the century progressed for migrants to come increasingly from the remote northern Highlands rather than just from neighbouring Argyllshire.[95]

The rise of temporary migration from the Highlands to help with the Lowland harvest was also a notable feature of the later eighteenth century,[96] due in part to growing population pressure and poverty within the Highlands and the increasing demand from the ever more commercialized farming systems of the Lowlands for casual labour at this crucial season in the agricultural year. Poverty in the Highlands generated flows of vagrants into the Lowlands seeking charity as well as migrants seeking casual work: contemporaries did not always distinguish between the two.[97] In some ways the Highlands were to Lowland Scotland what Ireland was to England in the eighteenth century, an increasingly impoverished and backward region which supplied streams of migrants to the towns and to the countryside in the more developed areas.

CONCLUSION: THE CHRONOLOGY AND CHARACTER OF MIGRATION IN SCOTLAND AND ENGLAND

Migration is a recurrent theme in the parish descriptions contained within the *Old Statistical Account of Scotland*, written during the 1790s. Some of the movement recorded there was clearly a response to recent changes in the economy: farm amalgamation and the reduction of cottar holdings coupled with substantial population growth in many rural areas were causing movement out of some country parishes while the creation of planned estate villages, often with concentrations of textile manufacture, were attracting people to others. The major manufacturing districts including old-established cities like Edinburgh, Glasgow, Dundee and Aberdeen along with newcomers like Paisley and Greenock which were rising rapidly up the urban hierarchy were drawing growing numbers from the countryside. However, there was comparatively little that was new in these patterns except, in some cases, their scale. Some types of population mobility – subsistence migration and vagrancy – declined from the early seventeenth century to the late eighteenth century while others, such as seasonal migration, increased. Others, such as migration to the towns and mobility within the countryside, were constant themes.

When the characteristics of migration in Scotland and England are compared the impression is that similar trends were occurring in both countries but with a clear time lag in Scotland that had become less noticeable by the later eighteenth century as their societies and economies converged increasingly. The change from the Tudor and early Stuart pattern of high levels of undifferentiated, long-distance, subsistence-oriented movement, to one characterized by more specialized migratory flows, which occurred in England during the later seventeenth century, is discernible in Scotland about a century later.[98] The decline of long-distance migration to the capital city with the rise of opportunities in other rapidly expanding industrial towns also took place in Scotland at a later period than in England, as did the rise of temporary migrant labour in agriculture. The countries were clearly on the same path. The elements which made Scotland's patterns of migration distinctive from those of England in the seventeenth century – the continuation of subsistence crises, the high levels of vagrancy, the impermeability of the Highland–Lowland boundary – were being steadily reduced in importance by the later eighteenth century.

The patterns identified have demonstrated how closely Scotland's experience corresponds with that of England. Although more detailed quantitative studies will be needed to confirm it, the indications are that the basic features of migration in Scotland were probably closer to the patterns which have been recorded for England than to the lower levels found in France.[99] The Highlands stand out as a region with a distinctive, more archaic social and economic structure, but even here the apparently static structure of clanship is misleading and levels of migration, if not as high as in the Lowlands, may have been greater than has been suspected. Movement from the Highlands nevertheless increased rapidly as the structure of clanship disintegrated in the later eighteenth century. More detailed community and local studies are needed to establish the distinctive features of Scottish migration patterns in more detail. In particular the possibility of regional variations within the Lowlands, the degree of mobility within Highland society before the mid-eighteenth century, and the nature of vagrancy in Scotland would be worth investigating. More detailed research on the structure of Scottish rural communities and urban society would probably highlight further interesting parallels and contrasts with England.

NOTES

1 The most recent summary of research in this field is P. Clark and D. Souden (eds), *Migration and Society in Early-Modern England*, London, 1987.
2 A. Macfarlane, *The Origins of English Individualism*, Oxford, 1978, pp. 64–6, 68–9.
3 T. A. Fischer, *The Scots in Germany*, Edinburgh, 1902; T. A. Fischer, *The Scots in Sweden*, Edinburgh, 1907; J. Harrison, *The Scot in Ulster*, Edinburgh, 1888; G. Donaldson, *The Scots Overseas*, Edinburgh, 1966.
4 R. A. Houston, 'Geographical mobility in Scotland 1682–1811', *Journal of Historical Geography* 11, 1985, pp. 379–94; I. D. Whyte and K. A. Whyte, 'Geographical mobility in a seventeenth-century Scottish rural community', *Local Population Studies* 32, 1984a, pp. 45–53; C. Withers, 'Highland migration to Dundee, Perth and Stirling 1753–1891', *Journal of Historical Geography* 11, 1985, pp. 295–318.
5 A. Macfarlane, 1978, op. cit., pp. 24–6.
6 T. C. Smout, *A History of the Scottish People 1560–1830*, Glasgow, 1972, pp. 39–43.
7 F. Braudel, *The Mediterranean and the Mediterranean World in the Age of Philip II*, London, 1972, vol. 1, pp. 44–7.
8 T. C. Smout, *Scottish Trade on the Eve of Union*, Edinburgh, 1963, p. 3.
9 A. J. Youngson, *After the Forty Five*, Edinburgh, 1973, pp. 11–12.
10 T. M. Devine, 'Highland migration to Lowland Scotland 1760–1860', *Scottish Historical Review* 72, 1983, pp. 137–49.
11 J. Thirsk, *England's agricultural regions and agrarian history 1500–1750*, London, 1987, pp. 49–50; J. Thirsk, 'Industries in the countryside', in F. J. Fisher (ed.), *Essays in the Economic History of Tudor and Stuart England*, London, 1961, pp. 70–88.
12 I. D. Whyte, *Agriculture and Society in Seventeenth-Century Scotland*, Edinburgh, 1979, pp. 19–22.
13 R. A. Dodgshon, *Land and Society in Early Scotland*, Oxford, 1981, pp. 214–17.
14 G. H. Tupling, *The Economic History of Rossendale*, Manchester, 1927; P. Hudson, 'Proto-industrialization: the case of the West Riding wool textile industry in the eighteenth and early nineteenth centuries', *History Workshop Journal* 12, 1981.
15 I. H. Adams, *Division of Commonty in Scotland*, unpublished Ph.D. Thesis, University of Edinburgh, 1967.
16 L. A. Clarkson. *Proto-industrialization: The First Phase of Industrialization*, London, 1985, pp. 20–1.
17 J. Pound, *Poverty and Vagrancy in Tudor England*, London, 1971; A. L. Beier, *Masterless Men: the Vagrancy Problem in England 1560–1640*, London, 1985.
18 P. Clark, 'The migrant in Kentish towns 1580–1640', in P. Clark and P. Slack (eds), *Crisis and Order in English Towns 1500–1700*, London,

1972, pp. 117–63.
19 M. P. Maxwell, *The Scottish Migration to Ulster in the Reign of James I*, London, 1973, pp. 26–7.
20 M. Flinn (ed.), *Scottish Population History*, Cambridge, 1977, pp. 116–49.
21 ibid., p. 13.
22 J. Wormald, *Court, Kirk and Community. Scotland 1470–1625*, London, 1981, pp. 16–17, 27–40; R. M. Mitchison, *Lordship to Patronage. Scotland 1603–1745*, London, 1983, pp. 80–2.
23 ibid.
24 R. M. Mitchison, 'North and south: the development of the gulf in poor law practice', in R. A. Houston and I. D. Whyte (eds), *Scottish Society 1500–1800*, Cambridge, 1989, p. 202.
25 R. A. Cage, *The Scottish Poor Law 1745–1845*, Edinburgh, 1981.
26 P. Clark, 'Migration in England during the late seventeenth and eighteenth centuries', in P. Clark and D. Souden, 1987, op. cit., pp. 213–52.
27 R. M. Mitchison, 'The making of the old Scottish poor law,' *Past and Present* 63, 1974, pp. 58–93.
28 P. Clark and D. Souden, 1987, op. cit., pp. 234–6.
29 However, see I. D. Whyte and K. A. Whyte, 1984a, op. cit.; I. D. Whyte and K. A. Whyte, 'The geographical mobility of women in early-modern Scotland', in L. Leneman (ed.), *Perspectives in Scottish Social History*, Aberdeen, 1988, pp. 57–60.
30 R. A. Houston, 1985, op. cit.
31 Sir John Sinclair, (ed.), *Statistical Account of Scotland*, 21 vols., Edinburgh, 1791–99, I p. 378, II p. 200, IV p. 474, VI p. 515, IX p. 476.
32 I. D. Whyte, 1979, op. cit., pp. 137–72; L. Timperley, 'The pattern of landholding in eighteenth-century Scotland', in M. L. Parry and T. R. Slater (eds), *The Making of the Scottish Countryside*, London, 1980, pp. 137–54.
33 I. D. Whyte, 1979, op. cit., pp. 141–52.
34 ibid., pp. 37–8.
35 R. A. Houston, 1985, op. cit.; I. D. Whyte and K. A. Whyte 1984a, op. cit.; D. G. Lockhart, 'Patterns of migration and movement of labour to the planned villages of north east Scotland', *Scottish Geographical Magazine* 98, 1982, pp. 35–47.
36 R. S. Schofield, 'Age-specific mobility in an eighteenth century rural English parish', *Annales de Démographie Historique*, 1971, pp. 261–74.
37 A. Kussmaul, *Servants in Husbandry in Early-Modern England*, Cambridge, 1981.
38 This is clear from the poll tax records of the mid-1690s. Those for Aberdeenshire and Renfrewshire have been published: J. Stuart (ed.), *List of Pollable Persons Within the Shire of Aberdeen, 1696*, 2 vols., Aberdeen, 1844; D. Semple (ed.), *Renfrewshire Poll Tax Returns*, Paisley, 1864. Manuscript records for some other areas including parts of the Lothians are available in the Scottish Record Office E70 series.
39 F. J. Shaw, *The Northern and Western Islands of Scotland: Their Economy and Society in the Seventeenth Century*, Edinburgh, 1980, pp. 191–2.
40 A. Kussmaul, 1981, op. cit.; T. M. Devine, *Farm Servants and Labour in Lowland Scotland 1770–1914*, Edinburgh, 1984.

41 P. Horn, *The Rural World 1780–1850*, London, 1980, pp. 23–4.
42 R. A. Houston, 1985, op. cit., pp. 384–5.
43 J. E. Handley, *Scottish Farming in the Eighteenth Century*, Edinburgh, 1953, p. 120.
44 I. D. Whyte and K. A. Whyte, 1984a., op. cit.; I. D. Whyte and K. A. Whyte, 'Continuity and change in a seventeenth-century Scottish rural community', *Agricultural History Review* 32, 1984b, pp. 159–69.
45 Poll tax records: see note 38.
46 I. D. Whyte and K. A. Whyte, 1984a, op. cit., pp. 47–9; 1984b, op. cit., pp. 163–4.
47 I. D. Whyte and K. A. Whyte, 1984b, op. cit., pp. 164–5.
48 I. D. Whyte, 'Written leases and their impact on Scottish agriculture in the seventeenth and eighteenth centuries', *Agricultural History Review* 27, 1979, pp. 1–9.
49 I. D. Whyte and K. A. Whyte, 1984a, op. cit., pp. 50–1.
50 I. D. Whyte and K. A. Whyte, 1984b, op. cit., pp. 166–7.
51 K. Wrightson, *English Society 1580–1680*, London, 1982, pp. 42–4.
52 I. D. Whyte and K. A. Whyte, 1984a, op. cit., pp. 47–8.
53 ibid., pp. 49–50; I. D. Whyte, 'Marriage and mobility in East Lothian in the seventeenth and eighteenth centuries', *Transactions of the East Lothian Antiquarian Society* 19, 1987, pp. 5–15.
54 P. Clark and D. Souden, 1987, op. cit., pp. 23–8.
55 I. D. Whyte, 'Urbanization in early-modern Scotland: a preliminary analysis', *Scottish Economic and Social History*, vol. 9, 1989, pp. 21–37.
56 ibid., pp. 21–2.
57 P. Clark (1972), op. cit.; P. Clark, 'Migration in England during the late seventeenth and early eighteenth centuries', *Past and Present* 83, 1979, pp. 57–90.
58 A. A. Lovett, I. D. Whyte and K. A. Whyte, 'Poisson regression analysis and migration fields: the example of the apprenticeship records of Edinburgh in the seventeenth and eighteenth centuries', *Transactions of the Institute of British Geographers*, New Series 10, 1985, pp. 317–32; I. D. Whyte 1988, op. cit., pp. 85–92.
59 J. Wareing, 'Changes in the geographical distribution of recruitment of apprentices to the London companies 1486–1750', *Journal of Historical Geography*, 6, (3) 1980, pp. 241–9.
60 A. A. Lovett, et al., 1985, op. cit., pp. 322–4; I. D. Whyte, 1988, op. cit., pp. 88–92.
61 I. D. Whyte, 'Population mobility', in R. A. Houston and I. D. Whyte (eds), *Scottish Society 1500–1800*, Cambridge, 1989, pp. 47–8.
62 I. D. Whyte and K. A. Whyte, 'Patterns of migration of apprentices to Aberdeen and Inverness during the seventeenth and eighteenth centuries', *Scottish Geographical Magazine* 102, 1986, pp. 81–91.
63 K. Wrightson, 1982, op. cit., pp. 144–5.
64 M. Flinn, 1977, op. cit., pp. 234–5.
65 R. A. Cage, 1981, op. cit.
66 R. Mitchison, 1974, op. cit.
67 M. Flinn, 1977, op. cit., pp. 170.
68 ibid., pp. 119–20; H. Armet, *Extracts from the Records of the Burgh of Edinburgh 1689–1701*, Edinburgh, 1962, pp. 208–10, 213, 228.

69 M. Flinn, 1977, op. cit., p. 170.
70 ibid., pp. 165–6.
71 R. M. Mitchison, 1989, op. cit., pp. 208–19.
72 Sir John Sinclair, 1791–9, op. cit., *passim.*
73 A. L. Beier, 1985, op. cit.
74 P. Slack, 1987, op. cit.
75 M. Flinn, 1977, op. cit., p. 170.
76 T. M. Devine, 'The Union of 1707 and Scottish development', *Scottish Economic and Social History*, vol. 5, 1985, pp. 25–6.
77 A. L. Beier, 'Vagrants and the social order in Elizabethan England', *Past and Present* 64, 1974, pp. 3–29.
78 A. Macfarlane, *The Justice and the Mare's Ale*, Oxford, 1981. The frequency with which weapons were carried in seventeenth-century Scotland has yet to be examined in detail but this is the general impression obtained from the sources.
79 M. Flinn, 1977, op. cit., pp. 123–6.
80 T. C. Smout, 1972, op. cit., p. 206.
81 A. L. Beier, 1985, op. cit., pp. 32–47.
82 I. D. Whyte, 1988, op. cit., p. 100.
83 M. Flinn, 1977, op. cit., p. 169.
84 P. Clark, 'Migrants in the city: the process of social adaptation in English towns 1500–1800', in P. Clark and D. Souden, 1987, op. cit., pp. 274–5.
85 I. D. Whyte and K. A. Whyte, 1984b, op. cit., p. 102.
86 The most recent survey of clanship is R. A. Dodgshon, ' "Pretense of Blude" and "Place of thair duelling": the nature of Scottish clans 1500–1745', in R. A. Houston and I. D. Whyte (eds), *Scottish Society 1500–1800*, Cambridge, 1989, pp. 169–98.
87 H. Jones, 'The evolution of Scottish migration patterns: a social relations of production approach', *Scottish Geographical Magazine* 102, 1986, pp. 151–64.
88 A. Macfarlane, 1978, op. cit., pp. 72–8, 88–93.
89 T. C. Smout, 1963, op. cit., pp. 3, 14.
90 R. A. Dodgshon, 1989, op. cit., p. 183.
91 A. G. Macpherson, 'Migration fields in a traditional Highland community 1350–1850', *Journal of Historical Geography* 10, 1984, pp. 1–14.
92 R. A. Dodgshon, 1989, op. cit., p. 183; R. A. Gailey, 'The mobility of tenants on a Highland estate in the early nineteenth century', *Scottish Historical Review* 40, 1961, pp. 136–45; E. Cregeen, 'The tacksmen and their successors. A study of tenurial reorganisation in Mull, Morvern and Tiree in the early eighteenth century', *Scottish Studies* 13, 1969, pp. 93–144.
93 F. J. Shaw, 1980, op. cit., pp. 191–2.
94 A. Lovett et al., 1984, op. cit.; I. D. Whyte (1988), op. cit., pp. 89–91.
95 I. D. Whyte, 1989, op. cit., p. 45.
96 T. M. Devine, 1983, op. cit., pp. 137–49.
97 ibid.
98 P. Clark, 1979, op. cit.
99 D. Hufton, *The Poor of Eighteenth-Century France*, Oxford, 1974.

6 The role of the family in the process of migration

Kevin Schurer

INTRODUCTION

The migration of populations in the past is no new topic of research. Much has been written on the volume, nature and processes of migration in an historical context.[1] It is now commonly accepted that in past times English society was very mobile. Results from 'turnover' studies, linking the inhabitants of a particular community for one year with those present in the same community at a subsequent date, point to high levels of movement for the nineteenth, eighteenth and seventeenth centuries, in both urban and rural areas.[2] Indeed, evidence from a unique set of tithing documents for late fourteenth-century Essex suggests that rates of turnover in the medieval period may well match those from the seventeenth century onwards.[3] It is also known that most of this migration was dominated by young, unmarried adults and adolescents. However, despite a wealth of research, little is known about the part played by the most basic and fundamental domestic institution, the family, in influencing the processes of migration. To what extent did the family play a role in determining patterns of migration?

In the large and growing literature on internal migration, kinship and family often go undiscussed. Indeed, these two institutions are seldom mentioned, and usually only in passing.[4] However, despite this omission, in the case of emigration overseas, the influence of the family has been acknowledged.[5] Moreover, it has been demonstrated that even if those moving within or as part of a family may not have constituted a numerical majority, the family continued to perform an essential social role, in terms of facilitating the passage and aiding the process of assimilation into a new community. Family and kin were important in supplying assistance, providing social introductions and creating employment opportunities.[6] In an attempt to guarantee

DOI: 10.4324/9781003172918-8

acceptance, many would-be settlers destined for North America, Australia and southern Africa would go to great lengths to demonstrate ties of kinship with those already settled, ties which seem to have prevailed above all others.[7]

If family and kin were so important in the process of emigration is it also plausible to expect them to have played a significant part in internal migration; or was it the case that the upheavals created by emigration were an exception to the general rule? In trying to answer this question it is interesting to reflect upon the recent work of Bailyn, and in particular his analysis of the Register of Emigrants for 1773–6.[8] Using this unique source to examine transatlantic emigration Bailyn suggests a two-fold type of movement, what the author terms 'the Dual Emigration'.[9] Upon examining the register it appears that some 70 per cent of those sailing across the Atlantic to a new home travelled alone, with only 30 per cent travelling in families. Yet when the data are broken down by region geographical differences become apparent. Whereas the south east of England recorded under 4 per cent travelling in families, and London and the Home Counties 7.5 and 7.3 per cent respectively, the north of Scotland recorded 80.5 per cent travelling in families and Perthshire 78.3 per cent, the overall figure for Scotland being 47.9 per cent compared to England's 19.9 per cent. Yet this was not simply an English–Scottish divide, but rather a southern England–northern England plus Scotland contrast; for instance, Yorkshire recorded 67.2 per cent family movement. At the heart of this geographical variation lies a socio-occupational difference. Migrants from south-eastern England included a large number of people employed in trades, crafts and merchandising, many of whom were highly skilled, whilst among migrants from Yorkshire and Scotland agricultural and labouring employment predominated.[10] In the words of Bailyn:

> The differences form a spectrum stretching from the urban concentration of London out to the remote northern provinces, and they are so great at the extremities . . . that at those two poles they form two quite different kinds of emigration, which may now be designated 'metropolitan' on the one hand and 'provincial' on the other . . . The metropolitan pattern . . . is typified by a young man, in his early twenties, who appears to be acting individually and who decides as an individual to migrate to America. He is not drawn from London's desperate, totally unskilled labourers sunk in absolute destitution . . . He is, rather . . . (a) young artisan or craftsman who has probably served an apprenticeship or otherwise learned some-

> thing of a trade . . . In (the) provincial pattern the predominant unit is not . . . an isolated male artisan . . . It is not even a person. It is, rather, a family, and a family that contains not only mature women but also small children . . . The provincial emigration was predominantly the transfer of farming families, whose heads were men of some small substance, or at least to some extent economically autonomous.[11]

This 'Dual Emigration' can perhaps be compared to the notion of 'subsistence' versus 'betterment' migratory movements put forward by Clark, in which those motivated by reasons of betterment – apprentices for example – moved in a deliberate, pre-determined and organized fashion over predominantly short distances, while those subsisting – vagrants and paupers for example – moved in a more transient, undirected fashion, more usually over longer distances.[12] In simpler terms the two types of transatlantic movement may be seen as being affected differently by 'push' and 'pull' factors. For the single migrants of the south the great demand for skilled workers in the growing industries of North America may have appeared as a dominant pull factor, while for the families of Scotland and the north of England general lack of prospects locally may have been a decisive push factor.

Whatever the situation, an important point is that within the same migratory flow, two types of movement, different in terms of both structure and motivation, co-existed. This may help to explain why a minority of researchers have pointed to the importance of family and kinship in the migration process, while others have virtually dismissed it. For example, it would be easy to make a distinction between migration into urban areas from rural districts and circular intra-rural movements, with the family role being different in these two extreme types. The disruption of leaving one's home to live and work in a town for the first time might, like emigration, have generated a set of circumstances in which it was favourable to call upon the support and assistance of family and kin.[13] Yet equally, it is easy to overestimate the process of assimilation for newcomers to an urban environment.[14] It need not be the case that urban–rural differences were the most significant factor. This point has been illustrated in a recent study of migration into the two nineteenth-century Lincolnshire towns of Grantham and Scunthorpe.[15] Both grew quickly from the mid-century, with in-migration a vital component. Yet the migration of families was almost twice as important in the case of the iron-producing town of Scunthorpe than was the case for the railway and engineering town of

Grantham. Ironically this situation is the reverse of what one might predict since family-based employment, as measured by the proportions of females and children employed in the town, was higher in Grantham.[16]

THE GEOGRAPHICAL FRAMEWORK

This study examines the incidence and nature of family migration and the significance of families in the migration process within a rural setting. Two contiguous groups of parishes have been selected. Both groups are located within Essex, one in the extreme east of the county, the other in the extreme west. The easterly group, hereafter collectively referred to as Dengie, is located on the Dengie peninsula, bounded by the River Blackwater to the north, the River Crouch to the south and the North Sea to the east, and comprises four parishes: Southminster, Steeple, Asheldham and St Lawrence. Covering in total some 5,200 hectares, the four parishes vary widely in area and population. In the core period chosen for study, the population of Dengie fluctuated between 2,379 in 1861, and 2,502 in 1871 and 2,217 in 1881.[17] Of these totals, the largest parish, Southminster, accounted for some three-fifths, numbering on average around 1,500. Of the remaining parishes, Steeple recorded an average population of around 500, with St Lawrence and Asheldham both maintaining populations of just under 200.

The second group of parishes, hereafter referred to as Hatfield, lies adjacent to the Hertfordshire–Essex border, only a few miles from the Hertfordshire market town of Bishop's Stortford. It too is dominated by a single parish, Hatfield Broad Oak, which accounted for around two-thirds of the total population, which averaged around 3,150.[18] Yet unlike Southminster, Hatfield Broad Oak comprised two distinct nuclear settlements of about equal size, Broad Oak to the north and Hatfield Heath to the south.[19] The remaining two parishes of the Hatfield group are Great and Little Hallingbury, the first retaining a population of around 650, the latter some 550.[20] The population of the Hatfield group of parishes remained relatively constant throughout the central twenty-year period of this study (1861–81), with small gains in Little Hallingbury being counterbalanced by small losses in Great Hallingbury.[21]

The economic and occupational structure of the two parish groups was dominated by agriculture, with arable farming being particularly important. The Dengie area was characterized by low-lying heavy clays, accompanied by large stretches of coastal marsh, often turned to grass and traditionally used for fattening livestock for the London markets.[22] In favourable conditions the clays gave good returns, yet the intensive capital and labour investment required to work them made the land vulnerable to adverse conditions.[23] Consequently, the series of wet summers between 1875 and 1879 were particularly devastating for the heavy clay lands of Essex. Indeed, Lord Ernle's gloomy appraisal of British agriculture during the following period of depression, although generally misleading, is in part a fair reflection of the situation in the south-eastern part of Essex.[24] The onslaught of depression in the 1880s brought with it falling land prices, depressed rental values, and the abandonment of farms.[25] In comparison, the lighter soils of the Hatfield area made it less vulnerable to the agricultural depression. Although arable farming was the dominant form of agriculture, it was possible to diversify into horticulture and animal husbandry. Indeed such activities increased as declines in grain prices made arable farming less attractive.[26] Apart from agriculture, the largest settlement in each area, Southminster and Hatfield Broad Oak respectively, acted as a local service centre, and consequently offered limited employment in trade and traditional craft occupations.[27] Yet any form of rural industry was absent from both areas. The land was the ultimate source of most income and employment.

DATA AND METHODS

The principal sources in this study are census enumerators' books of 1861, 1871 and 1881.[28] The nineteenth-century census is, of course, the only source available which systematically provides a complete enumeration of parish populations. Unlike other sources which have often been used to study migration patterns, for example, settlement examinations and apprenticeship records,[29] the census records all age groups, and of particular importance for this study, individuals are identified within their residential familial context.[30] Ever since the pioneering studies of Ravenstein, census information has been used to examine patterns of migration, at both an aggregated national and local level.[31] Within this corpus of work there has been a marked concentration on the birthplace information provided by the census and the study of 'lifetime' migration through the comparison of place of enumeration and place of birth.[32] Clearly, such a method has serious limitations. In examining lifetime migration one is in effect investigating two cross-sections, two days in a given individual's life; the day of birth and the day (or night) of the census, a migrant being defined as someone whose location changed between the two days.

Consequently, if an individual had moved after birth yet returned again by the time of the census enumeration this movement would go unrecorded. Equally, for those who had apparently moved after birth, nothing is known about subsequent movements, or their timing. Thus, one does not know if an individual moved directly from their place of birth to the place of enumeration, or at what age.[33] In addition, the analysis of lifetime migration only provides information on migration into an area and fails to examine those individuals, both natives and non-natives, moving out of an area. This, of course, is a major failing if the area under examination was one characterized predominantly by outward migration, as was the case for many rural areas of late nineteenth-century England and Wales.

A more appropriate method for the study of migration is to generate longitudinal records by linking the individuals recorded in one census year to those of the next. By doing this it is possible to observe those entering and leaving the study area during the intervening time period. However, the method is still not ideal since, in the English case, national censuses are only taken every ten years. Therefore, the age at which movement takes place in or out of the parish can only be calculated to within plus or minus five years.[34] Yet despite this drawback, as will be demonstrated in this chapter, the generation of longitudinal records provides a useful insight to the process of migration at both the individual and family level, one which is unobtainable from other sources.

There is little need to provide a lengthy description of the method of linking census data since a detailed description is provided elsewhere.[35] However, before discussing the results of the linking exercise, some basic points need to be made. First, it is essential to link not only one census with the following, but also to include the records of intervening marriages and deaths, in order that females changing their surname, and individuals dying, are properly identified and not mistaken as migrating away from the parish. This need is frustrated by the fact that access to the civil registers of births, marriages and deaths established in 1837 is officially barred, with the result that one has to rely on ecclesiastical parish registers instead. Clearly, due to problems of under-registration and the general failure to record non-conformists, in some cases these are not a totally satisfactory substitute.[36]

In order to test the degree of burial under-registration in this study, the number of linked burials was compared to the likely number expected as estimated from the construction of regional life-tables using information published in the annual reports of the Registrar General's office.[37] This exercise suggests that although all age groups were under-registered to a minor degree, significant levels of burial under-registration relate only to those aged less than 5.

MIGRATION: GENERAL TRENDS

The overall levels of migration for the two areas derived from the linking exercise are given in Table 6.1. This indicates that migration was more frequent in Dengie than Hatfield, and in both areas more important among females. These broad trends were true of both movement in and out of the study areas. The table also shows that the figures for the two study areas are broadly comparable with similar data available from other nineteenth-century census linking exercises, which suggest that a turnover rate of around 50 per cent of the population over ten years is not unreasonable. However, it should be noted that in comparison to figures available for the Essex parish of Elmdon, situated only some 25 km to the north of the Hatfield area, the two study areas appear to record quite high rates of out-migration.[38] Although it is not intended to discuss information relating to the individual parishes of the two study areas in detail, it is worth pointing out that the rates of migration in parishes of the Hatfield group were quite evenly distributed, while in Dengie the two smaller parishes (St Lawrence and Asheldham) displayed higher than average rates of migration, supporting Horn's suggestion that the more rural an area, the more likely it was to experience an outflow of population.[39]

In both regions there appears to be a relationship between the proportions of incomers and out-migration.[40] High rates of out-migration are matched by high rates of incomers and vice versa, a relationship evident at both a regional and parish level.[41] This situation may be suggestive of the existence of some notion of an optimum population size in which the levels of movers and incomers attempt to balance themselves. Thus a community can only sustain a large number of incomers if an appropriate number of vacancies have been created by those moving out. Just such a relationship was observed in Laslett's pioneering turnover study of seventeenth-century Clayworth, in which he states:

> what impresses the observer is continuity in the number of husbandmen and the number of labourers, and the continuity in the list of craftsmen and shopkeepers to be found in the village. When one man got old, or went to the bad and gave up or died, he was

Table 6.1 Movers, stayers and incomers in selected villages

Place	Date	Pop. 1	Movers G%	Movers N%	Stayers G%	Stayers N%	Incomers Pop. 2	Incomers %
Hatfield (males)	1861–71	1549	43	41	57	53	1634	25
Hatfield (females)	1861–71	1519	55	51	45	42	1522	32
Hatfield (males)	1871–81	1634	44	39	56	51	1582	21
Hatfield (females)	1871–81	1522	53	48	47	43	1551	30
Dengie (males)	1861–71	1181	55	51	45	42	1353	36
Dengie (females)	1861–71	1040	58	54	42	39	1138	36
Dengie (males)	1871–81	1353	61	58	39	36	1122	30
Dengie (females)	1871–81	1138	61	57	39	36	1029	33
Ashworthy[1]	1841–51	1096	35	31	65	59	1904	19
Laxton, Notts[2]	1851–61	534	48	42	52	46	500	26
Elmdon, Essex[3]	1851–61	528	40	36	59	52	520	19
Bolton Abbey, Yorks[4]	1851–61	519	45	39	55	49	506	34
	1861–71	506	49	45	51	47	484	35
Brenchley, Kent[5]	1851–61	2705	64	60	36	34	2867	51
	1861–71	2867	68	65	32	30	3365	57
Puddletown, Dorset[6]	1851–61	1296	59	54	41	38	1227	48
	1861–71	1227	61	56	39	36	1254	41
	1871–81	1254	67	62	33	30	1175	43
Clayworth, Notts[7]	1676–88	401	49	38	51	39	412	40
Cogenhoe, Northants[7]	1616–28	185	49	45	51	47	180	36

Sources: [1] = Williams, 1963, p. 128; [2] = Beckett and Foulds, 1985, p. 452; [3] = Robin, 1980, p. 190; [4] = Aslett et al., 1984, pp. 8–9; [5] = Wojciechowska-Kibble, unpublished, 1984, pp. 266–7; [6] = Wolniakowski, unpublished, 1976, pp. 93–4; [7] = Laslett, 1977, p. 98.

Notes: All the figures in this table have been recalculated from the original sources to account for migration gross and net of mortality. Research in publications for which the situation regarding mortality is unclear have been omitted.

Pop. 1 = Initial census population
Pop. 2 = Secondary census population
G% = Percentage gross of mortality
N% = Percentage net of mortality

replaced, so that there tended always to be a cooper at Clayworth, or two or three tailors, a butcher and a blacksmith.[42]

The operation of such a model of balanced migration flows seems logical if under normal circumstances the availability of resources, in terms of employment and housing stock, are finite. People simply cannot move into an area unless there is accommodation to house them and work to employ them. Thus the volume of incomers will be dependent on the volume of vacancies created. If new jobs are not being created and houses are not made available, then vacancies will only result from individuals moving away. However, if such a model of infill is to operate successfully and is not simply the result of chance, it would require, and indeed suggests, the existence of an extensive communication network to relay the relevant information of supply and demand. It is plausible to expect that family and kin connections could have fulfilled such a role.

From Table 6.1 it can also be seen that in the second period, 1871–81, in both Dengie and Hatfield, the ratio between incomers and outgoers increases in favour of those moving out. It is a simple point, yet one of great importance. Traditionally observers of the timing, nature and extent of nineteenth-century rural depopulation have concentrated on explaining the phenomenon by increased levels of rural out-migration.[43] This is not entirely surprising since such studies have concentrated on aggregate rural population changes. However, large-scale migration in rural areas was not new to the nineteenth century, rather it was a long-established phenomenon. Consequently, prior to the period of major depopulation, rural areas had always been characterized by a movement of people away from the parish. Yet as fast as these people moved out they were replaced by people moving into the parish. The process of migration was two-way, and can be seen as a mechanism for balancing the chief resource of the pre-mechanized countryside, people. It was a way of accounting for natural population imbalances: evening out sex ratios; finding a potential marriage partner, learning a trade or skill, taking up an inheritance.[44] The evidence from this study suggests that the significant transformation was not so much an increased tendency for people to move out of a parish, but rather a decreased tendency for people to move into the parish. Consequently, it appears that an important and overlooked feature of nineteenth-century rural depopulation was not the numbers of people moving out of rural parishes – there was nothing new about this – but instead the lack of people moving into rural parishes. This was the real change. In this case the prime cause of nineteenth-century rural depopulation can be seen not as significantly increased levels of out-migration from rural parishes, but simply a change in the direction of the migration flows. Rather than being a two-way process in which movements out of a parish were counter-balanced by movements in, a change in the destination of migrations from similar rural parishes to urban areas would invariably lead to depopulation.

LIFE-CYCLE MIGRATION

An initial indication of the participation of families in the migration process can be gained by studying the age profile of migrants. The age-specific migration rates for Dengie and Hatfield, both incomers and movers, depicted in Figures 6.1 and 6.2, show that although the overall volume of movement was dominated by young adolescents, migration was not restricted to these age groups alone. The situation was not one, as has been suggested by other researchers, in which the propensity to migration for those over 10 was in inverse linear correlation with age.[45] Rather, the pattern of age-specific mobility relates to an inverse s-shape or sigmoid function.[46] This overall feature is true of both incomers and movers, thus re-emphasizing the notion of compensatory flows. A low point in terms of migration occurs at around age 8 to 9. After this migration rates rise sharply, peaking at around age 20, then dropping steadily to about age 50, before flattening out and then increasing again for those aged 60 plus. Differences can be identified between males and females, in particular with females experiencing more marked and slightly earlier migration peaks in the adolescent age groups, yet the basic sigmoid function is still retained. The lack of a total collapse of migration rates after the peak in the late teens/early twenties, suggests that migration did not cease with marriage, but was maintained at reduced levels, reaching a low point towards the end of the child rearing period, to increase again in the latter stages of life. This last feature may be an indication of return migration following 'retirement', and may help to explain why researchers undertaking census-linking exercises often encounter a surplus of burials which cannot be linked to the previous census enumeration, even if taken only a few years previously.[47]

To gain a fuller understanding of the familial character of migration it is profitable to adopt a life-cycle approach. Taking only the core family members – heads of households, wives and unmarried children – the percentage of the family remaining after the relevant ten-year period has been calculated for various sized family groups by the age of the family head (Table 6.2).[48] It should be pointed out that the percentages in this table are calculated taking into account any deaths that may have occurred within the family, with individuals who died, and whose death was traced, being counted as stayers rather than movers. Consequently, in an extreme case, if all members of a family died in the ten-year time interval between the censuses the family would be counted as 100 per cent stable.[49]

Taking first the column and row totals in Table 6.2, it can be seen

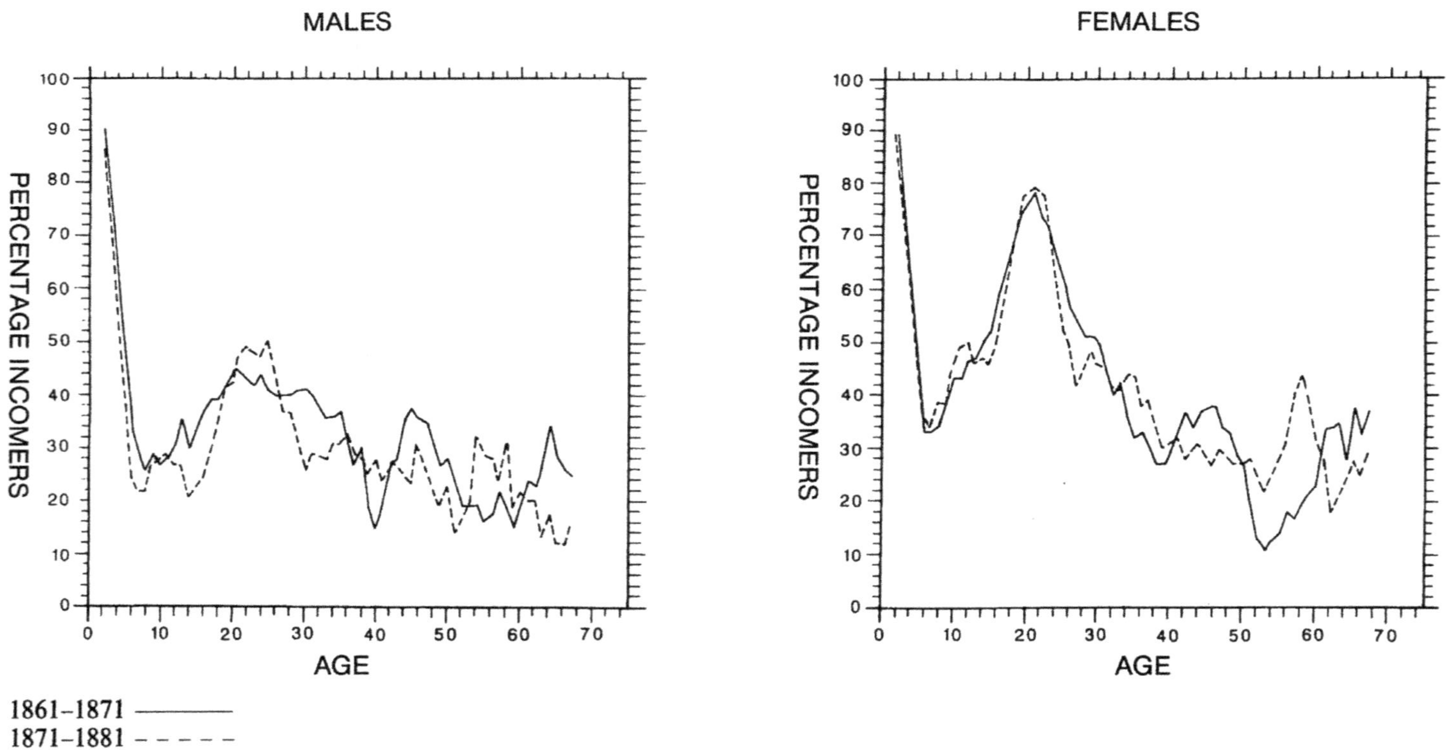

Figure 6.1a Incomers by age and sex: Hatfield 1861–81
Source: Census enumerators' books
Note: Curves are plotted as a nine-year moving average

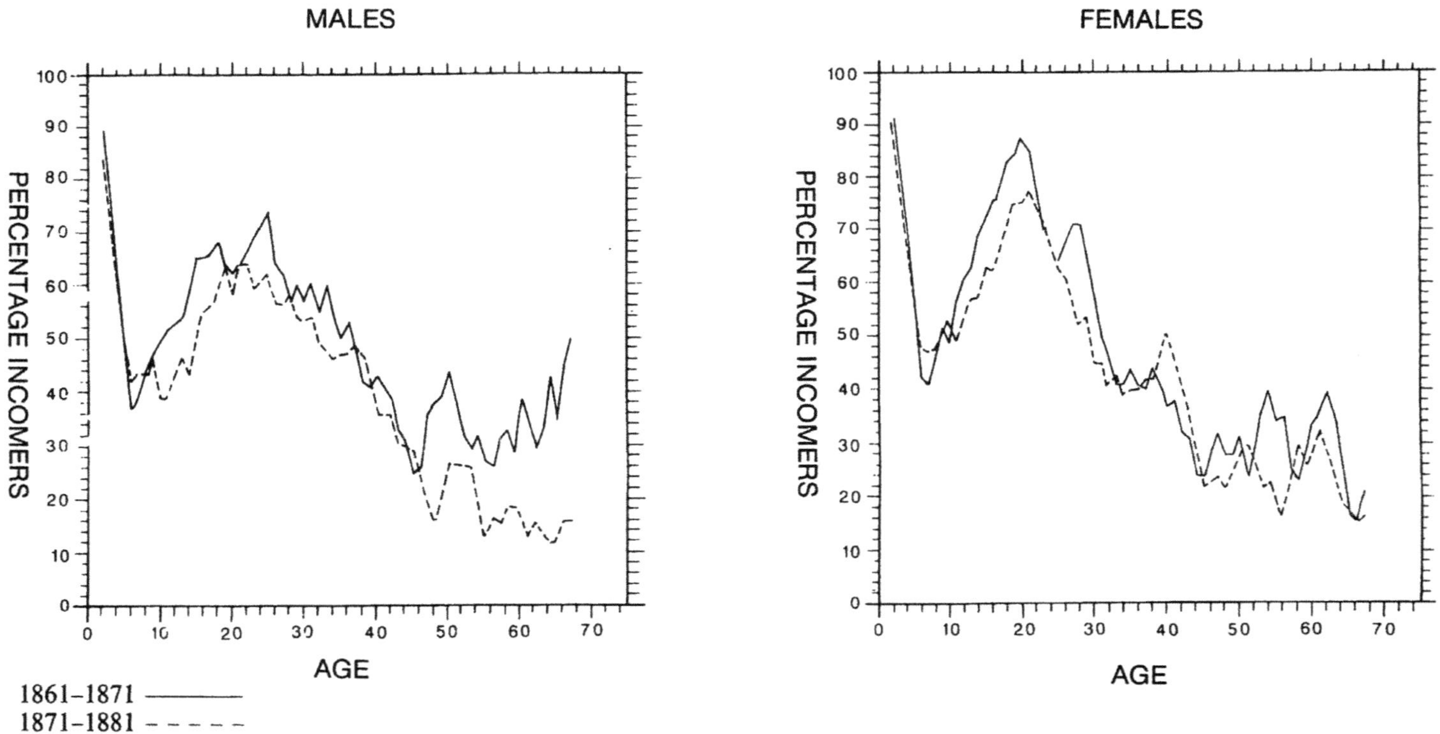

Figure 6.1b Incomers by age and sex: Dengie 1861–81
Source: Census enumerators' books
Note: Curves are plotted as a nine-year moving average

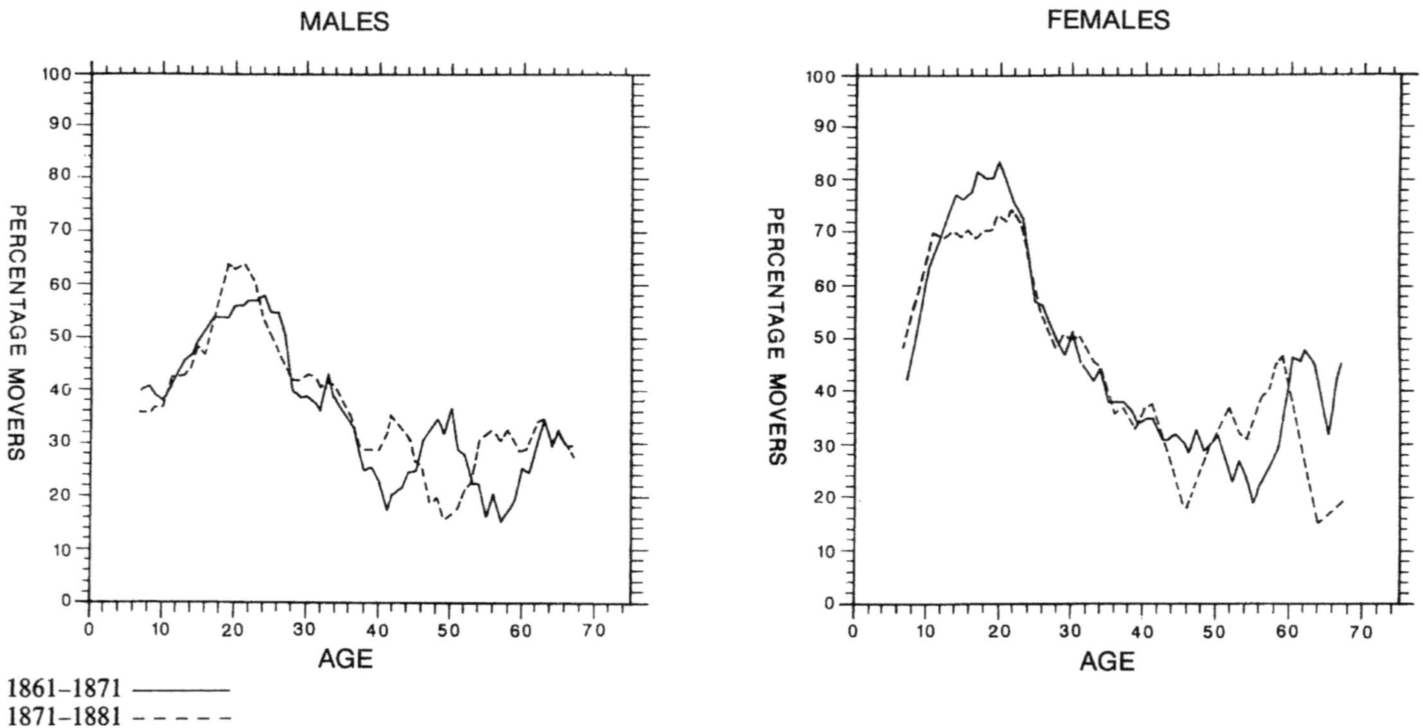

Figure 6.2a Movers by age and sex: Hatfield 1861–81
Source: Census enumerators' books
Note: Curves are plotted as a nine-year moving average

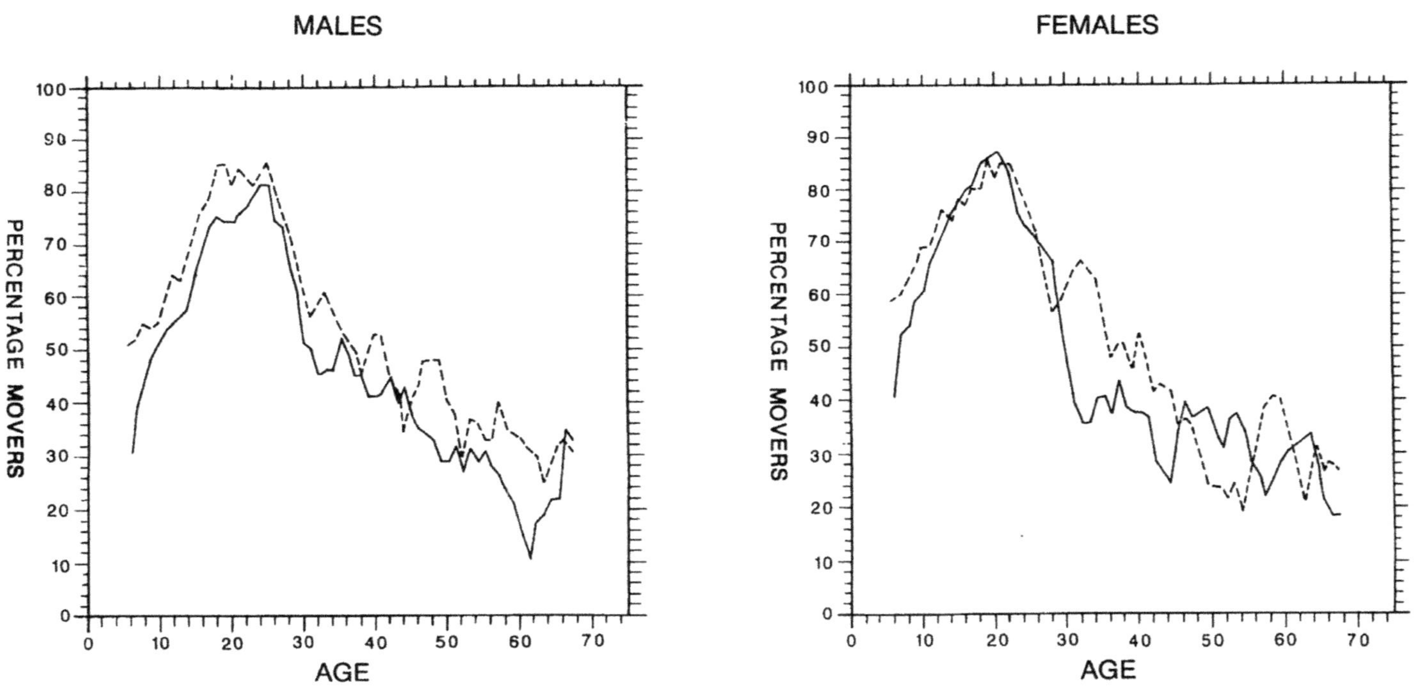

1861–1871 ———
1871–1881 - - - - -

Figure 6.2b Movers by age and sex: Dengie 1861–81
Source: Census enumerators' books
Note: Curves are plotted as a nine-year moving average

Table 6.2 Proportions remaining in family groupings: Hatfield and Dengie, 1861–81

a) Hatfield

	1861–71 Family size										1871–81 Family size									
	2–3		4–5		6–7		8+		Total		2–3		4–5		6–7		8+		Total	
Age of family head	(%)	(n)	(%)	(n)	(%)	(n)	(%)	(n)	(%)	(n)	(%)	(n)	(%)	(n)	(%)	(n)	(%)	(n)	(%)	(n)
25–34	67.4	46	59.1	30	66.7	1	.	.	64.1	77	51.5	45	70.4	32	38.1	7	.	.	57.6	84
35–44	63.9	30	61.3	35	61.7	41	60.6	16	62.0	122	62.6	37	50.3	46	60.9	42	58.4	11	57.5	136
45–54	68.1	35	52.9	26	50.6	28	51.7	33	56.4	122	64.7	34	57.8	29	57.9	45	53.0	25	58.7	133
55–64	65.2	55	63.8	31	48.6	19	47.9	11	60.4	116	48.0	42	68.3	25	51.0	16	54.5	10	54.7	93
65+	49.2	87	61.5	19	74.2	6	75.0	1	52.8	113	47.4	98	49.2	27	55.6	6	20.0	2	47.8	133
TOTAL	60.3	253	59.8	141	56.7	95	53.7	61	58.8	550	52.7	256	58.3	159	56.7	116	53.2	48	55.1	579

b) Dengie

	1861–71 Family size										1871–81 Family size									
	2–3		4–5		6–7		8+		Total		2–3		4–5		6–7		8+		Total	
Age of family head	(%)	(n)	(%)	(n)	(%)	(n)	(%)	(n)	(%)	(n)	(%)	(n)	(%)	(n)	(%)	(n)	(%)	(n)	(%)	(n)
25–34	60.4	32	53.2	17	50.0	1	.	.	57.8	50	35.0	41	35.1	22	11.1	3	75.0	1	34.5	67
35–44	59.6	38	50.1	38	43.9	26	48.6	8	51.8	110	39.1	23	32.9	34	44.5	31	36.2	13	38.3	101
45–54	61.1	30	60.9	35	47.1	31	36.9	19	53.3	115	56.5	28	41.6	28	42.9	28	54.8	24	48.7	108
55–64	66.2	38	39.7	20	68.0	7	62.5	2	58.4	67	55.6	36	41.9	24	47.0	14	42.5	8	48.8	82
65+	36.0	43	56.7	12	30.6	3	.	.	40.0	58	44.9	68	39.1	12	65.0	2	62.5	1	44.7	84
TOTAL	55.8	181	52.6	122	47.3	68	41.9	29	52.4	400	45.7	196	37.8	121	43.6	78	48.2	47	43.4	442

Source: Census enumerators' books.
Note: This table includes only male-headed families.

that in relation to male heads in both regions in the period 1861–71, the proportion of family members remaining declines inversely to the size of the family. Thus, the larger the family the lower the number of family members persisting. This relationship is not entirely surprising since the larger the family the more members it contained who were liable to move, the greater also the potential pressures of accommodation, and, of course, the greater the chance of having older children of an age to move away, to work and live elsewhere. Yet there is a marked difference between the two regions. Not only does Dengie return lower rates of persistence, the decline in persistence with family size is both greater and sharper. Over the range of family sizes, in Dengie the rates fell steadily by some 14 per cent (56–42 per cent), while in Hatfield the decline was by some 6 per cent only (60–54 per cent). Equally, in Hatfield the persistence levels of those families with two or three persons were much the same as those sized four or five. Only in the case of quite large families does the persistence rate decline. However, by 1871–81 the expected relationship between persistence and family size was disrupted. For example, in Hatfield the smallest families, those with two or three members, recorded the lowest rates of persistence, and in Dengie the largest families recorded the highest rates of persistence (48 per cent). Despite this change, the information in this study clearly contradicts the suggestion put forward by other researchers that persistency tended to increase with the size of the offspring group with childless families exhibiting low levels of persistence.[50]

Turning attention to the age of the household head, in the first period both regions experience high levels of persistence in the youngest age group (25–34), and the lowest rates of persistence in the oldest age group (65+). Apart from these two features the figures for the two regions are very mixed. However, the age group 45–54 does appear to be a low point in persistence in both regions. In comparison, by the second period structural changes in the pattern of migration appear to have taken place. In Hatfield the age group 45–54 displays the highest levels of persistence, although not much greater than the two age groups 25–44. In Dengie, although the levels of migration for the 65+ age group are quite low, there is a tendency for persistence to increase with age, the youngest age group 25–34 being the least stable. The most important factor to emerge from these patterns is that the increased levels of migration which occurred during the second half of the period investigated in this study were accompanied by structural changes in migration patterns.

Although the small numbers involved make it difficult to demonstrate any significant patterns, it is possible to detect further evidence in support of a structural change in the familial character of migration by an investigation of the individual cells of Table 6.2. Particularly striking are the high levels of persistence displayed by families of 6+ and headed by individuals in the 55–64 age group in Dengie in the first period. Although there were only nine families in these two groups, this was one of the most stable sections of Dengie society, and one of the few occasions when families in Hatfield were more mobile than their Dengie counterparts. The next most stable section of society in Dengie 1861–71 was the band of 65 families of between two and five members headed by a 45–54-year-old, returning persistence rates of around 61 per cent. This compares with a similar band of 86 families in Hatfield of the same size, yet headed by older men (55–64), who had a persistence rate of some 64 per cent. Yet by the second period these stable sections of society had disappeared in both regions. In Dengie all age groups and family sizes were relatively unstable, while in Hatfield a broad band of 108 families with between two and seven members appear quite stable: in the case of those families headed by a male aged 45–54 recording a persistency level of around 60 per cent.

The relatively high levels of family movement experienced in households headed by elderly persons may lead one to speculate that the death of a prominent family member, the head or perhaps a spouse, might act as a promoter of movement, perhaps as a result of changed employment needs. Indeed, in a recent study of the Berkshire parish of Binfield, 1790–1801, Escott suggests that death of the household head was an important influencing factor in residential mobility.[51] However, the evidence from this study is less conclusive. In both regions families affected by death experienced migration rates roughly the same as those unaffected.[52] Indeed, in the case of younger-headed families migration levels often tend to be lower for those affected by death. However, it must be pointed out that in the Binfield example many of the residential moves made following a mortality were made within the parish itself. If it were possible to include such moves in this study then death might appear as a more important promoter of migration. It may be that although death created the necessity to move, it was also a time when it was beneficial to be close to one's kin, neighbours and friends.[53]

THE MIGRATION OF FAMILIES

Although one can see broad similarities in the age and sex profiles of migrants across both study regions, the structure of movement in terms of the types of families affected, their size and position in the life cycle, appears diverse. However, although informative, the data in Table 6.2 do not give a clear indication of the actual number of families moving or staying in their entirety. For example, a persistence figure of say 50 per cent could be made up of half of the families staying in their entirety and the other half with all the family members leaving. Details of the percentage of families going or staying in their entirety, by the size of the family and the age of the head are given in Table 6.3.

Taking first the households of Dengie 1861–71, it can be seen that small families (two or three members) were not only the most stable, but also the most mobile. However, the types of families involved in these movements were at the opposite ends of the life cycle spectrum. Those staying were headed by younger men, while those leaving were headed by older men, indeed only those families headed by the most elderly (65+) were particularly mobile in this family size bracket.[54] As family size increases the tendency for families to stay decreases, yet this is balanced by 'mixed' moves; that is to say some, but not all, of the family members moving. This trend is not surprising since the mixed moves invariably represent offspring leaving home as the head of the household ages and the size of the family increases. However, what is perhaps less surprising is that the percentage of families with all members leaving does not show a similar tendency to decline with family size, the second highest proportion of total movers being recorded for the largest of family sizes. Indeed, although the most mobile are small families, invariably headed by older men, and to a lesser degree those under 45, whole families appear likely to migrate throughout the life cycle, with between a quarter and a third of all families being affected.

By the second period much of this pattern had changed as a result of the higher levels of migration. There was an increase in the volume of complete families moving throughout the life cycle, although this was especially marked in the case of those families headed by those aged less than 45. Overall the proportion of families headed by men aged 25–34 moving away in their entirety increased over the two periods from 34 per cent 1861–71, to 60 per cent 1871–81, while those headed by men aged 35–44 increased from 35 to 47 per cent respectively. Consequently, in the second of the two study periods, of those families that stayed in their entirety, some 80 per cent were small (two or three), and of these the dominant group were those headed by more elderly men, some 45 per cent of the total 'staying' families being small and headed by those over 55.

Despite the difference in the overall volume in movement between

Table 6.3 Movement of families: Hatfield and Dengie, 1861–81

a) Hatfield 1861–71

	Family size													
	2–3						4–5							
Age of family head	*All gone* (%)	(n)	*All stay* (%)	(n)	*Mixed* (%)	(n)	*All gone* (%)	(n)	*All stay* (%)	(n)	*Mixed* (%)	(n)	*All gone* (%)	(n)
25–34	30.4	14	65.2	30	4.3	2	30.0	9	36.7	11	33.3	10	.	.
35–44	26.7	8	53.3	16	20.0	6	28.6	10	40.0	14	31.4	11	17.1	7
45–54	25.7	9	57.1	20	17.1	6	26.9	7	19.2	5	53.6	14	17.9	5
55–64	27.3	15	56.4	31	16.4	9	12.9	4	25.8	8	61.3	19	10.5	2
65+	46.0	40	43.7	38	10.3	9	10.5	2	21.1	4	68.4	13	.	.
Total	34.0	86	53.4	135	12.6	32	22.7	32	29.8	42	47.5	67	14.7	14

(b) Dengie 1861–71

	Family size													
	2–3						4–5							
Age of family head	*All gone* (%)	(n)	*All stay* (%)	(n)	*Mixed* (%)	(n)	*All gone* (%)	(n)	*All stay* (%)	(n)	*Mixed* (%)	(n)	*All gone* (%)	(n)
25–34	34.4	11	53.1	17	12.5	4	35.3	6	35.3	6	29.4	5	.	.
35–44	36.8	14	55.3	21	7.9	3	36.8	14	28.9	11	34.2	13	26.9	7
45–54	30.0	9	50.0	15	20.0	6	17.1	6	28.6	10	54.3	19	32.3	10
55–64	23.7	9	50.0	19	26.3	10	30.0	6	5.0	1	65.0	13	.	.
65+	60.5	26	30.2	13	9.3	4	16.7	2	16.7	2	66.7	8	.	.
Total	38.1	69	47.0	85	14.9	27	27.9	34	24.6	30	47.5	58	25.0	17

c) Hatfield 1871–81

	Family size													
	2–3						4–5							
Age of family head	*All gone* (%)	(n)	*All stay* (%)	(n)	*Mixed* (%)	(n)	*All gone* (%)	(n)	*All stay* (%)	(n)	*Mixed* (%)	(n)	*All gone* (%)	(n)
25–34	44.4	20	44.4	20	11.1	5	25.0	8	56.3	18	18.8	6	57.1	4
35–44	32.4	12	54.1	20	13.5	5	34.8	16	23.9	11	41.3	19	21.4	9
45–54	29.4	10	55.9	19	14.7	5	20.7	6	17.2	5	62.1	18	15.6	7
55–64	40.5	17	33.3	14	26.2	11	8.0	2	32.0	8	60.0	15	12.5	2
65+	49.0	48	42.9	42	8.2	8	22.2	6	14.8	5	63.0	17	33.3	2
Total	41.8	107	44.9	115	13.3	34	23.9	38	28.9	46	47.2	75	20.7	24

d) Dengie 1871–81

	Family size													
	2–3						4–5							
Age of family head	*All gone* (%)	(n)	*All stay* (%)	(n)	*Mixed* (%)	(n)	*All gone* (%)	(n)	*All stay* (%)	(n)	*Mixed* (%)	(n)	*All gone* (%)	(n)
25–34	63.4	26	31.7	13	4.9	2	54.5	12	22.7	5	22.7	5	66.7	2
35–44	52.2	12	30.4	7	17.4	4	55.9	19	17.6	6	26.5	9	32.3	10
45–54	35.7	10	46.4	13	17.9	5	35.7	10	10.7	3	53.6	15	39.3	11
55–64	36.1	13	41.7	15	22.2	8	29.2	7	4.2	1	66.7	16	7.1	1
65+	51.5	35	39.7	27	8.8	6	30.8	4	7.7	1	61.5	8	.	.
Total	49.0	96	38.3	75	12.8	25	43.0	52	13.2	16	43.8	53	30.8	24

Table 6.3 (contd.)

a) Hatfield 1861–71

Family size										Total					
6–7						8+									
All stay		Mixed		All gone		All stay		Mixed		All gone		All stay		Mixed	
(%)	(n)	(%)	(n)	(%)	(n)	(%)	(n)	(%)	(n)	(%)	(n)	(%)	(n)	(%)	(n)
.	.	100.0	1	.	.	.	.	.	.	29.9	23	53.2	41	16.9	13
12.2	5	70.7	29	18.8	3	6.3	1	75.0	12	23.0	28	29.5	36	47.5	58
.	.	82.1	23	18.2	6	3.0	1	78.8	26	22.1	27	21.3	26	56.6	69
5.3	1	84.2	16	9.1	1	.	.	90.9	10	19.0	22	34.5	40	46.6	54
.	.	100.0	6	.	.	.	.	100.0	1	37.2	42	37.2	42	25.7	29
6.3	6	78.9	75	16.4	10	3.3	2	80.3	49	25.8	142	33.6	185	40.5	223

b) Dengie 1861–71

Family size										Total					
6–7						8+									
All stay		Mixed		All gone		All stay		Mixed		All gone		All stay		Mixed	
(%)	(n)	(%)	(n)	(%)	(n)	(%)	(n)	(%)	(n)	(%)	(n)	(%)	(n)	(%)	(n)
.	.	100.0	1	.	.	.	.	.	.	34.0	17	46.0	23	20.0	10
3.8	1	69.2	18	37.5	3	.	.	62.5	5	34.5	38	30.0	33	35.5	39
9.7	3	58.1	18	31.6	6	.	.	68.4	13	27.0	31	24.3	28	48.7	56
.	.	100.0	7	.	.	.	.	100.0	2	22.4	15	29.9	20	37.8	32
.	.	100.0	3	.	.	.	.	.	.	48.3	28	25.9	15	25.9	15
5.9	4	69.1	47	31.0	9	.	.	69.0	20	32.2	129	29.7	119	38.0	152

c) Hatfield 1871–81

Family size										Total					
6–7						8+									
All stay		Mixed		All gone		All stay		Mixed		All gone		All stay		Mixed	
(%)	(n)	(%)	(n)	(%)	(n)	(%)	(n)	(%)	(n)	(%)	(n)	(%)	(n)	(%)	(n)
28.6	2	14.3	1	.	.	.	.	.	.	38.1	32	47.6	40	14.3	12
21.4	9	57.1	24	9.1	1	.	.	90.9	10	27.9	38	29.4	40	42.6	58
11.1	5	73.3	33	16.0	4	.	.	84.0	21	20.3	27	21.8	29	57.9	77
.	.	87.5	14	20.0	2	.	.	80.0	8	24.7	23	23.7	22	51.6	48
16.7	1	50.0	3	50.0	1	.	.	50.0	1	42.9	57	35.3	47	21.8	28
14.7	17	64.7	75	16.7	8	.	.	83.3	40	30.6	177	30.7	178	38.7	224

d) Dengie 1871–81

Family size										Total					
6–7						8+									
All stay		Mixed		All gone		All stay		Mixed		All gone		All stay		Mixed	
(%)	(n)	(%)	(n)	(%)	(n)	(%)	(n)	(%)	(n)	(%)	(n)	(%)	(n)	(%)	(n)
.	.	33.3	1	.	.	.	.	100.0	1	59.7	40	26.9	18	13.4	9
6.5	2	61.3	19	46.2	6	15.4	2	38.5	5	46.5	47	16.8	17	36.6	37
.	.	60.7	17	12.5	3	.	.	87.5	21	31.5	34	14.8	16	53.7	58
.	.	92.9	13	25.0	2	.	.	75.0	6	28.0	23	19.5	16	52.4	43
.	.	100.0	2	.	.	.	.	100.0	1	46.4	39	33.3	28	20.2	17
2.6	2	66.7	52	23.4	11	4.3	2	72.3	34	41.4	183	21.5	95	37.1	164

Source: Census enumerators' books

the two regions, it is interesting that in the first period the pattern of family migration in Hatfield was quite similar to that of Dengie. The overall number of families staying was a little larger than in Dengie, and the overall number of movers a little lower, yet the *structure* of the family movement was much the same. The proportions of movers and stayers was in both cases greatest in the smallest-sized family group (two or three), yet it was predominantly the younger families who were staying and the older who were going. Proportions staying also decreased with family size, and the movement of entire families occurred throughout the life cycle, although in lower numbers than Dengie in the case of larger families (more than six). However, the change between the periods experienced in Dengie did not occur in Hatfield. An increase in the proportion of families moving entirely did take place in Hatfield, yet this was accompanied by very little structural change. Much of the increase took place in families headed by younger men (25–34), yet this primarily affected only the smaller families, relatively large increases in moving families also occurring in those families headed by older men over 50. Indeed, the proportion of families staying in their entirety in the broad-based band headed by those aged 35–54 remained constant throughout the two periods.

Although little can be stated concerning female-headed households/families due to the small numbers involved, a higher proportion of female-headed families moved in their entirety than did male-headed ones. With the general increase of mobility in Dengie in the second period this difference is less well defined, although in this region younger female heads (under 54) moved with their families more readily than their male counterparts. This may reflect a lack of employment opportunities enabling lone females to support a family, a lack which appears to have been greater in Dengie than in Hatfield.

When the data are broken down into occupational categories (Table 6.4) some interesting features emerge. In Hatfield, 1861–71, farmers display the greatest tendency to move as a complete family and labourers the least, yet there is little variation in the level of moving families between the three key occupation groups (23.7 per cent). However, farmers tend to experience less 'mixed' movement than the other groups, recording also the highest level of families staying intact, some 40 per cent of families compared to a third in the case of labourers and craftsmen. Another difference can be seen by the fact that total family movement peaks in the age group 45–54 for farmers (31 per cent) yet occurs rather later for labourers and craftsmen (aged 60+). Yet the movement of entire families is also important for younger age cohorts, particularly for craftsmen and to a lesser degree for labourers. Mixed family movements appear more important for labourers than the other two occupational groups, especially in the 35+ age groups.

By the second period the farmers of Hatfield had undergone a significant change. The proportion of families moving as a whole increases to 39 per cent, with the other two occupations remaining around a quarter. Particularly striking is the fact that this increase in family migration was achieved not at the expense of mixed moves, but rather of those staying.

In Dengie, 1861–71, the proportion of family migration was higher than in Hatfield for farmers (36 per cent) and labourers (33 per cent), but not so for craftsmen (25 per cent). Yet farming families remained intact to a much lesser extent than in Hatfield, with mixed migrations being rather more important. Indeed, with only a fifth of all families staying intact in Dengie, farmers recorded lower proportions of stayers than both labourers (27 per cent), and more especially craftsmen (41 per cent). For labourers family migration was most prominent in the case of younger heads (25–44), while the reverse was true for craftsmen. In the second period, although increased levels of family movement were recorded for all three occupations, craftsmen witnessed a dramatic turnround, with the result that in 1871–81 all three occupations recorded similar levels of total movement (41.3 per cent). This increase in the family migration of craftsmen was particularly noticeable in the case of younger headed families, labourers also experiencing increased numbers of young families migrating as a whole. In comparison, the family migration of farmers was distributed throughout all age cohorts. Instead, the most dramatic change affecting farming families over the two periods in Dengie was the virtual collapse of families staying in their entirety.

It can be seen, therefore, that the levels of family movement increased over time for all occupational groups in both regions, and that generally the levels of total family movement were relatively evenly distributed between the various occupations within the regions, especially in Hatfield between 1861–71 and Dengie, 1871–81. Increases in the levels of young families moving occurred in the second period, primarily in the case of labourers in Dengie and craftsmen in both regions. Farmers displayed distinctive patterns in both regions, the proportion of families staying intact dropping dramatically in both regions and the numbers moving in total rising sharply in Hatfield. Together with the feature of migration levels varying almost randomly with the age of the head in both regions, the migratory situation of farmers outlined above may reflect a reaction to the onslaught of

Table 6.4 Movement of families by occupation: Hatfield and Dengie, 1861–81

a) Hatfield

	1861–71							*1871–81*					
Crafts													
Age of family head	*All gone* (%)	(n)	*All stay* (%)	(n)	*Mixed* (%)	(n)	*Age of family head*	*All gone* (%)	(n)	*All stay* (%)	(n)	*Mixed* (%)	(n)
25–34	42.9	3	42.9	3	14.3	1	25–34	50.0	5	50.0	5	.	.
35–44	21.4	3	35.7	5	42.9	6	35–44	26.7	4	26.7	4	46.7	7
45–54	18.2	4	27.3	6	54.5	12	45–54	16.7	3	16.7	3	66.7	12
55–64	10.5	2	31.6	6	57.9	11	55–64	11.1	2	38.9	7	50.0	9
65+	50.0	9	38.9	7	11.1	2	65+	35.7	5	21.4	3	42.9	6
Total	26.2	21	33.7	27	40.0	32	Total	25.3	19	29.3	22	45.3	34
Farmers													
Age of family head	*All gone* (%)	(n)	*All stay* (%)	(n)	*Mixed* (%)	(n)	*Age of family head*	*All gone* (%)	(n)	*All stay* (%)	(n)	*Mixed* (%)	(n)
25–34	.	.	.	.	.	.	25–34	66.7	2	.	.	33.3	1
35–44	25.0	3	66.7	8	8.3	1	35–44	22.2	2	44.4	4	33.3	3
45–54	30.8	4	38.5	5	30.8	4	45–54	41.7	5	25.0	3	33.3	4
55–64	31.3	5	18.8	3	50.0	8	55–64	21.4	3	28.6	4	50.0	7
65+	21.4	3	42.9	6	35.7	5	65+	56.3	9	31.3	5	12.5	2
Total	27.3	15	40.0	22	32.7	18	Total	38.9	21	29.6	16	31.5	17

Labourers

Age of family head	*All gone*		*All stay*		*Mixed*		*Age of family head*	*All gone*		*All stay*		*Mixed*	
	(%)	(n)	(%)	(n)	(%)	(n)		(%)	(n)	(%)	(n)	(%)	(n)
25–34	26.2	16	54.1	33	19.7	12	25–34	24.1	13	57.4	31	18.5	10
35–44	18.3	15	26.8	22	54.9	45	35–44	19.4	18	33.3	31	47.3	44
45–54	21.6	16	16.2	12	62.2	46	45–54	17.8	16	20.0	18	62.2	56
55–64	18.6	13	34.3	24	47.1	33	55–64	24.5	13	18.9	10	56.6	30
65+	32.3	21	35.4	23	32.3	21	65+	41.6	32	36.4	28	22.1	17
Total	23.0	81	32.4	114	44.6	157	Total	25.1	92	32.2	118	42.8	157

Others

Age of family head	*All gone*		*All stay*		*Mixed*		*Age of family head*	*All gone*		*All stay*		*Mixed*	
	(%)	(n)	(%)	(n)	(%)	(n)		(%)	(n)	(%)	(n)	(%)	(n)
25–34	44.4	4	55.6	5	.	.	25–34	72.2	13	22.2	4	5.6	1
35–44	45.0	9	5.0	1	50.0	10	35–44	64.0	16	8.0	2	28.0	7
45–54	30.8	8	19.2	5	50.0	13	45–54	21.7	5	39.1	9	39.1	9
55–64	22.7	5	40.9	9	36.4	8	55–64	58.8	10	11.8	2	29.2	5
65+	50.0	15	30.0	9	20.0	6	65+	41.9	18	39.5	17	18.6	8
Total	38.3	41	27.1	29	34.6	37	Total	49.2	62	27.0	34	23.8	30

Table 6.4 Movement of families by occupation: Hatfield and Dengie, 1861–81 (*contd*)
b) Dengie

Crafts

	1861–71							*1871–81*					
Age of family head	*All gone*		*All stay*		*Mixed*		*Age of family head*	*All gone*		*All stay*		*Mixed*	
	(%)	(n)	(%)	(n)	(%)	(n)		(%)	(n)	(%)	(n)	(%)	(n)
25–34	14.3	1	71.4	5	14.3	1	25–34	61.5	8	38.5	5	.	.
35–44	24.0	6	44.0	11	32.0	8	35–44	64.7	11	23.5	4	11.8	2
45–54	18.8	3	50.0	8	31.3	5	45–54	5.6	1	27.8	5	66.7	12
55–64	30.0	3	20.0	2	50.0	5	55–64	30.0	3	10.0	1	60.0	6
65+	50.0	4	12.5	1	37.5	3	65+	66.7	6	11.1	1	22.2	2
Total	25.8	17	40.9	27	33.3	22	Total	43.3	29	23.9	16	32.8	22

Farmers

Age of family head	*All gone*		*All stay*		*Mixed*		*Age of family head*	*All gone*		*All stay*		*Mixed*	
	(%)	(n)	(%)	(n)	(%)	(n)		(%)	(n)	(%)	(n)	(%)	(n)
25–34	.	.	50.0	1	50.0	1	25–34	.	.	.	.	.	.
35–44	55.6	5	11.1	1	33.3	3	35–44	40.0	2	20.0	1	40.0	2
45–54	30.8	4	23.1	3	46.2	6	45–54	41.7	5	8.3	1	50.0	6
55–64	14.3	1	14.3	1	71.4	5	55–64	36.4	4	9.1	1	54.5	6
65+	50.0	4	25.0	2	25.0	2	65+	45.5	5	9.1	4	45.5	5
Total	35.9	14	20.5	8	43.6	17	Total	41.0	16	10.3	4	48.7	19

Labourers

Age of family head	*All gone* (%)	(n)	*All stay* (%)	(n)	*Mixed* (%)	(n)	*Age of family head*	*All gone* (%)	(n)	*All stay* (%)	(n)	*Mixed* (%)	(n)
25–34	41.9	13	41.9	13	16.1	5	25–34	57.1	24	26.2	11	16.7	7
35–44	31.7	20	28.6	18	39.7	25	35–44	43.9	25	10.5	6	45.6	26
45–54	24.6	16	18.5	12	56.9	37	45–54	36.8	21	10.5	6	52.6	30
55–64	28.2	11	25.6	10	46.2	18	55–64	27.9	12	20.9	9	51.2	22
65+	47.1	16	26.5	9	26.5	9	65+	48.9	23	38.3	18	12.8	6
Total	32.8	76	26.7	62	40.5	94	Total	42.7	105	20.3	50	37.0	91

Others

Age of family head	*All gone* (%)	(n)	*All stay* (%)	(n)	*Mixed* (%)	(n)	*Age of family head*	*All gone* (%)	(n)	*All stay* (%)	(n)	*Mixed* (%)	(n)
25–34	25.0	3	33.3	4	41.7	5	25–34	66.7	10	20.0	3	13.3	2
35–44	52.6	10	21.1	4	26.3	5	35–44	40.7	11	22.2	6	37.0	10
45–54	40.0	10	20.0	5	40.0	10	45–54	33.3	10	13.3	4	53.3	16
55–64	14.3	2	50.0	7	35.7	5	55–64	30.4	7	21.7	5	47.8	11
65+	41.7	5	41.7	5	16.7	2	65+	36.4	8	40.9	9	22.7	5
Total	36.6	30	30.5	25	32.9	27	Total	39.3	46	23.1	27	37.6	44

Source: Census enumerators' books

agricultural depression in the 1870s, increased but almost spasmodic family movement taking place as farms became unrealistic or uneconomic to run. Lastly, in the decade before the agricultural depression the farmers of Hatfield tended to be either stayers or movers, there was very little mixed movement of family members in between these extremes. This suggests that farming families tended to stick together, often all moving or all staying. This pattern stands in contrast not only to the other occupations, but also to the farmers of Dengie. This feature is clearly the result of differential policies in the migration of offspring away from the parental home. Not only did important differences in the process of leaving home occur between households and occupational groups, but fundamental structural changes in the operation of leaving home developed over time as the intensity of migration increased.

CONCLUSION

Many of the data presented in this chapter appear contrary to the fragmented evidence on family movement available from other studies. In particular, in relation to family migration from rural Brenchley, Wojciechowska-Kibble suggests that young childless families were the most dominant.[55] Similarly, in his study of migration from the surrounding rural districts into the growing industrial town of Lynn, Massachusetts, Dublin argues that the migration process was closely linked to family formation, moves often taking place following marriage, yet before the child-rearing stage of family life.[56] Although it is true that over time this type of family movement became more important in the regions examined in this study, clearly it was not the only form of family migration. However, as Darroch is at pains to point out, even in the case of individual movers it is the relationship and interplay between migrant and 'family' that was all-important.[57] It is the case that some migration which is individual in theory is, in reality, familial in nature. Much of this might be economically motivated, with individuals within a family migrating, yet maintaining a single collective 'family budget'. For example Brayshay has suggested evidence for miners emigrating to America from the depressed Cornish mines in the 1860s and 1870s travelling independently in search of a job and a home and later, once a settlement had been secured, sending for their wives and children.[58] Equally, in the same period, Beadle has pointed to unemployed Somerset miners tramping between villages in search of work, living in lodgings, and once settled bringing their families to join them.[59] One could also view seasonal migration, with migrants making journeys in search of temporary employment, in the same light.[60] Whatever the cause of, or motivation for, the movement, the evidence presented in this study echoes the sentiments expressed in the conclusion of Anderson's study of family and kinship in nineteenth-century Preston:

> It may be concluded then that, to a considerable extent, urban and rural kin, or at least some representatives of each and at least in the first generation of migrants, formed one kinship system at a functional level. Migrants moved along kinship channels into slots prepared for them by kin, and advice and assistance flowed along these channels in both directions. These services, and the need for them, plus the absence of any other immediately available source of assistance except for co-villagers seem, at the structural level, to be the main factors encouraging the considerable attempt made by migrants to maintain relationships with kin.[61]

From the information presented in this chapter it is clear that, at least in the case of the two study areas, the process of migration was often part of an integrated familial network, with the familial structure of migration changing in accord with fluctuating economic circumstances. However, despite this trend it is not always easy to distinguish any common pattern across either occupational or social groups, or between the two regions. To a certain extent this situation is similar to that described by Wall in his examination of the idealized nineteenth-century transition from a 'family economy' – in which the family was the unit of production and consumption with the household being a place to work and sleep – to a 'family wage economy' – in which the places of work and residence were separated and family members were wage earners, with the consequence that the constraint of accommodation was the only limit to the number of children who could live at home.[62] This transition was investigated by examining the structures of households in various occupational groups, in terms of the age structure, sex ratio, employment pattern and kin structure of their members, with Wall concluding that:

> Current theorizing about the family economy and the family wage economy proving inadequate for the conceptualization of these complex realities, it was proposed that the concept of an 'adaptive family economy' might prove a more appropriate model for societies where wage labour blended with proto-industrial activity and where some employers had the power to determine not only the place of work but also the residence of the employee.[63]

The key elements to the 'adaptive family economy' model are the varying strategies by which families attempt to 'maximize their economic well-being by diversifying the employments of family members'.[64] Although Wall only investigated the structure of members resident within individual households, it is clear from this study that the process of migration also played a significant role in the planning and flexibility of household economies and structures.

NOTES

1 For a recent survey of literature on historical patterns of migration see P. Clark and D. C. Souden, (eds), *Migration and Society in Early-Modern England*, London, 1987. For a broader view see also J. H. Jackson and L. P. Moch, 'Migration and the social history of modern Europe', *Historical Methods*, 22(1), 1989, pp. 27–36.

2 In the case of nineteenth-century rural parishes examples include: Elmdon, Essex; Laxton, Nottinghamshire; Brenchley, Kent; Bolton Abbey, Yorkshire; 'Ashworthy', a West Country village; and Berwick St James, Wiltshire. See J. Robin, *Elmdon: Continuity and Change in a North-West Essex Village 1861–1964*, Cambridge, 1980, p. 190; J. V. Beckett and T. Foulds, 'Beyond the micro: Laxton, the computer and social change over time', *Local Historian*, 16(8), 1985, pp. 451–6; B. Wojciechowska-Kibble, *Migration and the Rural Labour Market: Kent, 1841–71*, unpublished Ph.D. thesis, University of Kent at Canterbury, 1984, pp. 266–7; P. Aslett, et al., *Victorians on the Move: Research in the Census Enumerators' Books 1851–1881*, Thornborough, 1984, pp. 18–19; W. M. Williams, *A West Country Village: Ashworthy*, London, 1963, pp. 125–30 and P. R. A. Hinde, 'The population of a Wiltshire village in the nineteenth century: a reconstitution study of Berwick St James, 1841–71', *Annals of Human Biology*, 14(6), 1987, pp. 475–85. In the case of urban areas partial linking exercises, usually linking male heads of households only, have been carried out for Liverpool, Huddersfield and Leeds. A full and detailed turnover study has been made on a sample of households in the east London area of Bethnal Green. In addition, a sample of males aged over ten has been traced backwards rather than forwards for Preston. See R. Lawton and C. G. Pooley, *The Social Geography of Merseyside in the Nineteenth Century*, Final Report to the SSRC, Department of Geography, University of Liverpool, 1976; R. J. Dennis, 'Intercensal mobility in a Victorian city', *Transactions, Institute of British Geographers*, new series, 2(3), 1977, pp. 349–63; D. Ward, 'Environs and neighbours in the "Two Nations": Residential differentiation in mid-nineteenth-century Leeds', *Journal of Historical Geography*, 6, 1980, pp. 133–62; M. A. Clarke, 'Household and family in Bethnal Green, 1851–71: the effects of social and economic change', unpublished Ph.D. thesis, University of Cambridge, 1986, pp. 56–76 and M. Anderson, *Family Structure in Nineteenth Century Lancashire*, Cambridge, 1971, pp. 41–2. For earlier centuries see P. Laslett and J. Harrison, 'Clayworth and Cogenhoe', in H. E. Bell and R. L. Ollard (eds), *Historical Essays, 1600–1750, Presented to*

David Ogg, London, 1963, pp. 157–84 and J. Boulton, 'Residential mobility in seventeenth century Southwark', *Urban History Yearbook*, 1986, pp. 1-11.

3 L. R. Poos, 'Population turnover in medieval Essex: The evidence of some early fourteenth-century tithing lists', in L. Bonfield, R. M. Smith and K. Wrightson (eds), *The World We Have Gained: Histories of Population and Social Structure*, Oxford, 1986, pp. 1–22. The parishes in question are Margaret Roding, Great Waltham, Birdbrook and Messing. The first of these is located only some five kilometres to the south east of the Hatfield group of parishes detailed in this study.

4 A major exception to this trend, set mainly in the urban case, is A. G. Darroch, 'Migrants in the nineteenth century: fugitives or families in motion?', *Journal of Family History*, 6, 1981, pp. 257–77.

5 In particular two recent works on transatlantic emigration to early-modern north America have emphasized the importance of family networks in the migration process despite its apparent numerical shortfall: see H. Charbonneau, et al., *Naissance d'une population: Les Français établis au Canada au XVIIe siècle*, INED, Travaux et documents cahier No. 118, Montreal, 1987, pp. 41–5 and D. Cressy, *Coming Over: Migration and communication between England and New England in the Seventeenth Century*, Cambridge, 1987, pp. 263–91. See also B. Bailyn, *Voyagers to the West: Emigration from Britain to America on the Eve of the Revolution*, London, 1987, pp. 126–203 and C. Erickson, *Invisible Immigrants: The Adaptation of English and Scottish Immigrants in Nineteenth Century America*, Leicester, 1972, pp. 32–9.

6 See, for example, D. Cressy, 'Kinship and kin interaction in early modern England', *Past and Present*, 113, 1986, pp. 38–69.

7 ibid., pp. 44–8.

8 Bailyn, op. cit., pp. 126–39.

9 ibid., p. 126.

10 ibid., pp. 134–66. For the supposed cultural division between England and Scotland see also Houston, R. A., *Scottish Literacy and the Scottish Identity: Illiteracy and Society in Scotland and Northern England 1600–1800*, Cambridge, 1985.

11 ibid., pp. 201–3.

12 P. Clark, 'The migrant in Kentish towns 1580–1640', in P. Clark and P. Slack (eds), *Crisis and Order in English Towns 1500–1700*, London, 1972, pp. 117–63. The characteristics of these two types of movement have, however, rightly been challenged. Patten, for example, points out that much of what Clark classifies as betterment migration took place over relatively long distances and as subsistence over short distances, and that there were important temporal differences in relation to what might be termed betterment and subsistence movements; see J. Patten, *Rural-Urban Migration in Pre-industrial England*, Research Papers, No. 6, School of Geography, University of Oxford, 1973, pp. 8–11. Yet irrespective of these criticisms, the concept of distinctive types of movement, differing in structure and in terms of the migrants' perceived motivation for moving, is still an important one.

13 The most direct statement of this in the English case is to be found in M. Anderson, *Family Structure in Nineteenth-Century Lancashire*,

Cambridge, 1971, pp. 152–61. For the case of the Irish see L. H. Lees, 'Mid-Victorian migration and the Irish family economy', *Victorian Studies*, 20, 1976, pp. 25–43, and *Exiles of Erin: Irish Migrants in Victorian London*, Manchester, 1979. Examples from North America can be found in H. P. Chudacoff, 'Newlyweds and family extension: the first stage of the family cycle in Providence, Rhode Island, 1864–1865 and 1879–1880', in T. K. Hareven and M. A. Vinovskis (eds), *Family and Population in Nineteenth-Century America*, Princeton, 1978, pp. 179–205 and L. Glasco, 'Migration and adjustment in the nineteenth-century city: occupation, property, and household structure of natural-born whites, Buffalo, New York, 1855', ibid., pp. 154–178.

14 See, for example, M. Anderson, 'Urban migration in Victorian Britain: problems of assimilation?' in E. François (ed.), *Immigration et société urbaine en Europe occidentale, XVI–XX siècles*, Paris, 1985, pp. 79–91 and W. H. Sewell, *The Men and Women of Marseille, 1820–1870*, Cambridge, 1985.

15 M. B. White, 'Family migration in Victorian Britain: the case of Grantham and Scunthorpe', *Local Population Studies*, 41, 1988, pp. 41–50.

16 ibid. However, this study does suffer from various methodological problems. The findings are based on a single census study rather than a linking exercise, and in estimating the proportion of family migrants some 50 per cent of the population are discounted due to the uncertainty of their origin. In addition, the estimates are based on the assumption that natives and non-natives exhibit identical age-specific migration rates which seems unrealistic. See K. Schurer, 'Migration, population and social structure. A comparative study based in rural Essex, 1850–1900', unpublished Ph.D. thesis, University of London, 1988, pp. 291–2. (Hereafter abbreviated as Schurer, thesis).

17 Throughout this study aggregate population figures are taken from the appropriate published census reports of the nineteenth century. For a guide to these reports see M. Drake, 'The census, 1801–1891', in E. A. Wrigley (ed.), *Nineteenth-Century Society: Essays in the Use of Quantitative Methods for the Study of Social Data*, Cambridge, 1972, pp. 7–46.

18 The total population recorded for the Hatfield group was as follows: 1861, 3,149; 1871, 3,143; 1881, 3,157.

19 Details of this sub-division are given in Schurer, thesis, op. cit., pp. 24, 29–41.

20 The population of Great Hallingbury fluctuated as follows: 1861, 675; 1871, 651; 1881, 628; the comparable figures for Little Hallingbury being 514, 556 and 583.

21 See Schurer, thesis, op. cit., p. 139.

22 Details of the agricultural patterns of the two regions are discussed in Schurer, thesis, op. cit., pp. 87–115.

23 The intensive input needed to work the heavy claylands of Essex is described in G. E. Fussell, 'Essex Farmers of 1850. Men of enterprise and capital', *Essex Review*, 48(189), 1939, pp. 40–3 and 'Essex farmers a century ago', *Essex Review*, 65(258), 1957, pp. 53–9. See also W. L. Rham, *The Dictionary of the Farm*, London, 1850, pp. 194–5;

S. Applebaum, 'The Essex achievement', *Agricultural History Review*, 29(1), 1981, pp. 42–4 and Schurer, thesis, pp. 93–5.

24 Lord Ernle, *English Farming Past and Present*, London, 2nd edition, 1917, pp. 374–8; *British Parliamentary Papers*, 1881, XVI, Royal Commission on the depressed condition of the Agricultural interest, Part II; *British Parliamentary Papers*, 1894, XVI, Royal Commission on Agricultural Depression, Part I. Reports of Assistant Commissioners in certain districts: Ongar, Chelmsford, Maldon and Braintree.

25 *British Parliamentary Papers*, 1894, Royal Commission on Agricultural Depression, Part I, pp. 47, 246, 248, 251. See also P. J. Perry, *British Farming in the Great Depression, 1870–1914*, Newton Abbot, 1974; J. T. Coppock, 'The changing face of England, 1850–c.1900', in H. C. Darby (ed.), *A New Historical Geography of England*, Cambridge, 1973, pp. 295–373; T. W. Fletcher, 'The Great Depression of English agriculture, 1873–1896', *Economic History Review*, 2nd Series, 1960–1, p. 1.

26 One of the most famous diversifications of agriculture in this area of the county is the Elsenham jam factory established by Sir Walter Gilbey in 1889. See *The Victoria History of the Counties of England. A History of Essex*, vol. 2, London, 1907, pp. 476–72. See also Schurer, thesis, op. cit., pp. 97–9, 102–3.

27 For details see Schurer, thesis, op. cit., pp. 80–5.

28 The census enumerators' books of the nineteenth century have been so widely used that they do not require detailed description in this chapter. If necessary readers should refer to the various chapters of Wrigley, op. cit., or R. Lawton (ed.), *The Census and Social Structure: An Interpretative Guide to Nineteenth Century Censuses for England and Wales*, London, 1978. A recent book by Higgs provides a first class guide: E. Higgs, *Making Sense of the Census: The Manuscript Returns for England and Wales, 1801–1901*, London, HMSO, 1989.

29 See, for example, J. Patten, op. cit., and 'Patterns of migration of labour to three pre-industrial East Anglian towns', *Journal of Historical Geography*, 2, 1976, pp. 111–29; A. A. Lovett, I. D. Whyte and K. A. Whyte, 'Poisson regression analysis and migration fields: the example of the apprenticeship records of Edinburgh in the seventeenth and eighteenth centuries', *Transactions, Institute of British Geographers*, new series, 10, 1985, pp. 317–32; J. Wareing, 'Changes in the geographical distribution of the recruitment of apprentices to the London companies 1486–1750', *Journal of Historical Geography*, 6(3), 1980, pp. 241–9; A. Parton, 'Poor-law settlement certificates and migration to and from Birmingham, 1726–57', *Local Population Studies*, 38, 1987, pp. 23–9; D. M. Palliser, 'A regional capital as magnet: immigrants to York, 1477–1566', *Yorkshire Archaeological Journal*, 57, 1985, pp. 111–23.

30 The term 'residential' is important since the census, of course, records only the family members living together on the night of enumeration. It would be of particular interest to study the influence of the family in a broader context, tracing and examining kin beyond the census household, yet unfortunately this task is beyond the scope of this chapter. For an interesting attempt at studying migration in relation to kinship see R. C. Ostergren, 'Kinship networks and migration: a nineteenth-century Swedish example', *Social Science History*, 6(3), 1982, pp. 293–320.

31 E. G. Ravenstein, 'Census of the British Isles, 1871: birthplaces and migration', *Geographical Magazine*, 3, 1876, pp. 173–7, 201–6; 'Laws of migration: counties and general', *Geographical Magazine*, 3, 1876, pp. 229–33; 'The laws of migration', *Journal of the Statistical Society*, 48, 1885, pp. 167–227; 'The laws of migration', *Journal of the Royal Statistical Society*, 52, 1889, pp. 214–301. For examples of use of census data at an aggregate level see D. Friedlander and R. J. Roshier, 'A study of internal migration in England and Wales: Part I', *Population Studies*, 19, 1966, pp. 239–79; D. Baines, *Migration in a Mature Economy: Emigration and Internal Migration in England and Wales, 1801–1900*, Cambridge, 1985; R. Lawton, 'Population changes in England and Wales in the later nineteenth century', *Transactions, Institute of British Geographers*, 44, 1968, pp. 55–75 and 'Regional population trends in England and Wales, 1750–1971', in J. Hobcraft and P. Rees (eds), *Regional Demographic Development*, London, 1977, pp. 29–70.

32 As a guide see the appropriate entries in C. G. Pearce and D. R. Mills, *Census Enumerators' Books: An Annotated Bibliography of Published Work Based Substantially on the Nineteenth Century Census Enumerators', Books*, Milton Keynes, 1982. An extended and up-dated version of this bibliography is to be published in the Geo-books Historical Geography Research Series.

33 However, an analysis of the birthplace of children in relation to that of their mother can provide indications to the patterns of movement. See D. Bryant, 'Demographic trends in South Devon in the mid-nineteenth century', in K. J. Gregory and W. L. D. Ravenhill (eds), *Exeter Essays in Geography*, Exeter, 1971, pp. 125–41.

34 Yet to a certain extent in an urban environment this problem can be overcome by the use of directories which were sometimes published every two years; see Lawton and Pooley, op. cit. Alternatively, in his study of Leicester, Pritchard used electoral rolls to calculate migration rates; R. M. Pritchard, *Housing and the Spatial Structure of the City*, Cambridge, 1976, pp. 49–54. Rate books have also been used to investigate mobility in the case of nineteenth-century Ramsgate: R. S. Holmes, 'Ownership and migration from a study of rate books', *Area*, 5, 1973, pp. 242–51.

35 The linking process is described in Schurer, thesis, pp. 254–66. See also K. Schurer, 'Historical demography, social structure and the computer' in P. Denley and D. Hopkin (eds), *History and Computing*, Manchester, 1987, pp. 33–45. The same basic logic of linking is used in the suite of automated family reconstitution computer programs developed at the Cambridge Group for the History of Population and Social Structure, see K. Schurer, J. Oeppen and R. Schofield, 'Theory and methodology: an example from historical demography', in P. Denley, S. Fogelvik and C. Harvey, *History and Computing II*, Manchester, 1989, pp. 130–42.

36 The shortcomings of parish registers are discussed in J. T. Krause, 'The changing adequacy of English registration', in D. V. Glass and D. E. C. Eversley (eds), *Population in History*, London, 1965, pp. 379–93.

37 The information used to construct the life-tables relates to the Registration Districts of Dunmow and Maldon, 1861–80 and 1871–80, published in the *Supplement to the Thirty-Fifth Annual Report of the Register General of*

Births, Deaths and Marriages in England, London, 1875 and the *Supplement to the Forty-Fifth Annual Report . . .*, London, 1885. For the construction of life-tables see H. S. Shryock and J. S. Siegel, et al., *The Methods and Materials of Demography*, New York, 1976, pp. 249–59.

38 This difference might be even more marked since Robin suggests that the migration figures for Elmdon may be overstated due to the number of women who could not be traced in the 1861 census as a result of a change in surname due to marriage; Robin, op. cit., p. 192.

39 P. Horn, *The Rural World 1780–1850: Social Change in the English Countryside*, London, 1980, p. 256. It has also been argued that the proportions of native-born in a particular settlement are inversely correlated with the size of the settlement, see Bryant, op. cit.

40 In the case of incomers to the Dengie region it must be noted that the figures for Southminster are artificially too high for the period 1861–71 since the census of 1861 is under-enumerated as a result of pages lost from the enumerators' returns. A total of 127 persons missing from the 1861 enumeration, and therefore some of those counted as incomers between 1861 and 1871 would in fact have been present in the 1861 census had the enumeration been complete. Thus the figure of 34 per cent incomers recorded for the parish should be reduced. Since it is unlikely that all of the missing individuals would have persisted over the ten year period, one cannot simply take off the number of missing persons from the total of incomers and recalculate the figure. If, however, one estimates that the missing individuals migrated out of the area and died at roughly the same rate as the rest of the population, then the figures for incomers would be reduced to about 30 per cent for both males and females. Thus, the level of in-migration in Southminster for the period 1861–71 appears to be genuinely high, yet then declines in the second period particularly in the case of males. However, this situation is only to be expected given the fact that the population of the parish increased from 1,405 to 1,540 between 1861–71 and then fell to 1,244 by 1881.

41 It should be realized that these two figures cannot be directly compared to give the proportional increase or decrease of the parish populations. This is because the figure of those leaving the parish is calculated with the initial total population as the denominator and the figure of those entering the parish is calculated with the secondary census population as the denominator. In addition, whereas the figure for those migrating is compensated for those dying during the census interval, the figure for incomers does not include those born during the interval, some of whom would have been born outside the parish of residence in the secondary census. Therefore, one also needs to take into consideration the fact that in both regions throughout the period some 25.8 per cent of the total population was aged less than 10.

42 P. Laslett, *Family Life and Illicit Love in Earlier Generations*, Cambridge, 1977, pp. 74–5.

43 See, for example, J. Saville, *Rural Depopulation in England and Wales, 1851–1951*, London, 1957; G. B. Longstaffe, 'Rural Depopulation', *Journal of the Royal Statistical Society*, 52, 1893, pp. 380–442; A. L. Bowley, 'Rural population in England and Wales . . . a study of the changes of density, occupations and ages', *Journal of the Royal Statistical*

Society, 77, 1914, pp. 597–645; A. K. Cairncross, *Home and Foreign Investment 1870–1913: Studies in Capital Accumulation*, Cambridge, 1953; Lord Eversley, 'The decline in the number of agricultural labourers in Britain', *Journal of the Royal Statistical Society*, 70, pp. 267–303. The main argument between these authors is not on the occurrence of increased out-migration from rural areas but instead the timing and magnitude of the feature.

44 Fitting migration to the balancing of population imbalances is in some ways an extension of the ideas put forward by Wrigley in a highly original paper on the logic of fertility strategies in relation to inheritance: inheritance not only in the sense of capital goods bequeathed upon death but also the passing on of employment following retirement; E. A. Wrigley, 'Fertility strategy for the individual and the group', in C. Tilly (ed.), *Historical Studies of Changing Fertility*, Princeton, 1978, pp. 135–54. The ideas expounded in this essay have also been taken up in the introductory chapter of Clark and Souden, op. cit.

45 B. Wojciechowska, 'Brenchley: a study of migratory movements in a mid-nineteenth-century rural parish', *Local Population Studies*, 41, 1988, pp. 28–40; E. B. Wolniakowski, 'Family and population change in a nineteenth-century English village', unpublished Ph.D. thesis, Cornell University, 1976, pp. 105–6.

46 F. R. Oliver, 'Notes on the logistic curve for human populations', *Journal of the Royal Statistical Society*, Series A, 145, 1982, pp. 359–63. Model age-specific migration schedules for modern populations also take this form, see A. Rogers and L. J. Castro, *Model Migration Schedules*, Luxembourg, 1981.

47 Using the particularly detailed parish registers of Barming, Kent, Schofield has estimated that during the period 1788–1812 a third of the married adults buried in the parish were people who had lived and died outside the parish; R. S. Schofield, 'Traffic in corpses: some evidence from Barming, Kent (1788–1912)', *Local Population Studies*, 33, 1984, pp. 49–53. Snell also provides various examples of corpses being transported throughout the countryside in the seventeenth and eighteenth centuries. K. D. M. Snell, 'Parish registration and the study of labour mobility', *Local Population Studies*, 33, 1984, pp. 29–43. Interestingly, in her study of migration in rural Brenchley, Kent, Wojciechowska-Kibble linked only 146 of the 416 recorded burials (35 per cent) in the period 1851–61. The author, however, does not comment on this shortfall; Wojciechowska-Kibble, op. cit., p. 268. Equally, in relation to the linking of the repetitive listings of Clayworth, 1676–88, Laslett reported that 'Older people were also present in the village after 1676 and died there before 1688, and these deaths explain why the number of funerals in the parish registers during the twelve years is more than twice the number of persons named in the listing of 1676 who had been buried by 1688; Laslett, op. cit., p. 70. For a contemporary study of migration patterns of the elderly see E. Grundy, 'Migration and household change among the elderly in England and Wales 1971–1981', *Espace Population Sociétés*, 7(2), 1987, pp. 111–36.

48 Since the number of female-headed households in the two areas is too small for detailed discussion the table has been calculated for male-headed households only. The scant information on female-headed households is

discussed in Schurer, thesis, op. cit., pp. 315–9.

49 This may appear slightly odd but is correct in the sense that they did not appear to have migrated before death. However, although it could be suggested that they may have moved if they had survived, this is entering into the realms of pure speculation.

50 Wojciechowska-Kibble, op. cit., pp. 285–6; see also T. Dublin, 'Rural–urban migrants in industrial New England: the case of Lynn, Massachusetts in the mid-nineteenth century', *The Journal of American History*, 73(2), 1986, pp. 623–44.

51 M. Escott, 'Residential mobility in a late eighteenth-century parish: Binfield, Berkshire 1779–1801', *Local Population Studies*, 40, 1988, pp. 20–35.

52 For details see Schurer, thesis, op. cit., pp. 317–8.

53 See the discussion in J. Robin, 'Family care of the elderly in a nineteenth-century Devonshire parish', *Ageing and Society*, 4(4), 1984, pp. 506–16. Following the work of Mills it would be informative to trace inter-censual stayers to the actual cottages inhabited at the census dates in order to detect movement within the parishes. However, in the case of all parishes the address information given in the census enumerators' books is insufficient to locate cottages specifically. This is especially true of the censuses of 1861 and 1871, see D. R. Mills, 'The residential propinquity of kin in a Cambridgeshire village, 1841', *Journal of Historical Geography*, 4(3), 1978, pp. 265–76.

54 However, with this situation, one is reminded of the problem of potential under-registration in the elderly age groups, since if an elderly couple both died but their burial went unrecorded this would count as an entire family migration, as would the case of an elderly widowed person dying with the burial unrecorded and a remaining offspring then moving away subsequent to the death.

55 Wojciechowska-Kibble, op. cit. p. 286.

56 Dublin, op. cit.

57 Darroch, op. cit. The point is also made in relation to Dublin's study of Lynn as well as various other studies of migration into nineteenth-century American cities, see Dublin, op. cit., p. 629; Chudacoff, op. cit. and Glasco, op. cit.

58 W. M. Brayshay, 'The demography of three West Cornwall mining communities: a society in decline', unpublished Ph.D. thesis, University of Exeter, 1977, pp. 256, 264–6.

59 S. Beadle, 'Economic changes and the population of coalfields in the early nineteenth century, with special reference to the Somerset and St Helens coalfields', unpublished Ph.D. thesis, University of Liverpool, 1984, p. 227.

60 See in particular C. B. Brettell, 'Emigration and household structure in a Portuguese parish, 1850–1920', *Journal of Family History*, 13(1), 1988, pp. 33–57.

61 Anderson, 1971, op. cit. p. 160.

62 R. Wall, 'Work, welfare and the family: an illustration of the adaptive family economy', in L. Bonfield, R. M. Smith and K. Wrightson (eds), *The World We Have Gained: Histories of Population and Social Structure*, Oxford, 1986, p. 265.

63 Wall, op. cit., p. 294.
64 ibid., p. 265.

7 The longitudinal study of migration

Welsh migration to English towns in the nineteenth century

Colin G. Pooley and John C. Doherty

INTRODUCTION

Most geographical studies of nineteenth-century migration in Britain concentrate on the lifetime movement of aggregate populations and the impact such moves had on the regional redistribution of population.[1] Nineteenth-century census sources, despite their many imperfections,[2] lend themselves to such analysis and it is now possible to assemble a considerable body of evidence relating to aggregate nineteenth-century population migration in Britain.[3] Whilst some research has focused on the impact of immigration on particular towns and regions[4] or on the migration experiences of particular well-defined groups,[5] few studies examine the significance and meaning of migration for families and individuals or the impact of migration on localities which lost and gained population. This omission is not surprising, because the most readily available source, the population census, gives no direct information on these topics. The interpretation of migratory moves requires speculation from available evidence, but most census studies provide insufficient detail to support such speculation.

The only historical studies which have begun to tackle directly such questions as why people moved, when people moved and the social, economic and psychological effects of such moves are those based on oral evidence.[6] Letters and diaries can also provide relevant information about the impact of migration on the individual,[7] but such sources inevitably have a sporadic spatial distribution and may be subject to considerable bias. This chapter attempts to use a widely available source, the census enumerators' books for England and Wales, to create longitudinal migration histories of individuals which may then be used to speculate sensibly about the motives for, and effects of, population migration in the nineteenth century.

DOI: 10.4324/9781003172918-9

DEFICIENCIES IN CENSUS-BASED MIGRATION ANALYSIS

Although existing studies of nineteenth-century migration[8] provide a great deal of valuable information, most of them contain significant deficiencies. First, the majority of studies are static, concerned with a snapshot at one point in time on census night. As such they cannot hope to capture the true significance of the dynamic process of population movement. Although some studies have attempted to calculate inter-censal migration flows,[9] this has been done only at a very broad level of aggregation and such an approach necessarily makes a number of questionable assumptions about the age structure and mortality of migrants over an inter-censal period.

Second, almost all census-based migration studies have been essentially aggregate in nature. Although census enumerators' books provide detailed personal information, this has rarely been fully exploited. Whilst aggregate analyses do provide a useful description of the socio-economic profile of particular migrant groups, they do not provide an understanding of the motives for movement or the significance of migration for individual migrants. The size and structure of the county units used in most such studies also make sensible inferences about migration processes almost impossible.

Third, and most damning, most census-based studies of nineteenth-century migration have not been concerned with the migration process at all. Rather, they have based their analysis on the lifetime movement of people from place of birth to place of residence on census night, assuming that this arbitrary definition of mobility has some significance. There are obviously several respects in which this approach to migration studies is deficient. Information about the distance and direction of movement is divorced from any knowledge of the circumstances surrounding the move: an individual could have moved at any age, singly or as part of a family group, and through any set of migration paths. Moreover, the fact that a migrant was born in a particular locality does not mean that the migrant necessarily had social or cultural characteristics affected by that locality: yet almost all studies of Irish migration (for instance) define the Irish in terms of birthplace. Information can be refined by utilizing the birthplaces of children and other family members to infer the timing of movement and the migration paths taken.[10] However, this provides only a partial sample, and does not allow the process of migration to be related to the social and economic context in which it was set.

It is easy to understand why most historical geographers have concentrated on the aggregate analysis of static birthplace data in studies of migration in nineteenth-century Britain. The data are readily available and easy to handle, they can be given a spurious rigour through statistical analysis, and the results have broadly confirmed expectations derived from migration theory and contemporary accounts.[11] However, the extent to which such analyses have improved our understanding of the processes of nineteenth-century migration, of the impact of migration on different localities, and of the significance and meaning of migration for individual people must be severely questioned. Because of the limitations of the data used, most studies have not even attempted to tackle such themes.

KEY QUESTIONS IN THE STUDY OF MIGRATION

The methodology described in this chapter, which allows the construction of longitudinal migration profiles for individuals, is time-consuming and gives only limited returns on a large investment of effort. Before embarking on such research we thus need to be convinced that the data collected will allow us to answer significantly different and more important questions than can be answered from conventional aggregate analyses of migration. It is suggested that there are three areas in which our knowledge is deficient and where the construction of longitudinal migration histories can significantly aid understanding and historical interpretation.

First, we need to know more precisely the timing and location of moves undertaken by individual migrants so that we can try to explain particular migration decisions rather than the less meaningful concept of lifetime migration from place of birth. Second, we need to know the characteristics of mobile individuals and households both before and after migration. By comparing the ages, marital status, occupations and family circumstances of migrants before and after movement we can begin to assess the impact of the migration process on individuals. Aggregate descriptions of the characteristics of lifetime migrants found in a particular destination at an arbitrary point in time give no information about the changes which migration has produced for either individuals or groups of migrants. Third, we need to know the context in which the moves took place. What were the demographic, economic and social circumstances in the particular locality which the migrants left and how did these change after migration? Aggregate studies, that lump migrants together into broad county or regional groupings of origin areas, confuse the context of movement and lead to explanations that can be no more than bland generalizations.

From these three types of information, which are not available from most census-based studies of nineteenth-century migration, we can more accurately infer other aspects of the migration process, such as why migration occurred, the impact of migration on areas of origin and destination, and the ways in which migration affected the everyday lives of individual migrants. It must be stressed that the examination of motives and meanings will still be no more than inference, but inference based on a reasonably sound empirical base which relates to the actual circumstances of particular moves. If understanding of the motives behind, and effects of, nineteenth-century migration is to progress beyond rather obvious generalizations, such detailed longitudinal databases need to be assembled for large numbers of individual migrants.[12]

THE CONSTRUCTION OF LONGITUDINAL MIGRATION HISTORIES FROM CENSUS ENUMERATORS' BOOKS

The method used to construct migration histories is essentially straightforward. It involves the backward linkage of cohorts of migrants which can be identified in both their destination and origin areas. It should be noted that the definition of origin and destination areas is arbitrary and variable depending upon the migrants being studied: all localities will serve as both origin and destination areas for some migrants. The research methodology proceeds through a number of stages which are summarized in Figure 7.1.

It is first necessary to define the broad origin areas and the specific destination areas of interest to the particular research theme that has been identified. It is advantageous if additional archival data are also available for these areas. Census enumerators' books for the destination areas are then scanned for selected census years (say 1861, 1871, 1881) and details of all migrants born in the specified origin areas are recorded. This population could, for instance, consist of the entire Welsh-born population living in Manchester in 1871 and 1881; or simply the Anglesey-born population living in Manchester in those years. The population of interest must obviously be clearly defined, and in addition to those born in the areas of origin it is sensible to record details of all co-resident members of households containing a migrant from a specified origin. This provides additional information on migration paths and household composition. If required a control group of non-migrant households can also be recorded. Complete factual details of the population of interest are then entered into a computer database management system.

From analysis of the birthplace details of migrants located in

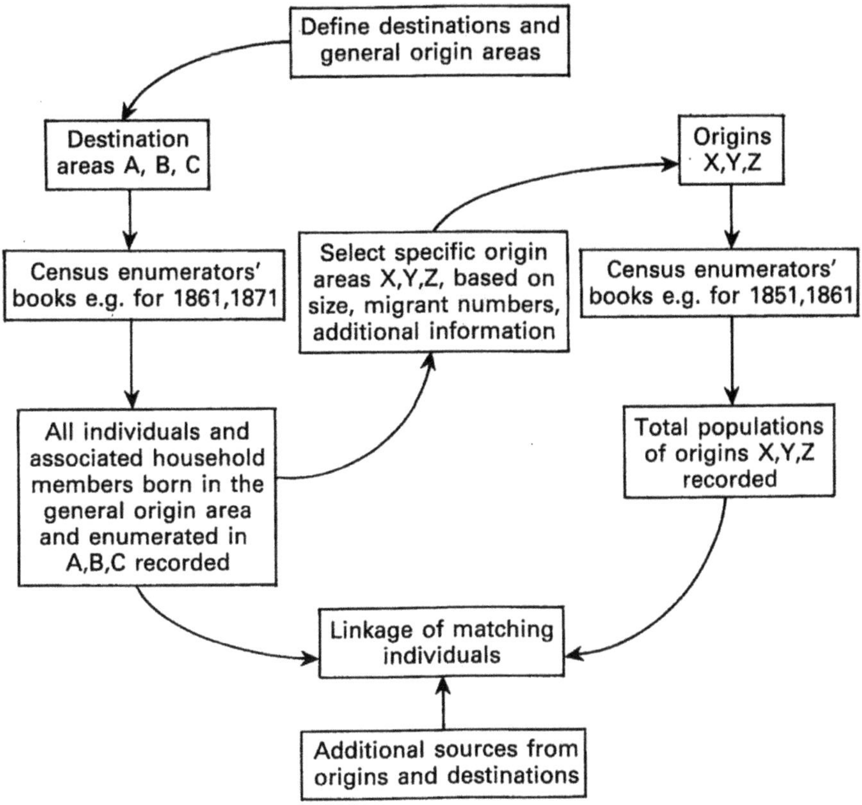

Figure 7.1 Flow diagram showing the process of nominal linkage to construct longitudinal migration profiles from census enumerators' books

destination areas, a series of smaller areas of origin are identified as suitable for detailed analysis. These are areas from which a reasonably large number of migrants had come and in which there is a reasonable probability of being able to trace migrants. The census enumerators' books for these origin areas are then examined for years prior to and overlapping with those used for the destination areas (say 1851, 1861, 1871), and details of the entire population of the selected origin areas are recorded. For instance this could consist of the entire population of Holyhead in 1861 and 1871. Again full factual details of all individuals are entered into the database management system.

The database management system is then used to sort both the origin and destination populations on specified variables, and produce listings from which individuals can be located in the destination area and in an origin area 10 or 20 years earlier. Thus, for instance, individuals may be identified in Manchester in 1881 and found also in Holyhead in 1871 or 1861. The actual linkage procedure is completed by hand, using name, age (plus census interval), and birthplace as the only linking variables. All other information could change as a result of migration. As it is just these changes that are of interest, using them for record linkage would produce a circular argument. The aim is to produce a file of linked migrants for whom we know the date of migration to within a maximum of ten years (for links between two adjacent censuses), the age, occupation and family circumstances before migration, and the changes in occupation and family circumstances that had occurred by the time of the first census to be taken after migration. Although imperfect, this methodology provides more information on the circumstances and effects of migration than can be gained from conventional migration studies. In addition we also have complete static data for all migrants in destination areas and the entire population of selected origin areas.

PROBLEMS IN THE CONSTRUCTION OF LONGITUDINAL MIGRATION PROFILES

It should be obvious that the methodology outlined above presents a number of problems, and only partially meets the objections to conventional migration analysis raised earlier in this chapter. Some of the major difficulties will now be examined in more detail.

First, the methodology is extremely time-consuming and requires the collection of a very large data set for a very small return in terms of linked migrants (Table 7.15, p. 163). This is particularly true for long-distance migration, and in cases where common names make linkage difficult.

Second, there are the practical problems involved in establishing whether or not a link is made. There is a sizeable literature on the problems of record linkage, including the development of computerized linkage procedures,[13] but for most practical purposes the establishment of a nominal link will require a subjective judgement. Given the idiosyncracies of census data[14] it is relatively rare to find a link in which the spelling of names and birthplaces matches precisely and the age difference exactly fits the census interval.

Third, the methodology and linkage procedure undoubtedly produces bias in the sample of linked migrants. Individuals with common names are less likely to be positively linked and women who married and changed their name between censuses are almost impossible to identify. Because of the corroborative evidence provided by other family members, the sample may also be biased towards family groups, but we do not consider this to be a serious problem.

Fourth, several inevitable problems arise from the use of census data which are only available at ten-year intervals. Although the move studied is based on actual origin and destination data, the identification of the migrant in the first instance is based on birthplace information. Thus, by definition, all migrants studied must be natives of the origin area and it is not possible to use this technique to study individuals who have moved through a variety of locations prior to the first census studied. Likewise, because the origin and destination data are ten years apart, it is not possible to determine whether a move was made directly or via an intermediate location. Information on children's birthplaces can help to fill in details, but this is only available for a small sub-set of the total migrants.

Fifth, there is a problem of establishing the representativeness of the migrants for whom links are made, not only with respect to the total specified migrant population, but also in relation to other migrant groups and non-migrants. Ideally, studies of specific migrant populations should include samples of migrants from a wide range of destinations and also samples of non-migrants to act as a control group. In this way features that are peculiar to the specific migration process under study can be separated from more general forces operating within nineteenth-century society. Although there is no theoretical reason why such control groups should not be established, it is extremely time-consuming to extract the necessary data.

Lastly, it must be emphasized that interpretation of the data still requires speculation even though the empirical data gathered for the sample of linked migrants is far superior to that available from most other sources. The method provides actual origin and destination data at ten-year intervals, information on the age, family circumstances and occupation of individual migrants before and after movement, and details of the social and economic context in which the move was set. However, from this we still have to infer the motives for movement and the significance of movement for individual migrants.

WELSH MIGRATION TO ENGLISH TOWNS: THE DESTINATION AREAS IN 1871

In a study of Welsh migration to English towns, three destination areas were chosen to represent a variety of types of migration and Welsh communities in England. Following analysis of published census data,[15] it was decided to examine Welsh migration to Shrewsbury, Liverpool and Middlesbrough. It was hypothesized from existing evidence that migration to Shrewsbury would consist mainly of

Table 7.1 Sample of Welsh population in English towns in 1871

English town	*Households with at least 1 Welsh member*	*Welsh-born population*	*Non Welsh-born population in Welsh households*	*Total population sampled*
Shrewsbury	783	1378	1990	3368
Liverpool (Part)*	754	1867	1723	3590
Middlesbrough#	310	956	719	1675

Source: Census enumerators' books, 1871

Notes:
* Drawn from the Welsh population of Everton, Toxteth and St Pauls.
# The Welsh population in Middlesbrough extracted from the census enumerators' books was smaller than that in the published census mainly due to the use of different areas.

short-distance rural to urban migration, movement to Liverpool would be large-scale and more varied in its composition (though mainly from North Wales), and migration to Middlesbrough would consist of long-distance occupation-specific migration flows. The remainder of this chapter describes the characteristics of the Welsh communities in these three English towns in 1871, the structure in 1861 of the origin areas from which substantial numbers of migrants had come, and the longitudinal migration profiles of individual migrants linked between origin and destination from 1861 to 1871.

The Welsh community in an English town can be defined in several ways. It may include only those born in Wales, those born in Wales and children subsequently born in England, or all those living in households containing a person born in Wales and thus having some contact with Welsh culture. For the purposes of this research the Welsh community in England was defined according to the third criterion, but the system of data extraction and recording allowed different elements to be easily identified. A statistical summary of the Welsh community in the three English towns is given in Tables 7.1–7.7, but these data were supplemented by a variety of archival sources.

In Shrewsbury, Welsh migrants were predominantly adult and there was a surplus of women over men. As in all of the towns the non-Welsh component mainly consisted of children born to Welsh parents, but in Shrewsbury this was slightly less dominant than in the other communities. The Welsh were relatively evenly distributed between

Table 7.2 Age structure of three Welsh migrant communities in England in 1871

English town		*Percentage in each age category* 0–19	20–39	40–59	60+	*Total population*
Shrewsbury	(A)	20.6	35.6	30.0	13.8	1378
	(B)	40.3	29.3	21.5	8.9	3368
	(C)	54.0	24.9	15.6	5.5	1990
Liverpool (Part)	(A)	18.1	46.1	29.0	6.8	1867
	(B)	42.0	35.0	18.7	4.3	3590
	(C)	67.9	23.0	7.7	1.4	1723
Middlesbrough	(A)	36.0	41.6	19.9	2.5	956
	(B)	48.2	34.3	15.5	2.0	1675
	(C)	64.5	24.5	9.7	1.3	719

Source: Census enumerators' books, 1871

Notes:
(A) = Welsh-born population living in each English town in 1871
(B) = Total population in households containing one or more Welsh-born person in 1871
(C) = Non Welsh-born population living in households containing one or more Welsh-born person in 1871

Table 7.3 Sex structure of three Welsh communities in England in 1871

English town		*Males*	*Females*	$\frac{\textit{Females}}{\textit{Males}} \times 100$
Shrewsbury	(A)	620	758	122.3
	(B)	1583	1785	112.8
	(C)	963	1027	106.7
Liverpool (Part)	(A)	977	890	91.1
	(B)	1845	1745	94.6
	(C)	868	855	98.5
Middlesbrough	(A)	539	417	77.4
	(B)	928	747	80.4
	(C)	389	330	84.8

Source: Census enumerators' books, 1871

Notes:
(A) = Welsh-born population living in each English town in 1871
(B) = Total population in households containing one or more Welsh-born person in 1871
(C) = Non Welsh-born population living in households containing one or more Welsh-born person in 1871

employment sectors, and there were few occupational differences between Welsh and non-Welsh, although the latter were more important in dealing and professional services. Most migrants, both Welsh and non-Welsh, had travelled over short distances from adjacent villages and towns. In most respects the Welsh community in Shrewsbury seemed well integrated into the social and economic structure of the town, although the existence of a Welsh Calvinistic Methodist Chapel in Shrewsbury since at least 1804,[16] and the close proximity of Shrewsbury to the Welsh border, meant that Welsh culture could easily be maintained in an English town.[17]

The Welsh community sampled in Liverpool was not totally representative of the town as a whole, as it was drawn only from three areas in Toxteth, Everton and the St Pauls district of the city. This sample probably under-represents female Welsh servants in non-Welsh households (because higher status areas of the city are excluded), but in other respects should reflect the characteristics of the community as a whole. This is confirmed by comparing this cluster sample with a 10 per cent systematic sample of the Welsh population in Liverpool in 1871 taken for other purposes.[18] The Welsh in Liverpool consisted mainly of young adults and the community was slightly male-dominated (which may be due to the omission of some servants from the sample). Over two-thirds of the non-Welsh living in 'Welsh' households were children, and in comparison with Shrewsbury it would seem that there was more movement of young single migrants from Wales. Although the Welsh were found in most employment sectors in Liverpool, they were particularly predominant in transport (shipping and on the docks) and building. The non-Welsh were particularly over-represented in manufacturing, and throughout the community there were fewer economically active women than in Shrewsbury. The Welsh influence on the building industry in Liverpool is well documented[19] and this formed an important focus for the Welsh community on Merseyside. This was further reinforced by the fact that most Welsh came (often by sea) from relatively accessible communities in North Wales, and by the network of Welsh chapels which operated on Merseyside. Although well integrated into the economic structure the Welsh community in Liverpool was close-knit and clearly defined in the nineteenth century.[20]

The Welsh community in Middlesbrough was rather different from those in Shrewsbury and Liverpool. Cut off by distance from Wales, the relatively small non-Welsh element in the households recorded suggests the community was more self-contained and mixed less with the non-Welsh population than in the other towns. The migrant

Table 7.4 Household composition of three Welsh migrant communities in England in 1871

		Percentage in each category							
English town		*Male household head*	*Female household head*	*Wife*	*Child*	*Other relative*	*Lodger*	*Servant*	*Total population*
Shrewsbury	(A)	25.7	8.7	20.8	17.2	6.2	10.8	10.6	1378
	(B)	18.4	5.0	16.0	38.8	5.4	8.5	7.9	3368
	(C)	13.3	2.4	12.8	53.8	4.9	6.9	6.0	1990
Liverpool	(A)	27.5	5.6	23.8	17.2	5.8	16.9	3.2	1867
	(B)	17.6	3.4	16.5	41.4	5.7	13.0	2.4	3590
	(C)	6.8	1.0	8.7	67.5	5.6	8.8	1.6	1723
Middlesbrough	(A)	22.6	1.3	19.6	38.2	4.1	12.3	1.9	956
	(B)	17.6	1.2	16.9	48.4	3.6	10.6	1.7	1675
	(C)	11.0	1.1	13.2	61.9	3.1	8.3	1.4	719

Source: Census enumerators' books, 1871

Notes:
(A) = Welsh-born population living in each English town in 1871
(B) = Total population in households containing one or more Welsh-born person in 1871
(C) = Non Welsh-born population living in households containing 1 or more Welsh-born person in 1871
Rows may not add to 100 per cent due to rounding up or down

Table 7.5 Male occupations of three Welsh migrant communities in England in 1871

English town		*Percentage of economically active population in each category*											
		Agriculture	*Mining*	*Building*	*Manufacture*	*Transport*	*Dealing*	*General industrial*	*Public and professional*	*Domestic*	*Independent*	*Total economically active*	*% males economically active*
Shrewsbury	(A)	10.6	0.8	9.0	26.8	13.5	15.4	11.7	3.7	7.9	0.6	519	83.7
	(B)	7.9	0.5	9.7	26.0	11.0	17.9	11.5	5.3	9.3	0.9	1059	66.9
	(C)	5.4	0.2	10.4	25.2	8.5	20.2	11.3	6.8	10.7	1.3	540	56.1
Liverpool	(A)	0.2	0.6	24.9	19.6	26.6	9.9	14.5	2.5	1.1	0.1	843	86.4
	(B)	0.4	0.5	21.1	22.5	26.0	10.5	14.9	2.5	1.4	0.2	1216	65.9
	(C)	0.8	0.3	12.3	29.2	24.7	11.8	15.8	2.7	2.1	0.3	373	43.0
Middlesbrough	(A)	—	0.7	2.7	82.7	1.5	0.7	10.3	0.7	0.7	—	409	75.9
	(B)	—	1.2	3.6	76.9	2.1	1.4	13.4	0.9	0.5	—	577	62.2
	(C)	—	2.4	5.9	63.1	3.6	3.0	20.8	1.2	—	—	168	43.2

Source: Census enumerators' books, 1871

Notes:
(A) = Welsh-born population living in each English town in 1871
(B) = Total population in households containing one or more Welsh-born person in 1871
(C) = Non Welsh-born population living in households containing 1 or more Welsh-born person in 1871

Table 7.6 Female occupations of three Welsh migrant communities in England in 1871

English town		*Percentage of economically active population in each category*											
		Agriculture	*Mining*	*Building*	*Manufacture*	*Transport*	*Dealing*	*General industrial*	*Public and professional*	*Domestic*	*Independent*	*Total economically active*	*% females economically active*
Shrewsbury	(A)	0.7	—	—	14.1	—	12.4	—	1.7	64.6	6.5	291	38.4
	(B)	0.6	—	—	18.3	—	13.3	0.4	1.6	58.7	7.1	547	30.6
	(C)	0.4	—	—	23.0	—	14.5	0.8	1.6	51.9	7.8	256	24.9
Liverpool	(A)	—	—	—	26.3	—	14.9	—	1.1	52.6	5.1	175	19.6
	(B)	—	—	—	28.8	—	16.0	0.4	2.5	48.0	4.3	281	16.1
	(C)	—	—	—	33.0	—	17.9	1.0	4.7	40.6	2.8	106	12.4
Middlesbrough	(A)	—	30.7	—	—	—	7.7	—	2.6	56.4	2.6	39	9.4
	(B)	—	20.0	—	8.3	—	8.3	—	1.7	60.0	1.7	60	8.0
	(C)	—	—	—	23.8	—	9.5	—	—	66.7	—	21	6.4

Source: Census enumerators' books, 1871

Notes:
(A) = Welsh-born population living in each English town in 1871
(B) = Total population in households containing one or more Welsh-born person in 1871
(C) = Non Welsh-born population living in households containing one or more Welsh-born person in 1871

Table 7.7 Birthplaces of the Welsh community (male and female)* in three English towns in 1871

English town	Percentage born in each area: Town of enumeration	Surrounding counties#	Elsewhere in England	Ireland	Scotland	North Wales	Central Wales	South Wales	Wales Not stated	Overseas	Total population
Shrewsbury	36.0	14.5	7.6	0.6	0.3	10.3	28.3	1.5	0.9	—	3368
Liverpool	38.5	3.2	3.8	1.3	0.8	34.4	3.4	2.9	11.3	0.4	3590
Middlesbrough	21.6	8.3	7.8	4.3	0.6	2.1	4.2	31.9	18.9	0.3	1675

Source: Census enumerators' books, 1871

Notes:
* defined as total population living in households containing one Welsh-born person
# For Shrewsbury = Rest of Shropshire
For Liverpool = Rest of Lancashire and Cheshire
For Middlesbrough = Rest of Yorkshire and Durham

community was predominantly young and male, and contained within it a large proportion of children who had been born in Wales, indicating recent family migration. The male employment structure was completely dominated by employment in iron manufacture, and very few females had any economic activity declared in the census. Most Welsh migrants came from South Wales and it is clear that they had been lured to Middlesbrough by specific employment opportunities in iron manufacture. Skills acquired in the South Wales valleys were directly transferable to the north east, and there were well-established links between the iron masters of South Wales and the iron industry of north-east England.[21]

WELSH MIGRATION TO ENGLISH TOWNS: THE ORIGIN AREAS IN 1861

Five origin areas in Wales were selected for detailed study, based on an examination of the birthplaces of Welsh migrants in Shrewsbury, Liverpool and Middlesbrough (Figure 7.2). They were chosen to be representative of the range of birthplace areas from which migrants came, to contain a sufficiently large number of potential migrants to yield a reasonable sample of linked individuals, and to be small enough to create a manageable data set. The data extracted consisted of the entire population of five settlements in 1861: it provides a detailed portrait of the characteristics of areas in Wales which

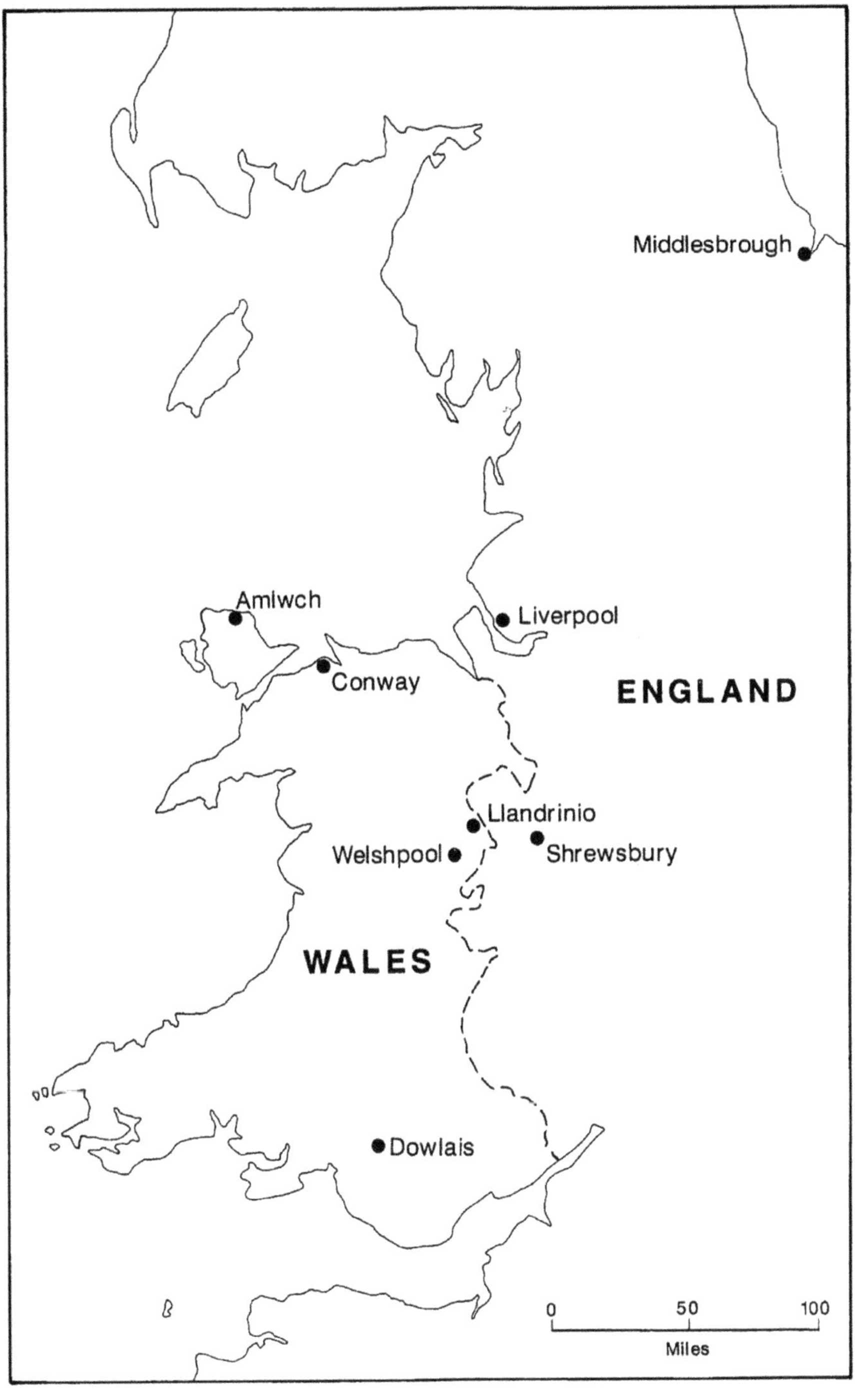

Figure 7.2 Location of origin and destination areas used in the study of Welsh migration to English towns

Table 7.8 Population of five Welsh communities in 1861

Community	*Households*	*Population*
Llandrinio	170	822
Welshpool	750	3650
Conway	367	1673
Amlwch	1235	4952
Dowlais	2100	10424

Source: Census enumerators' books, 1861

Table 7.9 Age structure of five Welsh communities in 1861

	Percentage in each age category				
Community	*0–19*	*20–39*	*40–59*	*60+*	*Total population*
Llandrinio	44.8	28.5	16.5	10.2	822
Welshpool	42.9	28.0	19.8	9.3	3650
Conway	43.3	31.2	17.0	8.5	1673
Amlwch	45.6	26.2	17.1	11.1	4952
Dowlais	48.2	32.2	15.8	3.8	10424

Source: Census enumerators' books, 1861

Table 7.10 Sex structure of five Welsh communities in 1861

Community	*Males*	*Females*	$\frac{Females}{Males} \times 100$
Llandrinio	426	396	93.0
Welshpool	1796	1854	103.2
Conway	796	877	110.2
Amlwch	2221	2731	123.0
Dowlais	5463	4961	90.8

Source: Census enumerators' books, 1861

migrants to Liverpool, Shrewsbury and Middlesbrough had left some time before 1871. Tables 7.8–7.14 provide a statistical summary of the characteristics of the areas and a brief description of each settlement is included below.[22]

Llandrinio in Montgomeryshire was a small village only 7 km from the English border and 22 km (by road) from Shrewsbury. There is little evidence of the effects of rural depopulation from the age and family structure, and male occupations were concentrated in agriculture, with a small number also employed in craft manufacture and the transport sector. There was relatively little female employment recorded in the census, and most migrants had come from the local area. A significant proportion of migrants had come from England, suggesting that although it was a small settlement Llandrinio could attract migrants in the mid-nineteenth century.

Welshpool was a much larger town 31 km from Shrewsbury, but in many respects its population structure was similar to that of Llandrinio. Despite a more diverse occupational structure, most employment was in craft industry and the service sector, and most migrants had travelled a short distance from elsewhere in Montgomeryshire or across the border from Shropshire.

Conway was a market town and a small port in North Wales some 135 km from Liverpool by road, but easily accessible to the Mersey by sea. It had a relatively young adult age structure and a predominance of females caused by many males being away at sea on census night. Employment was mainly in craft manufacture, building and transport (especially shipping), and most migrants were from elsewhere in North Wales.

Amlwch, on Anglesey, was larger than Conway but had similar demographic characteristics. The occupational structure of the town was quite broad, encompassing agriculture, fishing, copper mining, craft manufacture, shipping, and service trades. Birthplaces were highly localized, with 79 per cent of the male population having been born in Amlwch and 93.5 per cent on Anglesey. Amlwch was clearly a close-knit community and the main route of migration to Liverpool was almost certainly by sea.

Dowlais, Glamorganshire, was really an industrial suburb of Merthyr Tydfil. It grew around the iron works established in 1759[23] and expanded rapidly as the industrial town of Merthyr developed in the nineteenth century. The town had a young age structure, and the sex structure was dominated by males, most of whom were employed in the iron works and in coal mining. A very small proportion of women were economically active in this male-dominated economy, though some were working in local industries. Dowlais had attracted rather more migrants than the other Welsh settlements, with a substantial proportion travelling from outside Glamorganshire to take advantage of the employment opportunities in Dowlais. It is over 400 km from Dowlais to Middlesbrough and the two towns are linked only through their employment structure.

Table 7.11 Male occupations in five Welsh communities in 1861

	Percentage of economically active population in each category											
	Agriculture and Fishing	*Mining*	*Building*	*Manufacture*	*Transport*	*Dealing*	*General industrial*	*Public and professional*	*Domestic*	*Independent*	*Total economically active*	*% males economically active*
Llandrinio	50.4	—	5.7	13.2	16.4	4.6	1.8	2.5	3.9	1.4	280	65.7
Welshpool	15.9	0.5	10.6	29.1	9.5	10.6	9.2	5.4	8.7	0.6	1156	64.4
Conway	6.0	1.0	17.5	28.0	17.1	10.5	8.8	5.3	5.3	0.4	486	61.1
Amlwch	26.3	16.0	4.5	22.9	12.5	5.3	6.5	2.8	3.2	0.2	1333	60.0
Dowlais	0.6	29.3	4.6	44.0	7.3	5.1	6.9	1.0	1.1	0.1	3529	64.6

Source: Census enumerators' books, 1861

Note: Rows may not add to 100 per cent due to rounding up or down.

Table 7.12 Female occupations in five Welsh communities in 1861

Community	Percentage of economically active population in each category										
	Agriculture and Fishing	*Mining*	*Building*	*Manufacture*	*Transport*	*Dealing*	*General industrial*	*Public and professional*	*Domestic*	*Independent*	*Total economically active*	*% females economically active*
Llandrinio	23.9	—	—	3.4	—	5.7	—	3.4	62.5	1.1	88	22.2
Welshpool	4.1	—	0.2	21.1	0.2	9.3	0.2	5.4	55.6	3.5	462	24.9
Conway	2.5	—	—	12.8	—	21.7	—	2.5	58.1	2.5	203	23.1
Amlwch	11.1	1.7	—	25.8	0.2	11.1	—	2.0	46.3	1.7	592	21.7
Dowlais	0.3	15.5	0.2	29.5	0.8	8.1	3.4	2.9	38.7	0.9	657	13.2

Source: Census enumerators' books, 1861

Note: Rows may not add to 100 per cent due to rounding up or down.

Table 7.13 Male birthplaces in five Welsh communities in 1861

Community	*Percentage born in* *Community of enumeration*	*Elsewhere in county of enumeration*	*Elsewhere in Wales*	*Outside Wales*	*Total population (males)*
Llandrinio	43.4	31.9	3.3	21.4	426
Welshpool	46.4	33.6	3.0	17.0	1796
Conway	55.2	17.7	20.1	7.0	796
Amlwch	79.0	14.5	3.8	2.7	2221
Dowlais	39.0	15.7	34.8	10.5	5463

Source: Census enumerators' books, 1861

Table 7.14 Female birthplaces in five Welsh communities in 1861

Community	*Percentage born in* *Community of enumeration*	*Elsewhere in county of enumeration*	*Elsewhere in Wales*	*Outside Wales*	*Total population (females)*
Llandrinio	46.2	30.3	2.3	21.2	396
Welshpool	44.9	34.4	2.2	18.5	1854
Conway	51.5	20.9	18.9	8.7	877
Amlwch	80.2	14.4	3.2	2.2	2731
Dowlais	41.4	18.5	32.1	8.0	4961

Source: Census enumerators' books, 1861

WELSH MIGRATION TO ENGLISH TOWNS: THE LINKED MIGRANTS

The linkage procedure was carried out as outlined above, and 53 individuals in 30 different family groups were traced from an origin area in Wales in 1861 to one of the three English towns in 1871. This represents only 0.24 per cent of the total population of the five Welsh communities, but 18 per cent of all theoretical linkages and 34 per cent of those it was thought possible to trace taking into account age, sex and marital status (Table 7.15). Although a small sample, the detailed individual migration histories provide a wealth of information which is only briefly interpreted in this chapter.

Analysis of the linked migrants suggest that migration experience in the nineteenth century was varied, and did not always conform closely

Table 7.15 Linkage of migrants between Welsh origin in 1861 and English destination in 1871

Welsh origin (A)	*English destination (B)*	*Number linked A→B*	*Percentage of total from origin (A) in destination (B)*	*Percentage of estimated possible linkages*
Llandrinio	Shrewsbury	4	12.5	25.0
Welshpool	Shrewsbury	15	11.5	25.4
Conway	Liverpool	7	30.4	58.3
Amlwch	Liverpool	17	50.0	81.0
Dowlais	Middlesbrough	10	13.7	20.8
Total Linkages		53	18.2	34.0

Source: Census enumerators' books, 1861, 1871

to the stereotypical picture of young single migrants moving a short distance to the nearest town. Although there were only 11 family moves, as opposed to 19 single-person moves, no fewer than 34 of the 53 linked individuals who were traced migrated as part of a family group (Table 7.16). This was particularly the case for long-distance migrants from Dowlais to Middlesbrough, and only in the case of relatively short-distance movement from Welshpool to Shrewsbury did individuals moving in family groups form less than half of all moves traced. Although this conclusion must be treated with some caution due to the small size of the sample of linked migrants, and the fact that the linkage process is biased towards the identification of family groups, this interpretation is supported by the aggregate characteristics of all migrants in the three reception areas.[24]

Only rarely can the motives behind nineteenth-century migration be identified precisely, but the linkage of individuals from origin to destination allows the identification of employment change and thus inferences about the economic benefits of migration can be made. Perhaps the most striking conclusion to be drawn from the data is the relative lack of occupational change amongst the linked migrants (Table 7.17). The largest single group of migrants (mostly women) had no recorded occupation either before or after migration. As previously shown, female employment opportunities were limited in all areas studied and the need to find work for female family members was unlikely to have been a motive for migration. The second largest group were those (mostly children in the area of origin) who entered the labour market for the first time after migration. The move from a

Table 7.16 Classification of moves made by linked migrants 1861–71

Origin → Destination	*Number of migrants moving as a family**	*Number of families moving*	*Number of single migrants*	*Total number of linked migrants*
Llandrinio – Shrewsbury	3	1	1	4
Welshpool – Shrewsbury	5	2	10	15
Conway – Liverpool	4	1	3	7
Amlwch – Liverpool	13	4	4	17
Dowlais – Middlesbrough	9	3	1	10
Total	34	11	19	53
% of total linked migrants	64.2	—	35.8	100.0
% of total families and single migrants	—	36.7	63.3	

Source: Census enumerators' books, 1861, 1871

Note: * 'family' is defined as two related individuals moving together and co-resident at both origin and destination.

small to a large labour market should have increased employment opportunities: both for young single migrants and families with children the likelihood of increased employment opportunities open to those seeking work for the first time may have been a significant motive for migration.

Of those in work before migration, the majority remained in the same form of employment after moving, usually with little obvious advancement in status although there were likely to have been real or perceived economic gains for the individual. This was particularly true of migration from Dowlais to Middlesbrough where skills in iron manufacture were directly transferable and knowledge of relevant employment opportunities in the iron industry must have been a major spur to migration. However, the same pattern can also be discerned in other moves, and the only significant occupational change that occurred was a copper miner who migrated from Amlwch to Liverpool where he became a 'striker', presumably in an iron foundry. The overriding impression is one of migrants moving to carefully chosen destinations where their employment skills could be easily transferred to a different labour market. The economic benefits of migration were almost entirely in terms of the greater opportunities for advancement within one economic sector or through the employment of new workers in a larger labour market.[25]

Individual cases clearly illustrate these and other aspects of the

Table 7.17 Occupational change among linked migrants 1861–71

Origin – Destination	*Occupation → no occupation*	*No occupation → occupation*	*No occupation → No occupation*	*Occupation → same occupation and status*	*Occupation → same occupation but higher status*	*Occupation → different occupation*	*Total linked migrants*
Llandrinio – Shrewsbury	—	1	2	1	—	—	4
Welshpool – Shrewsbury	—	7	4	2	2	—	15
Conway – Liverpool	—	2	4	1	—	—	7
Amlwch – Liverpool	3	5	5	2	1	1	17
Dowlais – Middlesbrough	—	—	6	3	1	—	10
Total	3	15	21	9	4	1	53
% of total linked migrants	5.7	28.3	39.6	17.0	7.5	1.9	100.0

Source: Census enumerators' books, 1861, 1871

migration process. Just three examples are given in this chapter. Harriet and Ann Jones (Figure 7.3) provide interesting examples of young single migrants who left their home in Welshpool to seek work in domestic service in the nearby larger labour market of Shrewsbury. In 1861 the two girls (aged 14 and 15) lived at home in Welshpool in a farming family which employed two male farm servants. By 1871 they had migrated together to Shrewsbury and were both domestic servants in the household of a Shrewsbury-born cattle dealer. It can be suggested that in this case the motives for movement were clearly economic. Although not poor, Samuel Jones could presumably neither employ his teenage daughters on the farm nor support them at home. Shrewsbury offered better prospects in domestic service than Welshpool (there was little other female work available), and it is possible that Samuel Jones may have found employment for his daughters through a business link with the Shrewsbury cattle dealer Phillip Williams. The fact that the two girls remained together in Shrewsbury after migration emphasizes the importance of kinship links in providing a support mechanism in a new community. If Jones and Williams did have business connections then this, together with the close proximity of Welshpool to Shrewsbury, would have also enabled Harriet and Ann to maintain close links with their family in Wales.

The Roberts family (Figure 7.4) is a good example of a relatively mobile household which moved, probably by sea, from Conway to Liverpool between 1861 and 1871. Robert Roberts, a 'ship carpenter', had been born in Conway but had married a girl from Kent and had one daughter born in Kent in 1858. By 1859 they were back in Conway where a second daughter was born. Roberts was probably a carpenter on board a ship, and would have been easily able to move around the coast to different ports. The move to Liverpool was very likely stimulated by the desire to improve his economic prospects in a larger labour market where skills in shipbuilding and ship repairing were in demand. As a shipwright in Liverpool, Roberts may have worked in the ship repair yards along the Mersey or at sea, but in either case the opportunities for work in Liverpool were probably much better than those in Conway, and the Liverpool labour market allowed a direct transference of skill. Continued links by sea between North Wales and Liverpool would have meant that Roberts could also have kept in touch with family and friends in Conway if he wished.

The third case (Figure 7.5) exemplifies family migration from Dowlais to Middlesbrough. In 1861 John Davies was a recently married iron puddler in Dowlais with one baby son. Around 1864 the

Welshpool (1861)

Jones Samuel	Head	45	Farmer	Welshpool
Jones Sarah	Wife	47	None	Welshpool
Jones Harriet	Daughter	14	None	Welshpool
Jones Ann Sarah	Daughter	15	None	Welshpool
Pryce Edward	Servant	15	Agric. Lab.	Llanfair
Richards John	Servant	42	Agric. Lab	Buttington

Shrewsbury (1871)

Williams Phillip	Head	40	Cattle dealer	Shrewsbury
Jones Harriet	Servant	23	Servant	Welshpool
Jones Ann Sarah	Servant	25	Servant	Welshpool

Figure 7.3 Migration history of Ann and Harriet Jones, 1861–71
Source: Census enumerators' books, 1861, 1871

family (now with two children) moved to Middlesbrough where two more daughters had been born by 1871. The motives for the move were probably economic. As an iron puddler Davies had a relatively unskilled job in the iron industry, but by moving to Middlesbrough he was able to take advantage of the expanding employment opportunities, and by 1871 had advanced to the position of mill furnaceman. Although cut off from Wales by physical distance, John Davies was able to transfer to an employment sector with which he was familiar, and he would have become part of the well-established South Wales community which existed in Middlesbrough by 1871. Although it is impossible to be sure, it is quite likely that Davies had friends or kin already living in Middlesbrough, and he would almost certainly have

Conway (1861)		*Liverpool* (1871)
Roberts Robert	→	Roberts Robert
Head		Head
44		54
Ship carpenter		Shipwright
Conway Carn		Conway Carn
Roberts Margaret	→	Roberts Margaret
Wife		Wife
31		42
None		None
Kent		Kent
Roberts Elizabeth	→	Roberts Elizabeth
Daughter		Daughter
3		13
None		None
Kent		Kent
Roberts Jane	→	Roberts Jane
Daughter		Daughter
2		12
None		None
Conway Carn		Conway Carn
		Roberts Isaac
		Son
		3
		None
		Lancs.

Figure 7.4 Migration history of Roberts family, 1861–71
Source: Census enumerators' books, 1861, 1871

known about employment opportunities before migrating to the north east.

CONCLUSIONS

Three general conclusions can be drawn about the links between the individual migration process (described above) and wider social and cultural change. First, although economic motives can be inferred for most of the cases studied, this did not necessarily lead immediately to economic advancement. Most migrants who worked in the origin areas had similar employment both before and after movement, and more information about wage levels and relative costs of living in different areas is necessary before further conclusions can be drawn. Perhaps the main economic benefits were experienced by those entering the labour market for the first time but in the longer term the larger labour markets of the English towns could have offered a better

Dowlais (1861)	*Middlesbrough* (1871)
Davies John	Davies John
Head	Head
24	32
Iron Puddler	Mill Furnaceman
Dowlais	Dowlais
Davies Mary Ann	Davies Mary Ann
Wife	Wife
20	29
None	None
Dowlais	Dowlais
Davies Methusalah	Davies Methuselah
Son	Son
0	10
None	None
Dowlais	Dowlais
	Davies Jane
	Daughter
	8
	None
	Dowlais
	Davies Abigail
	Daughter
	6
	None
	Middlesbrough
	Davies Margaret
	Daughter
	0
	None
	Middlesbrough

Figure 7.5 Migration history of the Davies family, 1861–71
Source: Census enumerators' books, 1861, 1871

range of employment prospects for all migrants. Second, although any movement is potentially disruptive, especially where individuals have developed a close association with a particular place, there were many ways in which migrants could lessen the disruptive effects of migration. The large proportion of moves that took place in family groups meant that immediate contacts were not changed after migration, and movement into the same economic sector meant that work-place practices would remain familiar. It can thus be suggested that migration, even over long distances (such as that from Dowlais to Middlesbrough), was not necessarily traumatic or unduly disruptive to family life and everyday routine. Third, it is clear that adjustment to a new community was facilitated by a well-established network of contacts and institutions in those English towns which had substantial Welsh communities. Welsh families remained relatively self-contained in England, Welsh lodgers gravitated towards Welsh households, and the Welsh Calvinistic Chapel provided a focus for community involvement and social control. These and other factors allowed the maintenance of Welsh culture in England and meant that even long-distance migration did not necessarily cause great social and cultural change in the short term.

It might be questioned whether returns from the investment of effort in this project were worthwhile: 53 linked migrants is not a particularly impressive total. However, these 53 case histories should be viewed in the same light as oral evidence or diaries in which case the sample size becomes more acceptable. Moreover, the longitudinal migration profiles, although imperfect, do provide detailed case histories for a period when oral evidence is impossible and diaries or personal accounts are scarce and often unrepresentative. It is not suggested that this methodology replaces the aggregate study of census evidence, but it does provide important additional material which can significantly improve our understanding of the motives for and effects of migration.[26]

ACKNOWLEDGEMENTS

Research for this paper was mainly carried out during 1985 and 1986 with financial assistance from the ESRC (award number G00232176). Figures were drawn in the Cartographic Unit, Department of Geography, Lancaster University.

NOTES

1 For example, A. K. Cairncross, 'Internal migration in Victorian England', *The Manchester School*, 17, 1949, pp. 67–87; C. T. Smith, 'The movement of population in England and Wales in 1851 and 1861', *Geographical Journal*, 107, 1951, pp. 200–10; D. Friedlander and R. J. Roshier, 'A study of internal migration in England and Wales', *Population Studies*, 19, 1966, pp. 239–79; R. Lawton, 'Rural depopulation in nineteenth-century England', in D. R. Mills (ed.), *English Rural Communities*, London, 1973, pp. 195–219; S. Nicholas and P. Shergold, 'Internal migration in England 1818–39', *Journal of Historical Geography*, 13, 1987, pp. 155–68, D. R. Mills (ed.), *Victorians on the Move*, Milton Keynes, 1984; A. Redford, *Labour Migration in England 1800–1850*, Manchester, 3rd edition, 1976.

2 P. M. Tillot, 'Sources of inaccuracy in the 1851 and 1861 censuses', in E. A. Wrigley (ed.), *Nineteenth-century Society*, Cambridge, 1972; R. Lawton (ed.), *The Census and Social Structure*, London, 1978, especially chapter 4, D. E. Baines, 'Birthplace statistics and the analysis of internal migration'.

3 For Bibliographies see C. G. Pearce and D. R. Mills, *Census Enumerators' Books: an Annotated Bibliography of Published Work*, Milton Keynes, 1982; P. Clark and D. Souden, *Migration and Society in Early-Modern England*, London, 1987.

4 For example, B. Thomas, 'The migration of labour into the Glamorganshire coalfield 1861–1911', *Economica*, 10, 1930, pp. 275–94; H. C. Darby, 'The movement of population to and from Cambridgeshire between 1851 and 1861', *Geographical Journal*, 101, 1945, pp. 118–25; R. Lawton, 'Population movements in the West Midlands 1841–1861', *Geography*, 43, 1958, pp. 164–77; W. T. R. Pryce, 'Migration and the evolution of culture areas; cultural and linguistic frontiers in north east Wales 1750–1851'. *Transactions of the Institute of British Geographers*, 65, 1975, pp. 79–108; C. Withers, 'Highland migration to Dundee, Perth and Stirling, 1753–1891', *Journal of Historical Geography*, 11, 1985, pp. 395–418; M. Anderson, 'Urban migration in nineteenth-century Lancashire – some insights into two competing hypotheses', *Annales de Démographie Historique*, 1971, pp. 13–26; W. Tucker, 'Patterns of migration of textile workers into Accrington in the early nineteenth century', *Local Population Studies*', 30, 1983, pp. 28–34; P. Cromar, 'Labour migration and suburban expansion in the North of England in the 1860s and 1870s', in P. White and R. Woods, *The Geographical Impact of Migration*, London, 1980, pp. 129–51.

5 R. Lawton, 'Irish migration to England and Wales in the mid-nineteenth century', *Irish Geography*, 4, 1959, pp. 35–54; J. A. Jackson, *The Irish in Britain*, London, 1963, J. H. Johnson, 'Harvest migration from nineteenth-century Ireland', *Transactions of the Institute of British Geographers*, 41, 1967, pp. 97–112; C. Richardson, 'Irish settlement in mid-nineteenth-century Bradford', *Yorkshire Bulletin of Economic and Social Research*, 20, 1968, pp. 40–57; R. D. Lobban, 'The Irish community in Greenock in the nineteenth century', *Irish Geography*, 6, 1971, pp. 270–81; J. Werly, 'The Irish in Manchester', *Irish Historical Studies*, 18, 1973, 345–58; R. Dillon, 'The Irish in Leeds, 1851–1861', *Thoresby Society Publications Miscellany*, 16, 1974, pp. 1–28; L. H. Lees, *Exiles of Erin: Irish Migrants in Victorian London*, Manchester, 1979; B. Collins, 'Proto-industrialization and pre-famine emigration', *Social History*, 7, 1982, pp. 127–46; R. Swift and S. Gilley (eds), *The Irish in the Victorian City*, London, 1985; R. Swift and S. Gilley, *The Irish in Britain 1815–1939*, London, 1989; B. Williams, *The Making of Manchester Jewry 1740–1875*, Manchester, 1976; E. Jones, 'The Welsh in London in the seventeenth and eighteenth centuries', *The Welsh History Review*, 10, 1981, pp. 461–79; R. M. Jones, 'Welsh immigrants in the cities of north west England 1890–1930: some oral testimony', *Oral History*, 9, 1981, pp. 33–41; C. G. Pooley, 'Welsh migration to England in the mid-nineteenth century', *Journal of Historical Geography*, 9, 1983 pp. 287–305; E. Jones, 'The Welsh in London in the nineteenth century', *Cambria*, 12, 1985, pp. 149–69.

6 For example R. M. Jones, op. cit.; M. Mackay, 'Nineteenth-century Tiree emigrant communities in Ontario', *Oral History*, 9, 1981, pp. 42–8; R. B. Perks, 'A feeling of not belonging: interviewing European immigrants in Bradford', *Oral History*, 12, 1984, pp. 64–7; also K. Bartholomew, chapter 8 in this volume.

7 On the use of letters see C. Erickson, *Invisible Immigrants: The Adaptation of English and Scottish Immigrants in Nineteenth-century America*, London, 1972; P. O'Farrell, *Letters from Irish Australia, 1825–1929*, Sydney, 1984; also E. Richards, chapter 2 in this volume. On diaries and autobiographies see J. Burnett, *Useful Toil*, London, 1974; R. Lawton and C. G. Pooley, 'David Brindley's Liverpool: an aspect of urban society in the 1880s', *Transactions of the Historic Society of Lancashire and Cheshire*, 126, 1975, pp. 149–68; D. Vincent, *Bread, Knowledge and Freedom: a Study of Nineteenth-Century Working Class Autobiography*, London, 1981; J. Burnett, D. Vincent and D. Mayall (eds), *The Autobiography of the Working Class: An Annotated and Critical Bibliography*, Brighton, vol. 1 1984; vol. 2 1987; A. G. Parton, 'The travels of Joseph Smith, well sinker 1877–1897: a study in personal migration for work', *North Staffordshire Journal of Field Studies*, 20, 1980, pp. 33–40.

8 See notes 1, 4 and 5.

9 Friedlander and Roshier, op. cit.; D. Baines, *Migration in a Mature Economy*, Cambridge, 1986.

10 R. Lawton and C. G. Pooley, 'Problems and potentialities for the study of internal population mobility in nineteenth-century England', *Canadian Studies in Population*, 5, 1978, Special Issue, 1980, pp. 69–84.

11 D. Grigg, 'E. G. Ravenstein and the Laws of Migration', *Journal of Historical Geography*, 3, 1977, pp. 41–54.

12 See also related work on longitudinal analysis such as T. Hagerstrand, 'What about people in Regional Science?', *Papers and Proceedings of the Regional Science Association*, 24, 1970, pp. 7–21; T. Carlstein, D. Parkes and N. Thrift (eds), *Timing Space and Spacing Time*, London, 1978; A. Pred, 'The social becomes the spatial, the spatial becomes the social: enclosures, social change and the becoming of places in Skane', in D. Gregory and J. Urry (eds), *Social Relations and Spatial Structures*, London, 1985, pp. 337–65.

13 See E. A. Wrigley (ed.), *Identifying People in the Past*, London, 1973; also B. Wojciechowska, 'Brenchley: a study of migratory movements in a mid-nineteenth-century rural parish', *Local Population Studies*, 41, 1988, pp. 28–40.

14 Problems of handling census data for the study of migration are discussed in E. A. Wrigley (ed.), *Nineteenth-century Society*, Cambridge, 1972, pp. 311–35; R. Lawton (ed.), *The Census and Social Structure*, London, 1978, pp. 146–64.

15 C. G. Pooley 1983, op. cit.

16 A. T. Gaydon (ed.), *Victoria County History of Shropshire* vol. 2, University of London, 1973, p. 10. See also records of Hills Lane Calvinistic Chapel, Shrewsbury, in National Library of Wales, Aberystwyth (C.M.A. 13130).

17 For a general account of nineteenth-century Shrewsbury see B. Trinder (ed.), *Victorian Shrewsbury*, Shropshire Libraries, 1984.

18 C. G. Pooley, 'Migration, mobility and residential areas in nineteenth-century Liverpool', unpublished Ph.D. thesis, University of Liverpool, 1978.

19 J. R. Jones, *The Welsh Builder on Merseyside*, Liverpool, 1946.

20 See G. Davies, *Nationalism as a Social Phenomenon*, Liverpool, 1965; R. M. Jones, 1981, op. cit; R. M. Jones and D. B. Rees, *The Liverpool Welsh and their Religion*, Liverpool, 1984.

21 See entries in D. Jeremy (ed.), *Dictionary of Business Biography*, London, 1983–6; more generally on Middlesbrough see R. P. Hastings, 'Middlesbrough: a new Victorian boom town', *Bulletin of the Cleveland and Teesside Local History Society*, 30, 1976, pp. 1–20; J. W. Leonard, 'Urban development and population growth in Middlesbrough, 1831–71', unpublished Ph.D. thesis, Teesside Polytechnic, 1965; C. A. Hempstead (ed.), *Cleveland Iron and Steel*, Redcar, British Steel Corporation, 1979; T. Gwynne and M. Sill, 'Census enumerators' books: a study of mid-nineteenth-century migration', *Local Historian*, 12, 1976, pp. 74–9.

22 For more general information on Wales in the nineteenth century see D. Howell, *Land and People in Nineteenth Century Wales*, London, 1979; A. H. Dodd, *The Industrial Revolution in North Wales*, Cardiff, 1933; D. Smith (ed.), *A People and a Proletariat, Essays in the History of Wales 1780–1980*, London, 1980; W. T. R. Pryce 1975, op. cit. W. T. R. Pryce, 'Wales as a culture region: patterns of change 1750–1971', *Transactions of the Honourable Society of Cymmrodorian*, 1978, pp. 229–61.

23 H. Carter and S. Wheatley, *Merthyr Tydfil in 1851*, Cardiff, 1982.

24 See also M. B. White, 'Family migration in Victorian Britain: the case of Grantham and Scunthorpe', *Local Population Studies*, 41, 1988, pp. 41–50; A. G. Darroch, 'Migrants in the nineteenth century: fugitives or families in motion?', *Journal of Family History*, 6, 1981, pp. 257–77.

25 See also J. T. Jackson, 'Long-distance migrant workers in nineteenth-century Britain: a case study of the St Helens glass makers', *Transactions of the Historic Society of Lancashire and Cheshire*, 131, 1982, 113–37.

26 See also J. C. Doherty, 'Short-distance migration in nineteenth century Lancashire', unpublished Ph.D. thesis, University of Lancaster, 1986, where the same methodology was used. A much higher linkage rate was also achieved in this study of short-distance migration.

8 Women migrants in mind

Leaving Wales in the nineteenth and twentieth centuries

Kate Bartholomew

Margaret and her schoolfriend Alice, from Wrexham, left home in 1936, straight from school at the age of 17. Neither family was keen on the idea, although both fathers had been out of work for years, and had had quite a struggle to keep the girls on at school. The employment situation in Wrexham at the time was so bad that the town council had seventy applications when it advertised for an office junior.

However, it was agreed that they could go together, to Leicester, under a Ministry of Labour scheme that found them office jobs and approved lodgings, with supervision until they were 18, and which supplemented their small wages. Both girls were provided with travel warrants and a little blue book of advice, and they were met at Leicester station by 'a brisk young woman from the Juvenile Employment Office'.

They first saw Leicester from a tram, and were placed with two other girls from South Wales, in lodgings, run by a landlady who had 'a bit of fish and a glass of stout for her supper. Our Welsh upbringing recoiled in horror!' They had little money to spare, even for the three-halfpenny stamp for a letter home, but 'our fathers were unemployed, so pride kept us from writing home for financial help'. Of Leicester people, Margaret wrote:

> They made us welcome in their home . . . our accents may have been odd to them but some Leicester phrases were a foreign language to us. Our landlady 'mashed' the tea and there was a man who told us 'he wor frit'.

Margaret told of how her mother had gone into service in London when she was 17, as had her sisters, and 'it seems to have been quite the usual thing for Welsh girls to do'.[1]

DOI: 10.4324/9781003172918-10

Martha, from Ynyswen in the Rhondda Valley, left Wales in February 1929, to follow her husband who had gone to the Midlands about four months before in the hope of getting work when Bute Pit closed. His brother had got work in the Austin factory, but he had to settle for a job as a baker's roundsman, despite his qualifications and experience as a pit deputy.

Martha had a hard time settling in to two rooms in Halesowen, and soon had to cope with a young baby, and her husband losing his job because of pneumonia. She found the city a lonely place after her life in Wales in a family of ten, with 'crowds of cousins and friends'.

Martha's husband got a job at the Corona works, where he joined the male voice choir that was possible because of the large numbers of Welsh employees. Martha's company were her children, and then she met a woman from Tredegar, who persuaded her to join the Co-operative Women's Guild which, she wrote, was 'the beginning of my education'. During her long involvement with the Guild she held every office within it, and eventually became a magistrate, serving for eighteen years on the Birmingham Bench. Through her Party activities Martha chaired conferences, visited Budapest, Warsaw, Paris, Vienna, East Germany, Switzerland and Milan, and went on a Peace Caravan with Dora Russell to Moscow.

Leaving school at 13½ with no further opportunity for education Martha looked back on her life as having been both interesting and rewarding. She has been recently nursing her husband who has pneumoconiosis, his legacy from pit work 56 years earlier.[2]

Glenys left her home at Penryncoch, near Aberystwyth, on 12 April 1932, at the age of 19. Her father was a miner and, as one of seven children, she had decided to train as a nurse and go to the hospital that replied first to her application. She made the decision herself, went alone, and took only her personal clothing. She felt it was a great adventure, a journey to the unknown world. A neighbour said 'surely you are not taking a change of clothing, you will be back for that!' This helped her to stick it out.

Glenys went to Manor Hospital, Walsall, for training, where she found the language and dialect very difficult as she was, and is still, a Welsh speaker. She worked in the same hospital for over forty years until her retirement in 1973. She has maintained her contacts with Wales by letter and telephone, in Welsh, throughout the years.

She 'had a very satisfying job, and would happily go through it all again under the same conditions, which were very hard indeed in the 1930s. One thing in particular I noticed in my early days in England.

When I started to visit homes, I noticed that the *men* did far more in the home and were more domesticated in every way than men in Wales. I therefore decided I could never marry a Welshman as much as I thought of Wales.'[3]

Migration, as these personal accounts have shown, involves a move from one area to another, and usually requires abandoning one social setting and entering a different one. Migration takes place when an individual decides that moving is better than staying put. The process thus concerns not only the move itself, but also the decision-making that precedes it and the degree of assimilation or alienation which follows.

The use, in this chapter, of the testimony of migrant women, recognizes that they are in a unique position to provide evidence of the experience of migration. Autobiographical material can provide a new way of looking at migration through the eyes of the participants. It can be a corrective and a supplement to the more usual documentary and statistical sources and can open up new areas for consideration. Our picture of the world of the migrant can be enlarged, and migration theory illumined, by individual testimony. In particular, light can be shed on the motivation of migrants and the personal circumstances surrounding their moves. The richness of detail and immediacy provided by oral material is not available from other sources.

Interpretation of oral sources, and their use in historical studies, offers new problems and new possibilities. Biographical accounts make generalization difficult but can put flesh on the bones of analysis. Personal narratives, if grouped with care and sensitivity, can provide a variety of experiences around a theme that can overcome the unrepresentativeness of any one oral source. Individual descriptions of journeys and anecdotes of family contacts and support can be linked with theories concerning networks of information flows. The usual checks for bias and reliability apply as much to oral evidence as to documentary material, and evaluation of such sources takes place within the wider context of other sources.

One of the main difficulties in studying migration in an historical context is that of blending what can be discovered about individual actions with aggregate data. This problem is all the more difficult when there is a lack of statistical information as there is for Wales. Despite recent work which has produced a collection of Welsh historical statistics, gaps still remain.[4] These are often attributable to the practice of lumping Wales together with England, or of grouping together the counties of North Wales and South Wales, and showing

Monmouthshire separately. Aggregated figures obscure the county variations and fail to highlight the industrial/rural differences.

Other difficulties arise, when trying to measure net migration of women from Wales, from the way in which births were recorded in the Registrar General's Annual Reports. Information on women that can be culled from official sources is often fragmentary and incomplete. The methods by which the figures were compiled mean that, for our purposes, inadequacies abound in the enumeration of women, especially in regard to their participation in the economy.[5] This is all the more unfortunate, as there is some unanimity in migration literature about the importance of economic factors in the migration process. Migrants themselves say so, as we have already seen.

Population statistics from 1851 to 1921 afford a picture for Wales as a whole of growth and increase – from 1.1 million in 1851 to 2.6 million in 1921. Closer examination of the figures, county by county, shows that this growth was not evenly distributed. Growth points were localized, as were points of decline. The urban areas of Cardiff, Swansea and Pontypridd, linked to the expanding coal industry, show the most striking increases, especially during the period 1871 to 1881. The slate quarrying industry in Meirionnydd and Caernarfon was thriving in the decade 1871 to 1881, and the population growth in these areas gives testimony to the development of industrial Wales.

By contrast, rural Wales, in particular Montgomeryshire, Brecon and Radnor, were already by the mid-nineteenth century beginning to show a decline in population.[6] For Montgomeryshire this had begun in 1851, for Brecon in 1871 and for Radnor in 1881. The rapidly expanding valleys of the industrial south and the belt from Wrexham across the north east of Wales are in sharp contrast to the decline and depopulation evident in the rural areas of North- and Mid-Wales. Only in Denbigh do the population figures show unbroken increase throughout the period 1801–1971. Flint, of all the counties whose population declined, shows the smallest change in the decade 1881–1891, a total loss of only 3,000. Glamorgan shows the largest single loss of men in the period 1931–1951. By contrast, and of great interest to this study, in Meirionnydd in that period there was a net loss of women without a similar accompanying loss of men. Clearly these differences are attributable to reasons other than birth and death rates. Migration can be held as the cause, and these two examples suggest that, contrary to received opinion, the sexes did not always move together.

Wales was not, and is not, a homogeneous region economically. During the inter-war years it was consistently the worst performer in the United Kingdom in terms of percentage unemployed. In 1929 Wales had a figure of 19.3 per cent compared with 13.5 per cent in the north of England and 12.1 per cent in Scotland. In 1932 the comparable figures were 36.5 per cent, 27.7 per cent and 27.1 per cent. In 1937 the figures were 22.3 per cent, 13.8 per cent and 15.9 per cent.[7]

There were considerable variations between North, South and Mid-Wales, and even between different areas within these divisions. For example, in Merthyr the demand for steam coal fell dramatically during this period, leading to higher unemployment there than in the Swansea area, where the fall in demand for anthracite was not nearly so marked, and the consequences for employment levels less dire.

Separating out the specific employment position and patterns of women from the aggregate is more difficult for reasons already mentioned. However, there are distinct trends that are discernible. Before the First World War there was a decline in the relative employment opportunities for women.[8] This was marked in the industrial areas but absent from rural areas. The general background was one of a narrow range of occupations taken up by women, centred on agriculture and domestic service, which in 1911 accounted for 51 per cent of occupied females.

Activity rates of women in Wales show slow growth from 1921, but the picture is somewhat obscured by migration flows and changes in occupational groupings. However, there is some support for the suggestion that opportunities for women increased as the importance of mining in industrial Wales decreased.[9]

Social investigation in Wales in the 1930s examined rural community life, and from this we may learn something of women's occupations in rural Wales. Alwyn Rees, in his study of a parish in northern Montgomeryshire,[10] offers both implicit and explicit observations on the nature of women's work and their contribution to rural community life. The part women played in the small economic units of the farms, by way of dairy, pig and poultry produce, was important to the domestic economy, to supply the seasonal shortfalls between income from the main crops and farm expenditure through the year. However, the amount of this type of work, especially for small holdings, was limited, and its economic value diminished with the development of commercial production in larger, more specialized units. This point is confirmed by occupation statistics which show a decline in the number of women in agriculture before 1911.[11] Imbalances in employment opportunities had long been a feature of agricultural communities, and had led to seasonal, long-term and permanent movement of people to other areas. Several studies show that these movements had occurred, and for the Welsh had not necessarily been of the rural to urban, Wales to overseas, no-looking-back variety.[12] There was, and is, a great deal of looking back when individuals move from Wales. Indeed, it has been argued that the Welsh have specially strong characteristics that distinguish them as an identifiable ethnic group which retains coherence in their migration destination.[13]

One of the great deficiencies of any purely statistical approach to human actions is that counting charts discrete events. It is here that the weakness of the method for historical enquiry shows most clearly. For history is concerned with both change and continuity, and migration contains elements of both, because of the human dimension. Studies of migration from Wales to England and elsewhere demonstrate that migrants did not immediately shed all their traditional ways, and assume those of their new home. These studies show that Welsh people were willing to move long distances when employment opportunities were available. Indeed, this fact was appreciated in the early twentieth century by the Press, who ran detailed employment vacancies in half-page advertisements of information for intending migrants, which quoted wage rates and areas where female servants were required.[14]

Migration of women from Wales had been a feature of demographic change for several centuries. It had long been the practice for girls to leave home to seek work. Seasonal migration of women to the market gardens of England during the summer months in the eighteenth and nineteenth centuries offers evidence of long-distance movement.[15] The wages of women who had moved away from home provided a vital contribution, in the form of remittances, to the family budget, especially in times of recession in Wales. Economic necessity no doubt provided a spur, but other influences played their part, and the pull of the town, freedom from parental supervision, and the chance of an independent income were other elements.

There were debates in government and other circles about overseas migration early in the nineteenth century. Thomas Malthus, in evidence to a Select Committee in 1826,[16] had viewed government-directed emigration as a temporary check on overpopulation to be applied, with other measures, to Ireland. This opinion was supported by some, such as the then Under Secretary for War and the Colonies, Robert Horton, and opposed by others, such as Richard Sadler and William Cobbett, who rejected Malthus' 'redundant population' theory.[17]

Governmental concern, then as later, centred on regulation, restriction and control. Nineteenth-century preoccupations with moral and disciplinary conditions on board emigrant ships continued into the twentieth century, especially with regard to women emigrants. This concern found its manifestation in the voluntary sector in the formation of emigration societies whose aims chimed in with government policies regarding selection. Supervision was paramount, with concern for protection of female emigrants and family settlement and reunion. The societies operated countrywide, using contacts with other organizations such as the Girls' Friendly Society, in order to ensure that potential applicants for emigration could be helped through the paperwork, with pre-embarkation training where necessary, and on to successful emigration.[18]

This voluntary effort was mirrored in commercial and government departmental drives to recruit female workers from Wales to the expanding domestic service occupations of London and the South East and the industrial markets of the Midlands and the North. The Ministry of Labour's Industrial Transference Scheme offered free fare, lodging allowances, pocket money and loans at special rates which proved tempting to some from South Wales in the middle and late 1930s.[19] Employment agencies in London and the Midlands recruited women from Wales during the inter-war years for domestic work and factory production. Cadbury's recruited girls and women for their chocolate works and an agency in Marylebone Road prepared others for domestic service. Others, from Newtown, moved to Huddersfield when the textile mill they worked in was destroyed by fire.

Academic investigation has generally concentrated on male settlers and migrants. All-male samples have been investigated and theories proposed on the basis of them.[21] They can be used to illumine some of the more general aspects of the process of migration, and the influences operating on migrants. The extent of migration is accessible from historical statistics, and attempts to understand the nature and scope of the process are helped by understandings gleaned from sociological studies. Structural factors, such as employment patterns and economic features of contemporary society, have a bearing upon decisions to move.

But when the people are women and the place of origin is Wales, a wide range of tools has to be employed. It has been suggested that migration and emigration were part of 'a process of change already in progress in their own country',[22] for those women who chose to move, and that long-distance movement was an extension of domestic mobility of women, which Ravenstein observed when formulating his Laws of Migration one hundred years ago.[23] He identified trends in movement from rural areas to towns, that most moves were short-distance, that large centres of industry and commerce attracted migrants from a long way away, and that 'females are more migratory than males'.

It is possible to characterize motivational influences by reference to 'push' and 'pull' factors. Information sources can be discovered by looking at the various schemes operating, direct recruitment by firms, advertisements in the Press and the practices of agencies. Informal information networks existed and intending migrants could obtain details of opportunities in other places from friends, family and contacts there. The intervening obstacles, such as distance and cost, and the nature of jobs and housing at the destination could be assessed, and the strategies used to overcome them examined. These assume a view of migrant women as passive victims of circumstance, economic and social. Closer examination of motivation demands a move from the general to the specific which is made possible when consideration is given to the meaning these decisions had for the individuals involved.

The question of motivation is central because it could be argued that economic and social factors operated on all those living in a certain place at a certain time, to a greater or lesser extent, but did not necessarily result in migration. Why did some decide to leave and others not? Who made the decision? Were they particular types of people? Did they have particular ambitions, aspirations, discontents and experiences? Are there identifiable strands in occupational backgrounds, skills, patterns of family organization and size, age, place of origin? Having made the first decision, that they would move, how did they decide on the destination? Attempts to ask these questions should properly be directed at individuals who move.

The problems attending obtaining answers are immense. Finding women to ask is the first problem. Those women who moved from Wales in the inter-war years are now in their seventies and eighties or as one of them chose to put it 'either compost or *non compos mentis*!'[24] Recollections of past events are, for an individual, coloured by subsequent life experiences, and memory can be incomplete and details inaccurate. But the richness of detail and immediacy that is available from such sources is not possible from anywhere else. Biographical accounts of important events for individuals present not only a narrative of their lives, but also, by the way in which women typically tell their stories in terms of their relationship with others, inform us about family networks and how economic and social factors bore upon their lives.

In order that motivation could be more fully explored, letters were sent to provincial newspapers in England in an attempt to make contact with some of the women who had left Wales in the inter-war years. Initial responses were followed by a more detailed questionnaire, which asked direct questions about dates and destinations, and allowed respondents to provide such further information about their motivations, feelings and memories as they thought important and relevant to their experience of migration. Over 150 detailed responses were received from all over England. Whilst not representative in a statistical sense, because this selection was not a properly-drawn sample of female migrants from Wales during the inter-war years, they are none the less of value as direct testimony, as the voices of migrants speaking of their perceptions of the process of migration.

What emerges from the stories are the concerns of migrants, what influenced their decisions to move, the help they received, and how they now view that move. Of those contacted, over 70 per cent made the journey on their own. But this does not mean that these were independent decisions made and carried out by individuals acting alone, for their stories show that over half of them were met at their destination by someone they knew, or had somewhere to stay with people they knew.

> Mother had friends who found us somewhere to live.[25]

> Met by some people my mother knew in Birmingham.[26]

Many migrants from Wales moved from counties and communities with a long tradition of migration and emigration. The existence of networks of contacts and information is documented in earlier studies of migration from Wales[27] with earlier waves of settlers and extended family contacts in the place of destination. Family gatherings brought distant relatives together and information was exchanged and support of various kinds given.

> My brothers paid for all my Nursing, medical and surgical books. My grandmother and aunts paid for training school dresses. An Uncle – my railway fare. My mother's eldest sister in North Wales contacted her brother-in-law who lived in Portsmouth, who met me at the station.[28]

Decision-making was often a family affair:

> After many family conferences, I was allowed to embark upon a nursing career.[29]

Official concern about the levels of unemployment amongst young women in Wales at the time is mentioned by several respondents.

> We had our names down at the local Labour Exchange some months before we were to leave. School authorities told us that if we did not get employment we could go back to school in the autumn.[30]

Teachers and Ministers in the rural communities used their wider networks and contacts to find work and training places for young women and girls. Work placements and glowing testimonials helped women to find jobs and enrol for training not available to them in Wales.

The complex nature of migration emerges clearly from the stories related by respondents in the study. There were many factors that may have influenced an individual's decision to leave home. Lack of employment prospects for women in many parts of Wales are mentioned as being decisive:

> Blaenau Ffestiniog had nothing to offer women.[31]

> The employment situation at the time was critical and I felt it necessary to move away to ease the burden at home.[32]

> My father had been unemployed for a long time and there was no hope of employment in the Rhondda for anyone at the time.[33]

For others the closed nature of Welsh life, unhappiness at home and a wish for more freedom were considered the most pressing reasons:

> In Wales there was too much class distinction – snobbery.[34]

> Home life was love-less – I would not wish any child to have a childhood like mine – EMPTY.[35]

> Some say Wales is more friendly – I found it completely different.[36]

> In Bangor everyone knew almost everyone else's business.[37]

> I looked forward to making up my own mind as to free time.[38]

The feelings these women remembered having on leaving home were varied, ranging from depressed and apprehensive to excited and thrilled. No doubt these recollections are coloured, to some extent, by the subsequent events and experiences of individuals. Memories tend to be selective, the more so perhaps at a distance of forty or fifty years, but they do recall contrasts between country life and that of the towns and cities the women moved to. Many write of the 'cold reserve' and unfriendliness of the English, and of communication difficulties caused by unfamiliarity with the English language or the regional accents encountered. However, some of the non-Welsh speaking women felt that their move was from an area where they had felt alien to one where they soon felt at home. This reminds us of the immigrant nature of much of the population of the Welsh coal-mining areas which had, a generation earlier, attracted labour from all over Britain. Many of the respondents, second-generation settlers, found they had no place in the land of their birth, and did not know where their future lay:

> No first year teachers could apply to Welsh schools.[39]

> In Wales I was looked upon as an English person, in England I was regarded as different, consequently there was always a feeling of 'not belonging'.[40]

Lack of knowledge of the Welsh language provided a strong reason for some to leave Wales, where they had felt unfairly rejected.

Accounts of the journeys and what was taken vary considerably according to whether a family was on the move, or an individual. Lone travellers typically took only what they could carry on the train, whilst families tended to travel with household furniture and effects to join the father, who had gone on ahead to secure accommodation. Most respondents expressed some degree of shock on arrival, commenting on the perceived increased pace of life and on the contrasts between a depressed and a thriving community.

The speed at which new arrivals settled also varied with some making a new home and life quickly and others still yearning to return, and doing so on retirement many years later. The flatness of the land and the people were commented on – 'no dramatization in communication' is how one woman puts it.

Keeping in touch with Wales is a feature of the majority of the stories, by the weekly letter, and later by regular annual visits with their children. Some speak warmly of the shared activities of the Welsh societies and chapels in their destination, which enabled them to maintain contact with their cultural identity. Others, recognizing the material improvements for them and their families, chose not to look back.

> I would never want to go back there . . . my roots are here now with my children and grandchildren.[41]

The complex of social relationships and contacts examined by Rees[42] in Montgomeryshire in the 1930s have an echo in Welsh expatriate social organization, and have direct relevance to the communication and support networks that were involved in facilitating the movement of people from their home area. Traditions of visits and reciprocal favours afforded by community contacts and co-operation carried over to migrant communities, and geographical dispersion did not necessarily lead to either social isolation or ghettos in the place of destination.[43] Migrants were distributed throughout England, but they kept contact with each other and with their cultural roots through understandings based on common interests and the common culture that had its provenance in the hospitality and exchange, the business and social transactions of Welsh communities of origin, cementing the idea of Welsh identity.

These recollections can help us to understand the process of migration for a group of migrants usually invisible or under-represented in aggregated data. The record they provide of the motivations and actions of women support the points made elsewhere about the decision-making which preceded migration, and the careful weighing of potential advantages of moving for individuals and families with children. The testimonies also confirm the existence and illustrate the efficiency of networks and information flows over long distances.

It is in the light shed on the process of migration for single, lone female migrants that these testimonies are particularly useful, for this group has remained elusive or indistinct by other methods because of gaps in statistics and name changes on marriage. The question of what is the appropriate unit for the study of migration is raised again, for discerning patterns is a difficult task when there are such a number of variables to examine. These women provide, through their recollections, the fullest range of financial inducements, family considerations, individual choices, economic and social factors, destinations, timings and motivations that operated on them. The picture that is revealed is rich and detailed, such that only participants can give.

NOTES

1 Respondent 111.
2 Respondent 150.
3 Respondent 64.
4 L. J. Williams, *Digest of Welsh Historical Statistics*, Cardiff, 1987.
5 P. Allin and A. Hunt, 'Women in official statistics', in V. Beechey (ed.) *The Changing Experience of Women*, Milton Keynes, 1982.
6 Census Reports 1801–1971, HMSO.

7 H. P. Fogarty, *Prospects of the Industrial Areas of Great Britain*, London, 1945.
8 L. J. Williams and T. Boyns, 'Occupations in Wales 1851–1911', *Bulletin of Economic Research*, University College of Wales, Aberystwyth, 1977.
9 ibid.
10 Alwyn Rees, *Life in a Welsh Countryside*, Cardiff 1961.
11 ibid.
12 J. Saville, *Rural Depopulation in England and Wales 1851–1951*, London 1957.
13 J. Williams Davies, '*Merched y Gerddi*: a seasonal migration of women from Wales', *Folk Life*, 15, 1972, pp. 12–23; E. Jones, 'The Welsh in London in the seventeenth and eighteenth centuries', *Welsh History Review*, 10, 1981; R. M. Jones, 'Welsh immigrants in the cities of North West England 1890–1930: some oral testimony', *Oral History*, 9, 1981; C. Pooley, 'Welsh migration to England in the mid-nineteenth century', *Journal of Historical Geography*, 9, 1983.
14 *Rhondda Leader*, January 9, 1904 and April 8, 1905.
15 Williams Davies, op. cit.
16 Report of Select Committee on Emigration from the United Kingdom, 1826, vol. 4, CMD 404.
17 E. G. Wakefield, *A View of the Art of Colonization in Letters Between a Statesman and a Colonist*, Oxford, 1914.
18 Una Monk, *New Horizons: 100 Years of Women's Migration*, London, 1963.
19 A. D. K. Owen, 'Social consequences of the Industrial Transference Scheme', *Sociological Review*, XXIX, 1937.
20 Respondent 111.
21 K. Young, 'Sex Specificity in Migration: A Case from Mexico', International Migration Review, vol. 14, no. 1, 1980.
22 M. Morokvasic, 'Women in migration: beyond the reductionist outlook', in A. Phizacklea (ed.), *One Way Ticket*, London, 1983.
23 E. G. Ravenstein, 'The laws of migration' in *Journal of the Royal Statistical Society*, XLVIII, 1885.
24 Respondent 109.
25 Respondent 070.
26 Respondent 064.
27 Pooley, op. cit.
28 Respondent 024.
29 Respondent 039.
30 Respondent 111.
31 Respondent 023.
32 Respondent 107.
33 Respondent 015.
34 Respondent 074.
35 Respondent 023.
36 Respondent 074.
37 Respondent 070.
38 Respondent 004.
39 Respondent 017.
40 Respondent 013.

41 Respondent 112.
42 Rees, op. cit.
43 C. G. Pooley, 'Migration, mobility and residential areas in nineteenth century Liverpool', Ph.D. thesis, University of Liverpool, 1978.

Part III
Immigration to Britain

9 Historians and immigration

Colin Holmes

INTRODUCTION

In considering migration and British society, we should guard against concentrating exclusively upon emigration. In other words, apart from asking 'Who left Britain and where did they go?', we need to ask 'Who came to Britain and what were the experiences of such groups after their arrival?'.

If we begin from this standpoint, and concentrate essentially on the last one hundred years, it soon becomes clear that historians have paid little attention to immigration history. This lack of interest is strikingly evident in texts by Taylor, Bédarida, Stevenson and Robbins.[1] However, if the footprints of historians are weak, those left by sociologists are heavy. Indeed, sociologists have dominated academic research on immigration into Britain. However, this sociological literature does not convey any impression of immigration as a continuing process; moreover, the weight of emphasis in these enquiries has centred upon Black and Asian immigrations since 1945. A dissatisfaction with this state of affairs provides some of the motivation for this discussion of historians and immigration. It is also influenced by the reflected experience of writing *John Bull's Island*, published in the summer of 1988, which attempted to construct the first comprehensive history of immigration into Britain, concentrating on the years between 1871 and 1971.[2] In writing this type of book, an awareness gradually develops of those issues which need to be kept in mind in future research activity.

NEGLECTED AREAS: THE IRISH

Let us begin by noticing areas of immigration which would repay further attention. The last major general survey of Irish immigrants

DOI: 10.4324/9781003172918-12

appeared in 1963, and, to reinforce one of the introductory emphases, it was written by J. A. Jackson, a sociologist.[3] Since that date a number of studies of the Irish minority have been published, including the works of L. P. Curtis, Lynn Lees, Roger Swift and Sheridan Gilley and the useful synthesizing article of M. A. G. O' Tuathaigh.[4] However, apart from the last item, these writings are specific studies of parts of the Irish experience in Britain and heavily weighted towards the 'crown of thorns' period in the mid-nineteenth century. The subsequent history of Irish groups has been almost totally ignored. In recovering more of it we should be recapturing details on the largest single immigrant minority living in Britain during the last hundred years.[5] The fact that this fragment of statistical information is not widely known or appreciated is itself significant.

THE CONTINENTAL EUROPEAN DIMENSION

If a wider glance is cast at European groups in Britain other holes soon become visible. But after making this point a degree of qualification is in order. The Jewish immigrants from Russian Poland in the late nineteenth century and the refugees from the Greater Germany in the 1930s have been the subject of numerous enquiries, even if some features of these immigrations still remain obscure.[6] Jewish communities have tended in most countries to recover their history and in Britain the efforts of individual scholars, of varying ideological persuasions, and institutional activity, have all contributed to this process.

Other groups, however, have been less well-served. If we retreat into the late nineteenth century, until 1891 the Germans constituted the largest single continental European immigrant minority in Britain. The weight of enquiry into the experiences of Russian Polish Jews has obscured this fact. The result is that we need to know more regarding the reasons behind this movement from Germany. If the lives of certain individuals such as Ludwig Mond[7] and the history of specific groups, particularly that of German clerical workers,[8] have provided some evidence on this question, we still await information on German pork butchers, those Germans who worked in the salt industry in Cheshire, indeed, on the majority of working-class Germans, including the impoverished German governesses, and also on the ubiquitous German bands who formed a familiar feature of British society before the Great War. A recent study, written incidentally by a specialist in English literature, is helpful in bringing into focus the intellectual and political émigrés who came to Britain from Germany before 1914, but it does not assist us much outside these groups.[9] Furthermore, it is only within the last few years that we have started to construct the history of responses towards the German minority during the First World War.[10] The gap which at present exists between the level of such recovery and the relatively lavish treatment of the Jewish refugees from the Greater Germany in the 1930s remains enormous.

If we switch from the Germans to the Italians we soon encounter important omissions. Until recently the Italians in Scotland had been better served by researchers. However, with the appearance of Lucio Sponza's work some of this ground has been clawed back.[11] Even so, none of this research has touched upon the more recent history of the Italians, the fifth largest immigrant minority in the 1950s and early 1960s when the migration flow from Italy was relatively strong. At the moment, the fullest account of these Italians, but a study almost certain to remain unpublished, arises from the efforts of an anthropologist.[12]

At this point it is worth observing that if the Jews who left the Tsar's Empire and settled in Britain have had their history substantially recovered, the same cannot be said of the other smaller groups who left the Russian Empire in the late nineteenth and early twentieth century. A start has been made on piecing together the history of the predominantly Catholic Lithuanian minority but the resulting picture of this group, who developed a particularly vibrant community in Lanarkshire, remains patchy and incomplete.[13] Furthermore, in spite of the interest shown by sociologists in Britain's post-war experience of immigration we are still some time away from the likely appearance of any large-scale comprehensive studies of the post-war Polish exiles. The European Volunteer Workers of various nationalities who were recruited by the British Government to assist in the post-war recovery of Britain have also been neglected. Published studies of the Polish minority have been dominated until very recently by a process of sociological enquiry which has been re-worked and revised on a number of different occasions. The recent publication of an historical investigation into the post-war Polish group marks a step in the right direction of recovery even though this particular study takes 1950 as its outer chronological limit.[14] As for the European Volunteer Workers, no full-scale study has appeared since 1958 when a Civil Servant who had been involved in various EVW schemes worked on the official papers under a privileged access arrangement.[15] Interest has been revived recently in the EVWs, however, partly on account of the possible presence of war criminals among their ranks.[16] Independently of this enquiry, an ESRC-funded exercise led by sociologists at Glasgow University, has also begun to investigate the lives of those men and women who exchanged the dreariness of Displaced Persons camps in Europe for a new uncertain start in Britain.

NEGLECTED AREAS: IMMIGRATION FROM BEYOND EUROPE

If we direct our attention to those groups who come from 'beyond the oceans',[17] it is a sobering thought that for many years the most comprehensive historical study of Blacks in Britain, in other words those groups of Afro-Caribbean origin, came from a social anthropologist, Kenneth Little, whose book *Negroes in Britain*, first published in 1948, constituted the pioneer study of what we might call 'the Edinburgh school'.[18] Work carried out at a later date by Jim Walvin has added to our understanding of the history of the Black minority[19] and paved the way for Peter Fryer's *Staying Power*, which now constitutes the fullest historical account of Blacks in Britain and is particularly useful for its emphasis on the varied but often neglected contributions made by Black men and women to the development of British society.[20] In the case of the minorities from the Indian subcontinent the most comprehensive historical study is the recently published work by Rozina Visram.[21] The books by Fryer and Visram have their strengths and weaknesses. However, both surveys must be welcomed and the fact that these books have been written by people outside the academic world underlines the fact that for many academic historians Blacks and Asians remain invisible people.[22] Such social invisibility applies even more to the Chinese, on whose presence in Britain there is no history.

Where historians have been reluctant to engage in any commitment, sociologists have been particularly busy and their interest in solving social problems has drawn them particularly to the study of Blacks and Asians since 1945. We have noticed as much. In now considering their activity in more detail, it is worth observing that the bulk of their work is characterized by assumptions, claims and perspectives against which historians need to be on their guard. Three interrelated emphases have some claim on our attention. In accounting for the hostility experienced by Blacks and Asians, sociological enquiries have placed considerable emphasis upon the role of the folkways, the cultural conditioning process, which is presented as one legacy of the colonial imperial epoch. In short, it has been emphasized that these groups did not step into a neutral ideological world when they arrived in Britain but entered into a society where colonialism and imperialism had nourished impressions of white supremacy. This emphasis has been particularly pronounced in the work of John Rex and his followers.[23] If we can accept the possibility that such cultural conditioning might be important, we are still left with a number of problems which sociologists have done little to resolve and to which historians should address more attention. For example, are there specific strands within this general set of images upon which we should direct our attention? In addition, can we assess the influence of the weight of the past in relation to the weight of the present in analysing the causes of conflict? In other words, the blanket use of the past as an all-enveloping influence needs to be resisted; at the moment its deployment smacks heavily of speculation.[24]

Closely related to this emphasis on the persistence of the past is the gregarious use of the term racism to describe the hostility encountered by Blacks and Asians. Too often it remains undefined and in many cases has degenerated into little more than a catch-all concept, or in its ultimate degenerative form, into a term of mere abuse. There is also a failure in many accounts to recognize that racism possesses its own complex history and that its definition and social significance change over the course of time.[25]

Finally, and related to this emphasis, when sociologists in the course of their studies indulge in their token reference to historical precedents, they have shown a remarkable tendency to assess the past exclusively through the values of the present. This 'presentism' acts as a distorting mirror to the historical dimension of their work.[26] In short, historians need to be constantly on guard – borrowing indiscriminately from sociologists is a high-risk exercise.

THE NUMBERS GAME

But do any of these questions and criticisms relate to a significant strand of the British experience? Is it not a fact that the country lacks a tradition of immigration? It has been hinted already that this assumption would be difficult to sustain and at this juncture it can be directly rebutted. In considering such immigration we are not dealing with an episodic phenomenon; on the contrary, we can trace a continual process of entry. Furthermore, we are not restricted to a limited range of immigrant and refugee groups; instead, we can point to a wide range of newcomers. These perspectives need to be emphasized and understood.[27]

So does a qualifying perspective. Over the past one hundred years

Britain has tended to be a net exporter of population. At certain times, in the early 1930s and in the years preceding the Commonwealth Immigrants Act in 1962, for example, an opposite pattern can be detected. Nevertheless, the general trend of outward movement which in itself has encouraged an interest in the history of emigration, cannot be gainsaid.[28] Popular remarks dwelling on the prospect of over-population in Britain as a consequence of immigration are often heard. However this emphasis, and the related imagery of such discussions, expressed in references to 'waves', 'flooding' and 'swamping', conveniently overlook the net loss factor, the other side of what must be regarded as a two-way process. Even so, we need to return to the emphasis which recognized the continual process of immigration and lay claims to its intrinsic historical importance. After all, which historian would restrict significance to a purely quantitative level? There are in addition other substantial grounds for studying immigration. A consideration of its impact upon the development of British society and a discussion of the responses towards immigration which emerged in Britain, raise points of more than a parochial significance.[29]

THE IMPACT OF THE NEWCOMERS

Many existing discussions of immigrant and refugee groups celebrate the virtues of the newcomers and stress their influence in shaping the contours of British society. In other words we encounter a fair dose of hagiography. Indeed, at times we might be forgiven for thinking that an effete and sinking Britain had been rescued and restored to an even keel by various groups of newcomers. The history of German Jews in Britain provides an excellent illustration of this tendency.[30] It can be readily understood why these emphases emerge. By advancing such claims members of a particular group are saying, in effect, to the majority: 'Look how useful we are; tolerate us.' But it is not only writers drawn from within various immigrant and refugee minorities who offer such emphases. The general transformation in the image of the Ugandan Asian minority is one of the most remarkable developments in recent British social history. This group, which initially ran into widespread opposition, has been showered more recently with lavish praise as the epitome of those qualities of hard work, diligence and self-help which at present are being strongly asserted in Britain.[31] It is not difficult to understand why minorities are content to bask in this admiring light. In more cautionary vein, however, we should recognize that no minority possesses a permanent guarantee of admiration. Public opinion can shift with changes in circumstance. Moreover, dangers can lurk in developing the view that the only worthwhile minorities are those which can lay claim to conventional forms of success.

Even so, it cannot be denied that immigrants and refugees have contributed to the development of British Society. This observation can be sustained both in relation to the economy and the nation's cultural life.

In concentrating on the theme of economic impact, uncertainties nevertheless continue to surround a number of issues. The role played by the Irish in the industrialization of Britain is a case in point. On the one hand, they have been regarded as indispensable agents in this change: in his general survey Jackson stressed their central role in the industrialization process.[32] A historian's later assessment has sounded a note of caution.[33] The resolution of this difference and the extension of the debate from the period of the Industrial Revolution into later years has not yet been attempted. The economic role of labour from Southern Ireland in the war industries between 1935 and 1945 is one area where more work is required. But it is not only the economic activity of the Irish which remains uncertain. We are told that during the First World War Black workers undertook an important role in the munitions industry.[34] Did they? Where is the evidence of this? What can we unearth on the role of Black workers in the merchant shipping industry in the same period beyond the observation that an increase occurred in their employment?[35] It would not be difficult to provide evidence on similar uncertainties relating to other groups and different periods.

If we move from economic to social or cultural themes, gaps are equally present. The role of the Irish in the Roman Catholic church would repay more attention: it is particularly disappointing that a recent study of the Roman Catholic minority contains only passing reference to the Irish and nothing at all on the Italians and the Ukrainians.[36] Furthermore, the influence of Blacks and Asians upon English literature,[37] to which might be added the contribution of such minorities to the arts in general, continues to escape any systematic historical enquiry.

Any attempt to assess economic or cultural impact poses acute problems, not least because impact is a slippery concept, but that is not a sufficient reason for avoiding the challenge. Studies which have already been completed on the role of Jews in business activity and the number of Jewish scientists admitted to Fellowships of the Royal Society[38] need to find their equivalents in surveys of other groups.

Until we engage in such work our understanding of the history of immigration and its relationship to broader currents in British society remains significantly incomplete.

RESPONSES

In considering the responses which newcomers faced we soon encounter the image of Britain as a tolerant society. Such sentiment forms the stuff not only of much popular and official opinion: its echo can also be found among immigrant and refugee minorities. Hence the observation by Kitty Pistel, a child-refugee from Vienna: 'I am so happy in this free, friendly country, where I experienced so much kindness that it is my biggest wish to remain here for ever'.[39] We shall need to return to this emphasis at a later point. At this juncture, however, it is more germane to remark that one task of the historian is to shift the discussion of response patterns from an emotive on to a cognitive level. In doing so we need to probe into the emphasis on toleration.

A comprehensive historical survey of immigrant and refugee minorities in Britain provides a procession of evidence indicating that such groups have encountered hostility, whether at the level of ideas or in the shape of discriminatory action. In its most dramatic fashion it surfaced in various incidents of collective violence. The years between 1911 and 1919, which witnessed attacks on the Chinese in Cardiff in 1911, on the Jews in Tredegar in the same year, on the German minority in 1914–15, the Russian Poles in 1917 and the Black minority in 1919 provide some of the most graphic testimony on this score.[40] Violence, however, has not been confined to this period. A group of sociologists, prompted by events in Bristol in 1980, revealed some awareness of this wider canvas but even their account is characterized by a limited chronological range and a concentration upon a restricted range of minority groups.[41] The theme of racial and ethnic violence in Britain still awaits its historian.

CONCLUDING COMMENT

A consideration of the responses encountered by immigrants and refugees not only provides an opportunity to qualify the image of Britain as a centre of liberal toleration, it also brings to the surface an issue within the academic profession which needs to be aired. There are historians who regard any work on immigration as a diversion.

'Why concentrate on the periphery when there are important tasks at the centre?' is their theme. The study of class conflict is academically respectable: the history of racial and ethnic conflict has not yet attained such status. This negative perception is one reason why so much more work on immigration has been conducted by sociologists, social anthropologists and geographers. Historians who focus on immigrants, refugees and minorities run the risk of being blocked in an intellectual cul-de-sac notwithstanding the fact that the distinction between mainstream and peripheral history which some attempt to draw is a false antithesis. In order to be effective at the level of analysis the history of immigration needs to be located within the broader swirls and currents of society. For example, the widespread hostility encountered by Russian Polish Jews in the East End in the late nineteenth century cannot be divorced from the complex changes which affected the housing market during these years. Furthermore, the countrywide attacks on the Irish in Britain in 1882 need to be related to events in Ireland in that year and the broader theme of Irish nationalism. Finally, if the roots of the 1962 Commonwealth Immigration Act are complex and at the moment particularly uncertain since the official papers are still shielded from public inspection, nevertheless it can be safely claimed that an understanding of the measure needs to transcend the debate over 'race relations' and take on board wider issues such as Britain's retreat from the Commonwealth in favour of a future in Europe and the changing needs of the labour market.[42]

If we do accept the claim that immigration and related issues are proper, respectable neighbourhoods for historians to inhabit, is it possible now to provide some guidelines as to the precise areas into which their research priorities might take them?

'Recover more on the history of European groups' should be one major consideration. Apart from repeating the need to recapture large chunks of the recent history of groups such as the Irish, two examples, drawn from continental European groups, further help to underline the importance of the European perspective. During the First World War, between August 1914 and the Spring of 1915, over 200,000 Belgian refugees poured into Britain. The size of this group alone should result in a degree of reflection. The influx of Belgians exceeded the number of Russian–Polish Jews who settled in Britain between 1881 and 1914. Yet the history of the gallant Belgians still retains its blank spots. The fullest study, published only recently, is more concerned with the evolution of social policy in the shape of refugee relief work than it is with a rounded study of the refugees.[43] Nevertheless, we should be grateful for what we have on the Belgians: it is not difficult to think of other groups who came to Britain on account of a well-founded fear of persecution, on whom even less information exists. The 21,000 Hungarians who entered after the uprising in 1956 constitute one such neglected case.

In recovering this European dimension one general theme also deserves our attention. In contrast to the reiterated importance of the Colonial–Imperial tradition as a force directing hostility towards Blacks and Asians, the tracing of a tradition through which the British perceived their superiority over Europeans still remains neglected by historians. How closely did the industrialization of Britain influence such perceptions? Can we detect any suggestion of a general hierarchy of toleration? Can it be said that northern Europeans were more likely to be tolerated than southern Europeans? Did further sub-divisions exist within these broad groups?[44] At the same time as probing into these questions, we need to assess the influence of such inherited stereotypes alongside immediate pressures, or what Americans often call situational influences, in trying to disentangle and understand the roots of the hostility which European groups have experienced in Britain.

In view of the fact that other social scientists have concentrated their attention almost exclusively on the years since 1945, an important role can also be envisaged for those historians interested in Blacks and Asians. Much more needs to be known about these groups before this period and the same observation applies to those other minorities who came to Britain from beyond Europe. 'Concentrate on recovering the historical dimension of these groups' might be dispensed as timely advice. After all, there is little likelihood of this activity being undertaken by others. In Sociology, particularly, the current lack of interest in the historical dimension is likely to be aggravated even more as the subject becomes increasingly policy-orientated.

'Recover more on the history of minorities in Britain' is another emphasis worth bearing in mind, considering the fact that Scotland and Wales have been particularly neglected. Comprehensive studies of those Lithuanians and Jews who lived north of the border have yet to appear. The history of the Irish in Scotland is also in need of revitalization and synthesis.[45] In view of this state of affairs it is to be hoped that the recently established Centre for Migration Research at Glasgow, attached to the Sociology Department, will not neglect the historical dimension of its work. In the case of Wales, there are patches of exhaustive recovery – the history of Blacks and other minorities in Cardiff, particularly those aspects relating to the collective violence of 1919 and the disputes in the shipping industry in the inter-war years, have received detailed attention.[46] However, other groups, such as the Irish, the Jews and the Poles, have been less well-served.

In the case of England, the intending researcher should be urged particularly: 'Recover the history of communities outside London.' The concentration on the capital is understandable. During most periods London has functioned as a magnet, drawing into itself both immigrants and refugees. The East End in particular has recruited many groups of such newcomers over the last hundred years. It is hardly surprising therefore that, for example, we have studies of the Irish in the capital but it is worth noting that Lees' book, *Exiles of Erin*, one of the best-known, follows a familiar pattern in concentrating on the mid-nineteenth century Irish.[47] In the case of the Jewish East End we need to notice Lloyd Gartner's pioneer study *The Jewish Immigrant in England 1870–1914*[48] and, more recently, and from a different perspective, David Feldman's Cambridge Ph.D. thesis.[49] Moreover, anyone interested in East End Jewry must take account of the works of Bill Fishman who, more than any other historian, has recaptured the ambience of Jewish East London.[50] Sponza's recent work on the Italians reveals that the history of other minorities in the capital has also caught the attention of historians.[51] Even so, it is surprising that, as yet, no one has attempted to construct a general history of immigrants and minorities in London.

Nevertheless, whatever remains to be written on London even more work is needed on the history of other cities. Bradford is a case in point. Scattered fragments can be found on the Irish and on the more recent history of minorities originating in the New Commonwealth.[52] However, none of this work possesses the feel of completeness. In addition, we certainly need to ask what has happened to the history of the Germans in Bradford, a group celebrated by J. B. Priestley, one of the city's sons, and the visible symbols of whose heyday can still be seen in Little Germany? A similar darkness has settled upon the history of the Poles and the European Volunteer Workers who came to the city after the Second World War. Oral recollections from these and other groups have been compiled by the Bradford Heritage Recording Unit but a historian's firm hand is needed to pull together such material into a coherent whole.[53] This focus upon Bradford is not because it provides a unique case of supporting evidence for the particular argument which is now being advanced. A similar case can be constructed if our focus is shifted towards other great northern cities such as Liverpool and Manchester. However, the newly established Institute of Irish Studies at Liverpool University should swell our knowledge of the important Irish minority in that city. As for Manchester, one of the most cosmopolitan cities in Britain, an important gap would be plugged by the appearance of the second volume of Bill Williams' history of Manchester Jewry: without it we are lacking information on one of the city's important minority groups.[54] If we leave aside the specifically Jewish dimension of Manchester's history and focus on a more general perspective, it is also surprising that, as yet, there is no overall history of the immigrants and refugees who found their various ways to the city. On standing back from such observations, and reflecting for a moment, we can also envisage the possibility of a potentially important comparative study of Bradford, Liverpool and Manchester, as centres of immigration into Britain.

'Recover the history of immigration warts and all but with a due regard for the complexity of that history', might be presented as a final consideration. We need to ask ourselves whether we can remain content with celebratory studies which dilate upon the deeply etched virtues of Britons true, contemplate the pleasure of the country's civilization, and rejoice in the triumph of decency over evil. These assumptions and claims, sometimes shared, it has been noticed, by immigrants and refugees, have acted as a distorting agency in many accounts of immigration. In particular, such work underplays the realities of group conflict which cannot be written out of the script. Indeed, its extent should not be underestimated. Opposition towards immigrants and refugees has surfaced not only from individuals and groups but has also in official policies. In other words, the state has disrupted the hopes, aims and aspirations of such groups whether through immigration control, internment, the powers it has assumed over deportation, or through the consequences of these developments, in the course of which immigrants and refugees often become stereotyped as 'problem groups'.[55]

Over the past few years considerable emphasis has been placed upon the weight of institutional opposition pressing upon the lives of Blacks and Asians.[56] However, in recognizing the significance of this observation and extending it to other groups, a degree of caution is in order. Some accounts of such hostility towards Blacks and Asians have displayed a particularly *farouche* dimension. A certain wildness of judgement has also extended beyond this particular theme. We can easily lay our hands on texts which portray Britain as a society in which hostility towards immigrants and refugees has been rampant and universal and remains so. In fact, however, attitudes and actions at both official and popular level have often displayed a complexity which cautions against any simple categorization of responses.[57]

If we tackle this issue of complexity from a different angle, liberal writers anxious to promote the view of immigration as a positive force in British society have paid too little attention to the role that immigrants and refugees might have played in the development of hostility.[58] A due degree of caution and a sensitivity to detail and argument are essential in any such exercise but, as in other areas of immigration, the difficulty of the task should not lead to its avoidance. This last observation is also relevant to the themes of inter-minority and intra-minority conflict; these phenomena pose particularly awkward questions which many investigators are inclined to side-step.[59]

The overall thrust of this discussion has been to draw attention to gaps, problems and difficulties which face historians interested in immigration. In order to meet these challenges successfully, at a fundamental level historians need to believe in the intrinsic worth of their endeavours. They should resist any tendency to operate from an academic ghetto, whether self-imposed or as a consequence of pressure from other historians. At the same time, they should reach out towards other social sciences and draw discreetly and selectively rather than slavishly upon the insights offered by these disciplines, particularly by sociology and psychology, but without forgetting the additional relevance of political science and geography. By travelling along such lines of enquiry we shall build upon existing strengths. Furthermore, by using whatever material is at hand, whether it comes in the form of traditional printed sources or in the varied shapes of oral and visual artefacts, irrespective of whether these materials are conventionally regarded as 'appropriate' for the historian's task, we shall be able to construct an academic springboard capable of launching us into a 'consistently comparative'[60] analysis, which sets the British experience of immigration against that of other countries. If that point is still some way off and other threads need to be knitted together first, comparative work, the difficulty of which cannot be underestimated needs to be firmly in our sights in a longer term vision. After all, the study of immigration is hardly conducive to the perpetuation of an insular tradition of history. Perhaps that is an additional reason why some historians avoid the topic or reduce it to a residual insignificance? However, the pursuit of that particular argument will have to wait for another occasion.

NOTES

1 See A. J. P. Taylor, *English History 1914–1945*, Oxford, Oxford University Press, 1985; F. Bédarida, *A Social History of England 1851–1975*, London, Methuen, 1979; K. Robbins, *The Eclipse of a Great Power: Modern Britain 1870–1975*, London, Longman, 1983; J. Stevenson, *British Society 1914–45*, London, Allen Lane, 1984.

2 C. Holmes, *John Bull's Island, Immigration and British Society 1871–1971*, London, Macmillan, 1988.

3 J. A. Jackson, *The Irish in Britain*, London, Routledge & Kegan Paul, 1963. Some observers prefer to regard the Irish as migrants but custom and practice has the Irish minority in Britain classified as immigrants.

4 L. P. Curtis, *Anglo-Saxons and Celts: A Study of Anti-Irish Prejudice in Victorian England*, Bridgeport, Conn., New York University Press, 1968; L. P. Curtis, *Apes and Angels, The Irishman in Victorian Caricature*, Newton Abbot, David & Charles, 1971; L. H. Lees, *Exiles of Erin: Irish Migrants in Victorian London*, Manchester, Manchester University Press, 1979; R. Swift and S. Gilley (eds), *The Irish in the Victorian City*, London, Croom Helm, 1985; M. A. G. Ó'Tuathaigh, 'The Irish in nineteenth century Britain: problems of integration', *Transactions of the Royal Historical Society*, vol. 31, 1981, pp. 149–73.

5 *Census 1981, Great Britain, Country of Birth*, London, HMSO, 1983, p. 2.

6 The role of women in both movements would repay more attention.

7 J. Goodman, *The Mond Legacy*, London, Weidenfeld & Nicolson, 1982.

8 G. Anderson, *Victorian Clerks*, Manchester, Manchester University Press, 1976 and his 'German clerks in England 1870–1914: another aspect of the Great Depression debate', in K. Lunn (ed.), *Hosts, Immigrants and Minorities. Historical Responses to Newcomers in British Society, 1870–1914*, Folkestone, Dawson, 1980, pp. 201–21.

9 R. Ashton, *Little Germany. Exile and Asylum in Victorian England*, Oxford, Oxford University Press, 1986.

10 P. Panayi, 'Germans in Britain during the First World War', Ph.D. thesis, Sheffield University, 1988.

11 L. Sponza, *Italian Immigrants in Nineteenth-Century Britain: Realities and Images*, Leicester, Leicester University Press, 1988.

12 R. C. G. Palmer, 'The Britalians. An anthropological investigation', Ph.D. thesis, Sussex University, 1981.

13 See K. Lunn, 'Reactions to Lithuanian and Polish immigrants in the Lanarkshire coalfield 1880–1914', in Lunn, op. cit., pp. 308–42; J. D. White, 'Scottish Lithuanians and the Russian Revolution', *Journal of Baltic Studies*, vol. 6, 1975, pp. 1–8; M. Rodgers, 'The Anglo-Russian Military Convention and the Lithuanian immigrant community in Lanarkshire, Scotland 1914–20', *Immigrants and Minorities*, vol. 1, 1982, pp. 60–88.

14 S. Patterson, 'The Poles: An exile community in Britain', in J. L. Watson (ed.), *Between Two Cultures. Migrants and Minorities in Britain*, Oxford, Basil Blackwell, 1977, pp. 214–41; K. Sword et al., *The Formation of the Polish Community in Great Britain*, London, School of Slavonic and East European Studies, 1989.

15 J. A. Tannahill, *European Volunteer Workers in Britain*, Manchester, Manchester University Press, 1958.
16 See *War Crimes. Report of the War Crimes Enquiry*, Cm.744, London, HMSO, 1989.
17 V. G. Kiernan, 'Britons old and new', in C. Holmes (ed.), *Immigrants and Minorities in British Society*, London, Allen & Unwin, 1978, p. 54.
18 K. Little, *Negroes in Britain. A Study of Racial Relations in English Society*, London, Kegan Paul, Trench, Trubner, 1948: re-issued 1972. Little, Michael Banton, Sidney Collins and Sheila Patterson are among those researchers associated with Edinburgh University in the early years after the Second World War.
19 See J. Walvin, *Black and White. The Negro in English Society 1555–1945*, London, Allen Lane, 1973, re-issued 1988.
20 P. Fryer, *Staying Power. The History of Black People in Britain*, London, Pluto Press, 1984.
21 R. Visram, *Ayahs, Lascars and Princes. Indians in Britain 1700–1947*, London, Pluto Press, 1986.
22 One recalls Ralph Ellison's novel *Invisible Man*, London, Victor Gollancz, 1953.
23 J. Rex, *Race Relations in Sociological Theory*, London, Weidenfeld & Nicolson, 1970, pp. 106 ff. and his *Race, Colonialism and the City*, London, Routledge & Kegan Paul, 1973. For an attempt to tackle a specific issue against this perspective, see R. May and R. Cohen, 'The interaction between race and colonialism: a case study of the Liverpool race riots of 1919', *Race and Class*, vol. 16, 1974–5, pp. 111–26.
24 M. Banton, 'The beginning and the end of the racial issue in British politics', *Policy and Politics*, vol. 15, 1987, p. 41, commenting on one specific treatment of the role of the slave trade in fostering images of white supremacy.
25 M. D. Biddiss, 'Myths of the blood', *Patterns of Prejudice*, vol. 9, 1975, pp. 11–19.
26 M. Banton, *Racial Theories*, Cambridge, Cambridge University Press, 1987, pp. xii, xvii and in other publications.
27 See Holmes, *John Bull's Island.*
28 R. K. Kelsall, *Population*, London, Longman, 1979 edition, pp. 29–30, 115.
29 C. Holmes, 'The Impact of immigration on British society, 1870–1980', in T. Barker and M. Drake (eds), *Population and Society in Britain 1850–1980*, London, Batsford, 1982, pp. 177–79.
30 H. Loebl, 'Government-financed factories and the establishment of industries by refugees in the special areas of the north of England 1937–1961' M.Phil. thesis, Durham University, 1978. See also C. C. Aronsfeld, 'German Jews in Victorian England', *Leo Baeck Yearbook*, vol. 6, 1962, pp. 313–29.
31 The initial history can be gleaned from E. N. Swinerton, W. G. Kuepper and G. L. Lackey, *Ugandan Asians in Great Britain*, London, Croom Helm, 1975.
32 Jackson, op. cit., p. 93.
33 E. H. Hunt, *British Labour History 1815–1914*, London, Weidenfeld & Nicolson, 1981, pp. 172–74.

34 Little, op. cit., p. 56; Walvin, op. cit., p. 205.
35 Little, op. cit., p. 56.
36 M. Hornsby-Smith, *Roman Catholics in England. Studies in Social Structure since the Second World War*, Cambridge, Cambridge University Press, 1987.
37 S. Rushdie, 'The Empire writes back with a vengeance', *The Times*, 3 July 1982.
38 H. Pollins, *Economic History of the Jews in England*, London and Toronto, Farleigh Dickinson University Press, 1982; R. N. Salaman, 'The Jewish Fellows of the Royal Society', *Miscellanies of the Jewish Historical Society of England*, Part 5, 1948, pp. 146–75.
39 Harris House Diary. Testimony of Kitty Pistel from Vienna: MS 2845. Manchester Central Reference Library.
40 See Holmes, *John Bull's Island*, chapters 1 and 2.
41 H. Joshua et al., *To Ride the Storm: The 1980 Bristol 'Riot' and the State*, London, Heinemann, 1983.
42 C. Holmes, *Anti-Semitism in British Society 1876–1939*, London, Edward Arnold, 1979, chapter 2 on the East End and *John Bull's Island*, pp. 41, 58 and 60 (on the Irish) and 261–63 (on the 1962 Act).
43 P. Cahalan, *Belgian Refugee Relief Work During the Great War*, New York, Garland Press, 1982.
44 M. D. Biddiss, 'Racial ideas and the politics of prejudice, 1850–1914', *Historical Journal*, vol. 15, 1972, p. 572.
45 The pioneer work of J. E. Handley, including *The Irish in Scotland 1798–1845*, Cork, Cork University Press, 1943; *The Irish in Modern Scotland*, Cork, Cork University Press, 1947 and *The Navvy in Scotland*, Cork, Cork University Press, 1970, constitute an excellent base.
46 By Neil Evans, particularly in 'The South Wales race riots of 1919', *Llafur*, vol. 3, 1980, pp. 5–29, and 'Regulating the Reserve Army: Arabs, Blacks and the local state in Cardiff 1919–45', *Immigrants and Minorities*, vol. 4, 1985, pp. 68–115.
47 Lees, op. cit.
48 L. P. Gartner, *The Jewish Immigrant in England 1870–1914* Detroit, Wayne State University Press, 1960.
49 D. Feldman, 'Immigrants and workers: Englishmen and Jews: Jewish Immigration to the East End of London, 1880–1906', Ph.D. thesis, Cambridge University, 1985.
50 W. J. Fishman, *East End Jewish Radicals 1875–1914*, London, Duckworth, 1975, *The Streets of East London*, London, Duckworth, 1979 for text and photographs and *East End 1888*, London, Duckworth, 1988.
51 Sponza, op. cit.
52 See, for example, C. Richardson, 'Irish settlement in mid-nineteenth century Bradford', *Yorkshire Bulletin of Economic and Social Research*, vol. 20, 1968, pp. 40–57 and M. Le Lohé, 'The effects of the presence of immigrants upon the local population in Bradford 1945–77', in R. Miles and A. Phizacklea (eds), *Racism and Political Action*, London, Routledge & Kegan Paul, 1979, pp. 184–203.
53 R. B. Perks, '"A feeling of not belonging": interviewing European immigrants in Bradford', *Oral History*, vol. 12, 1984, pp. 64–7, provides a sample of oral evidence.

54 B. Williams, *The Making of Manchester Jewry 1740–1875*, Manchester, Manchester University Press, 1976.
55 See Holmes, *John Bull's Island* on these various points and his *A Tolerant Country? Immigrants, Refugees and Minorities in Britain*, London, Faber, 1991.
56 K. Leech, '"Diverse reports" and the meaning of "Racism"', *Race and Class*, vol. 28, 1986, pp. 82–8.
57 Recognized by Paul Rich in his review of *John Bull's Island* which is described as 'a sober historical assessment of an emotive issue which has frequently given rise to polemics', *History Today*, vol. 39, April 1989, p. 48.
58 Following the guideline of J. Higham, 'Anti-semitism in the gilded age', *Mississippi Valley Historical Review*, vol. 43, 1957, p. 566.
59 See Holmes, *John Bull's Island*, p. 413, note 172 for a number of examples.
60 Higham, op. cit., p. 569.

Bibliography

A Holograph Memoir of Capt. Charles Bagot of the 87th Regiment, Adelaide, 1942.

Adams, I. H., 'Division of commonty in Scotland', unpublished Ph.D. thesis, University of Edinburgh, 1967.

Aldcroft, D. H., *The Inter-War Economy: Britain 1919–1939*, London, Batsford 1970.

Allin, P. and Hunt, A., 'Women in official statistics' in Beechey, V. (ed.), *The Changing Experience of Women*, Milton Keynes, 1982.

Amery, L. S., 'Migration within the Empire', *United Empire*, 13, April 1922, pp. 206–18.

An Teachdaire Gaidhealach, Hobart, 1 August, 1857.

Anderson, G. L., *Victorian Clerks*, Manchester, 1976.

Anderson, G. L., 'German clerks in England 1870–1914: another aspect of the Great Depression debate', in K. Lunn (ed.), *Hosts, Immigrants and Minorities. Historical Responses to Newcomers in British Society, 1870–1914*, Folkestone, 1980.

Anderson, M., *Family Structure in Nineteenth-Century Lancashire*, Cambridge, 1971.

Anderson, M., 'Urban migration in nineteenth-century Lancashire – some insights into two competing hypotheses', *Annales de Démographie Historique*, 1971, pp. 13–26.

Anderson, M., 'Urban migration in Victorian Britain: problems of assimilation?' in E. François (ed.), *Immigration et société urbaine en Europe occidentale, XVI–XXe siècles*, Paris, 1985, pp. 79–91.

Applebaum, S., 'The Essex Achievement', *Agricultural History Review*, 29(1), 1981, pp. 42–4.

Armstrong, A., review of R. Arnold's *Farthest Promised Land* in *Agricultural History Review*, 32, 1984, pp. 106–7.

Aronsfeld, C. C., 'German Jews in Victorian England', *Leo Baeck Yearbook*, vol. 6, 1962.

Ashton, R., *Little Germany. Exile and Asylum in Victorian England*, Oxford, 1986.

Ashworth, W., *The Genesis of Modern British Town Planning*, London, 1954.

Aslett, P. et al., *Victorians on the Move: Research on the Census Enumerators' Books 1851–1881*, Thornborough, 1984.

Bagnell, K., *The Little Immigrants: the Orphans Who Came to Canada*, Toronto, 1980.
Bailyn, B., *The Peopling of British North America*, London, 1987.
Bailyn, B., *Voyagers to the West: Emigration from Britain to America on the Eve of the Revolution*, London, 1987.
Baines, D. E., 'Birthplace statistics and the analysis of internal migration', in R. Lawton (ed.), *The Census and Social Structure*, London, 1978.
Baines, D. E., *Migration in a Mature Economy: Emigration and Internal Migration in England and Wales; 1861–1900*, Cambridge, 1985.
Baker, M., 'A migration of Wiltshire agricultural labourers to Australia in 1851', *Journal of the South Australian Historical Society*, 14 1986.
Banton, M., 'The beginning and the end of the racial issue in British politics', *Policy and Politics*, 15, 1987.
Banton, M., *Racial Theories*, Cambridge, 1987.
Barker, T. and Drake, M. (eds), *Population and Society in Britain 1850–1980*, London, 1982.
Beadle, S., 'Economic changes and the population of coalfields in the early nineteenth century, with special reference to the Somerset and St Helens coalfields', unpublished Ph.D. thesis, University of Liverpool, 1984.
Bean, P. and Melville, J., *Lost Children of the Empire*, London, 1989.
Beckett, J. V. and Foulds, T., 'Beyond the micro: Laxton, the computer and social change over time', *Local Historian*, 16(8), 1985, pp. 451–6.
Bédarida, F., *A Social History of England 1851–1975*, London, 1979.
Beechey, V. (ed.), *The Changing Experience of Women*, Milton Keynes, 1982.
Beier, A. L., 'Vagrants and the social order in Elizabethan England', *Past and Present*, 64, 1974, pp. 3–29.
Beier, A. L., *Masterless Men: the Vagrancy Problem in England 1560–1640*, London, 1985.
Berg, M., *The Age of Manufactures 1700–1820*, London, 1985.
Biddiss, M. D., 'Racial ideas and the politics of prejudice, 1850–1914', *Historical Journal*, 15, 1972.
Biddiss, M. D., 'Myths of the blood', *Patterns of Prejudice*, 9, 1975.
Blakeley, B. L., 'Women and imperialism: the colonial office and female emigration to South Africa, 1901–10', *Albion*, 13, 1981, pp. 131–49.
Blakeley, B. L., 'The Society for the Oversea Settlement of British Women and the problems of Empire settlement, 1917–1936', *Albion*, 20, 1988, pp. 421–44.
Bloomfield, G. T., *New Zealand: a Handbook of Historical Statistics*, Boston, 1984.
Bonfield, L., Smith, R. M. and Wrightson, K. (eds), *The World We Have Gained: Histories of Population and Social Structure*, Oxford, 1986.
Booth, General W., *In Darkest England and the Way Out*, London, Salvation Army, 1890.
Booth, General W., 'Our emigration plans', *Proceedings of the Royal Colonies Institute*, 37, 1905–6, pp. 137–54.
Boulton, J., 'Residential mobility in seventeenth-century Southwark', *Urban History Yearbook*, 1986, pp. 1–11.

Bowley, A. L., 'Rural population in England and Wales . . . a study of the changes of density, occupations and ages', *Journal of the Royal Statistical Society*, 77, 1914, pp. 597–645.
Bowman, I. (ed.), *Limits of Land Settlement: a Report on Present-Day Possibilities*, New York, Council on Foreign Relations, 1937.
Brabazon, Lord, *State-Directed Colonization – Its Necessity*, London, Stanford, 1886.
Braudel, F., *The Mediterranean and the Mediterranean World in the Age of Philip II*, London, 1972, 2 vols.
Brayshay, W. M., 'The demography of three West Cornwall mining communities: a society in decline', unpublished Ph.D. thesis, University of Exeter, 1977.
Brettell, C. B., 'Emigration and household structure in a Portuguese parish, 1850–1920', *Journal of Family History*, 13(1), 1988, pp. 33–57.
Brown, B. H., *The Tariff Reform Movement in Great Britain 1881–95*, New York, 1943.
Bruce, M., *The Coming of the Welfare State*, London, 1961.
Bryant, D., 'Demographic trends in South Devon in the mid-nineteenth century', in K. J. Gregory and W. L. D. Ravenhill (eds), *Exeter Essays in Geography*, Exeter, 1971, pp. 125–41.
Buckley, S., 'British female emigration and imperial development: experiments in Canada 1885–1931', *Hecate*, 3, 1977, pp. 26–40.
Burnett, J., *Useful Toil*, London, 1974.
Burnett, J., *Destiny Obscure*, London, 1982.
Burnett, J., Vincent, D. and Mayall, D. (eds), *The Autobiography of the Working Class: An Annotated and Critical Bibliography*, Brighton, 1, 1984, 2, 1987.
Burroughs, P., *Britain and Australia 1831–1855*, Oxford, 1967.
Cage, R. A., *The Scottish Poor Law 1745–1845*, Edinburgh, 1981.
Cahalan, P., *Belgian Refugee Relief Work During the Great War*, New York, 1982.
Cairncross, A. K., 'Internal migration in Victorian England', *The Manchester School*, 17, 1949, pp. 67–87.
Cairncross, A. K., *Home and Foreign Investment 1870–1913: Studies in Capital Accumulation*, Cambridge, 1953.
Carlstein, T., Parkes, D. and Thrift, N. (eds), *Timing Space and Spacing Time*, London, 1978.
Carrothers, W. A., *Emigration from the British Isles*, London, 1929.
Carter, H. and Wheatley, S., *Merthyr Tydfil in 1851*, Cardiff, 1982.
Charbonneau, H. et al., *Naissance d'une population: les Français établis au Canada au XVIIe siècle, INED,* Travaux et documents cahier, No. 118, Montreal, 1987.
Charlewood, D., *The Long Farewell*, Melbourne, 1981.
Checkland, O., *Philanthropy in Victorian Scotland*, Edinburgh, John Donald, 1980.
Chudacoff, H. P., 'Newlyweds and family extension: the first stage of the family cycle in Providence, Rhode Island, 1864–1865 and 1879–1880', in T. K. Hareven and M. A. Vinovskis (eds), *Family and Population in Nineteenth-Century America*, Princeton 1978, pp. 179–205.

Clark, D., *The Irish in Philadelphia - Ten Generations of Urban Experience*, Philadelphia, 1973.
Clark, P., 'The migrant in Kentish towns 1580–1640', in P. Clark and P. Slack (eds), *Crisis and Order in English Towns 1500–1700*, London, 1972, pp. 117–63.
Clark, P., 'Migration in England during the late seventeenth and early eighteenth centuries', *Past and Present*, 83, 1979 pp. 57–90, reprinted in P. Clark and D. Souden (eds), *Migration and Society in Early-Modern England*, London, 1987.
Clark, P., 'Migrants in the city: the process of social adaptation in English towns 1500–1800', in P. Clark and D. Souden (eds), *Migration and Society in Early-Modern England*, London, 1987.
Clark, P. and Slack, P. (eds), *Crisis and Order in English Towns 1500–1700*, London, 1972.
Clark, P. and Souden, D. (eds), *Migration and Society in Early-Modern England*, London, 1987.
Clarke, M. A., 'Household and family in Bethnal Green, 1851–71: The effects of social and economic change,' unpublished Ph.D. thesis, University of Cambridge, 1986.
Clarke, P., *The Governess; Letters from the Colonies, 1862–1882*, London, 1985.
Clarkson, L. A., *Proto-industrialisation: The First Phase of Industrialisation*, London, 1985.
Clements, R. V., 'Trade unions and emigration, 1840–80', *Population Studies*, 9, 1955–6, pp. 167–80.
Collins, B., 'Proto-industrialization and pre-famine emigration', *Social History*, 7, 1982, pp. 127–46.
Collins, E. J. T., 'Migrant labour in British agriculture in the nineteenth century', *Economic History Review 2nd Series*, 36, 1976, pp. 38–59.
Constantine, S., *Unemployment in Britain Between the Wars*, London, 1980.
Constantine, S., 'Amateur gardening and popular recreation in the nineteenth and twentieth centuries', *Journal of Social History*, 14, 1981, pp. 387–406.
Constantine, S., *The Making of British Colonial Development Policy 1914–1940*, London, 1984.
Constantine, S. (ed.), *Emigrants and Empire: British Settlement in the Dominions between the Wars*, Manchester, 1990.
Cooke, S., *The Maiden City and the Western Ocean*, Dublin, 1961.
Coppock, J. T., 'Agricultural changes in the Chilterns, 1875–1900', *Agricultural History Review*, 9, 1961, pp. 1–16.
Coppock, J. T., 'The changing face of England, 1850–c. 1900', in H. C. Darby (ed.), *A New Historical Geography of England*, Cambridge, 1973, pp. 295–373.
Cregeen, E., 'The tacksmen and their successors. A study of tenurial re-organisation in Mull, Morvern and Tiree in the early eighteenth century', *Scottish Studies*, 13, 1969, pp. 93–144.
Cressy, D., 'Kinship and kin interaction in early modern England', *Past and Present*, 113, 1986, pp. 38–69.
Cressy, D., *Coming Over: Migration and Communication Between England and New England in the Seventeenth Century*, Cambridge, 1987.

Cromar, P., 'Labour migration and suburban expansion in the North of England in the 1860s and 1970s', in P. White and R. Woods, *The Geographical Impact of Migration*, London, 1980, pp. 129–51.
Culshaw, M. Owen, 'Empire migration and settlement: Salvation Army methods and aims', in H. E. Harper (ed.), *Empire Problems*, London, 1939, pp. 166–7.
Curtis, L. P., *Anglo-Saxons and Celts: A Study of Anti-Irish Prejudice in Victorian England*, Bridgeport, Conn., 1968.
Curtis, L. P., *Apes and Angels. The Irishman in Victorian Caricature*, Newton Abbot, 1971.
Darby, H. C., 'The movement of population to and from Cambridgeshire between 1851 and 1861', *Geographical Journal*, 101, 1945, pp. 118–77.
Darby, H. C. (ed.), *A New Historical Geography of England*, Cambridge, 1973.
Darroch, A. G., 'Migrants in the nineteenth century: Fugitives or families in motion?', *Journal of Family History*, 6, 1981, pp. 257–77.
Darwin, J., 'Imperialism in decline? Tendencies in British imperial policy between the wars', *Historical Journal*, 23, 1980, pp. 657–79.
Davies, G., *Nationalism as a Social Phenomenon*, Liverpool, 1965.
Denley, P. and Watson, D. (eds), *History and Computing*, Manchester, 1987.
Denley, P., Fogelvik, S. and Harvey, C., *History and Computing II*, Manchester, 1989.
Dennis, R. J., 'Intercensal mobility in a Victorian city', *Transactions Institute of British Geographers*, new series, 2(3), 1977, pp. 349–63.
Dennis, R. J., 'Distance and social interaction in a Victorian city', *Journal of Historical Geography*, 3(3), 1977, pp. 237–50.
Devine, T. M., 'Highland migration to Lowland Scotland 1760–1860', *Scottish Historical Review*, 72, 1983, pp. 137–49.
Devine, T. M. (ed.), *Farm Servants and Labour in Lowland Scotland 1770–1914*, Edinburgh, 1984.
Devine, T. M., 'The union of 1707 and Scottish development', *Scottish Economic and Social History*, 5, 1985, pp. 25–6.
Dickson, R. J., *Ulster Emigration to Colonial America, 1718–1785*, Belfast, Ulster Historical Foundation, 1976.
Dillon, R., 'The Irish in Leeds, 1851–1861', *Thoresby Society Publications Miscellany*, 16, 1974, pp. 1–28.
Dodd, A. H., *The Industrial Revolution in North Wales*, Cardiff, 1933.
Dodgshon, R. A., 'Land and society in early Scotland', Oxford, 1981.
Dodgshon, R. A., '"Pretense of Blude" and "Place of thair duelling": the nature of Scottish clans 1500–1745', in R. A. Houston, and I. D. Whyte (eds), *Scottish Society 1500–1800*, Cambridge, 1989, pp. 169–98.
Doherty, J. C., 'Short-distance migration in nineteenth-century Lancashire', unpublished Ph.D. thesis, University of Lancaster, 1986.
Donaldson, G., *The Scots Overseas*, Edinburgh, 1966.
Drake, M., 'The census, 1801–1891', in Wrigley, E. A. (ed.), *Nineteenth-Century Society: Essays in the Use of Quantitative Methods for the Study of Social Data*, Cambridge, 1972, pp. 7–46.
Drudy, P. J. (ed.), *The Irish in America*, Cambridge, 1985.
Drummond, I. M., *British Economic Policy and the Empire 1919–1939*, London, 1972.

Drummond, I. M., *Imperial Economic Policy 1917-1939*, London, 1974.

Dublin, T., 'Rural-urban migrants in industrial New England: the case of Lynn, Massachusetts, in the mid-nineteenth century', *The Journal of American History*, 73(2), 1986, pp. 623-44.

Ekirch, A. R., *Bound for America: the Transportation of British Convicts to the Colonies, 1718-1775*, Oxford, 1987.

Elliott, B. S., *Irish Migrants in the Canadas*, Kingston, 1988.

Ellison, R., *Invisible Man*, London, 1953.

Erickson, C., 'The encouragement of emigration by British trade unions, 1850-1900', *Population Studies*, 3, 1949-50.

Erickson, C., *Invisible Immigrants: The Adaptation of English and Scottish Immigrants in Nineteenth-Century America*, London, 1972.

Ernle, Lord, *English Farming Past and Present*, London, 2nd edition, 1917.

Escott, M., 'Residential mobility in a late eighteenth-century rural parish: Binfield, 1779-1801', *Local Population Studies*, 40, 1988, pp. 20-35.

Evans, N., 'The South Wales race riots of 1919', *Llafur*, 3, 1980.

Evans, N., 'Regulating the Reserve Army: Arabs, Blacks and the local state in Cardiff 1919-45', *Immigrants and Minorities*, 4, 1985.

Eversley, Lord, 'The decline in the number of agricultural labourers in Britain', *Journal of the Royal Statistical Society*, 70, 1907, pp. 267-303.

Fairbridge, K., *The Story of Kingsley Fairbridge by Himself*, Oxford, 1927.

Fairbridge, R., *Pinjarra: the Building of a Farm School*, London, 1937.

Fedorowich, K., 'The assisted emigration of British ex-servicemen to the Dominions, 1914-1922', in S. Constantine (ed.), *Emigrants and Empire: British Settlement in the Dominions between the Wars*, Manchester, 1990.

Fay, C. R. and Fay, H. C., 'The Allotment Movement in England and Wales', *Year Book of Agricultural Co-operation*, Cambridge, 1942.

Feldman, D., 'Immigrants and workers: Englishmen and Jews: Jewish immigration to the East End of London 1880-1906', unpublished Ph.D. thesis, Cambridge University, 1985.

Field, K. P., 'Migration in the later Middle Ages: the case of the Hampton Lovett villeins', *Midland History*, 8, 1983, pp. 29-48.

Fischer, T. A., *The Scots in Germany*, Edinburgh, 1902.

Fischer, T. A., *The Scots in Sweden*, Edinburgh, 1907.

Fisher, F. J. (ed.), *Essays in the Economic History of Tudor and Stuart England*, London, 1961.

Fishman, W. J., *East End Jewish Radicals 1875-1914*, London, 1975.

Fishman, W. J., *The Streets of East London*, London, 1979.

Fishman, W. J., *East End 1888*, London, 1988.

Fitzpatrick, D., 'Irish emigration in the later nineteenth century', *Irish Historical Studies*, 22(86), September 1980.

Fletcher, T. W., 'The Great Depression of English agriculture, 1873-1896', *Economic History Review*, 2nd series, 13, 1960-1, pp. 417-32.

Fletcher, T. W., 'Lancashire livestock farming during the Great Depression', *Agricultural History Review*, 9, 1961, pp. 17-42.

Flinn, M. (ed.), *Scottish Population History*, Cambridge, 1977.

Fogarty, M. P., *Prospects of the Industrial Areas of Great Britain*, London, 1945.

Forsyth, W. D., *The Myth of Open Spaces*, Melbourne, 1942.
Friedlander, D. and Roshier, R. J., 'A study of internal migration in England and Wales', *Population Studies*, 19, 1966, pp. 239–79.
Froude, J. A., *Oceana*, London, 1886.
Fryer, P., *Staying Power. The History of Black People in Britain*, London, 1984.
Fussell, G. E., 'Essex farmers of 1850. Men of enterprise and capital', *Essex Review*, 48(189), 1939, pp. 40–3.
Fussell, G. E., 'Essex farmers a century ago', *Essex Review*, 65(258), 1957, pp. 53–9.
Gailey, R. A., 'The mobility of tenants on a Highland estate in the early nineteenth century', *Scottish Historical Review*, 40, 1961, pp. 136–45.
Gartner, L., *The Jewish Immigrant in England 1870–1914*, Detroit, Wayne State University Press, 1960; 2nd edition, London, 1973.
Gaydon, A. T. (ed.), *Victoria County History of Shropshire*, vol. 2, London, 1973.
Giddens, A., *A Contemporary Critique of Historical Materialism*, London, 1981.
Gilbert, B. B., *British Social Policy 1914–1939*, London, 1970.
Gjerde, J., *From Peasants to Farmers: The Migration from Balestrand, Norway, to the Upper Middle West*, Cambridge, 1985.
Glasco, L., 'Migration and adjustment in the nineteenth-century city: occupation, property, and household structure of natural-born whites, Buffalo, New York, 1855', in T. K. Hareven and M. A. Vinovskis (eds), *Family and Population in Nineteenth-century America*, Princeton, 1978, pp. 41–54.
Glass, D. V. and Eversley, D. E. C. (eds), *Population in History*, London, 1965.
Goodman, J., *The Mond Legacy*, London, 1982.
Gothard, J., 'The healthy, wholesome British domestic girl: single female migration and the Empire Settlement Act, 1922–1930', in S. Constantine (ed.), *Emigrants and Empire: British Settlement in the Dominions Between the Wars*, Manchester, 1990.
Greenwood, W., *There was a Time*, London, 1967.
Gregory, D., 'Areal differentiation and post-modern human geography', in D. Gregory and R. Walford (eds), *Horizons in Human Geography*, London, 1989, pp. 67–96.
Gregory, D. and Urry, J. (eds), *Social Relations and Spatial Structures*, London, 1985.
Grigg, D. B., 'E. G. Ravenstein and the Laws of migration', *Journal of Historical Geography*, 3, 1977, pp. 41–54.
Grundy, E. 'Migration and household change among the elderly in England and Wales 1971–1981', *Espace Population Sociétés*, 7(2), 1987, pp. 111–36.
Gwynne, T. and Sill, M., 'Census enumerators' books: a study of mid-nineteenth-century migration', *Local Historian*, 12, 1976, pp. 74–9.
Hagerstrand, T., 'What about people in Regional Science?', *Papers and Proceedings of the Regional Science Association*, 24, 1970, pp. 7–21.
Haines, R., 'Therapeutic emigration: Australia, the last resort', unpublished BA Honours thesis, Flinders University, 1987.

Hamilton, P. and Gothard, J., 'The Other Half? Sources on British female emigration at the Fawcett Library, with special reference to Australia', *Women's Studies International Forum*, 10, 1987, pp. 305–9.
Hammerton, A. J., *Emigrant Gentlewomen: Genteel Poverty and Female Emigration, 1830–1914*, London, 1979.
Handley, J. E., *The Irish in Scotland 1798–1845*, Cork, 1943.
Handley, J. E., *The Irish in Modern Scotland*, Cork, 1947.
Handley, J. E., *Scottish Farming in the Eighteenth Century*, Edinburgh, 1953.
Handley, J. E., *The Navvy in Scotland*, Cork, 1970.
Hardy, J., *Stories of Australian Migration*, Sydney, 1988, p. 47.
Hareven, T. K. and Vinovskis, M. A. (eds), *Family and Population in Nineteenth-century America*, Princeton, 1978.
Harper, H. E. (ed.), *Empire Problems*, London, 1939.
Harris, J., *Unemployment and Politics*, Oxford, 1972.
Harrison, J., *The Scot in Ulster*, Edinburgh, 1888.
Harrison, P., *The Home Children: Their Personal Stories*, Winnipeg, 1979.
Hastings, R. P., 'Middlesbrough: a new Victorian boom town', *Bulletin of the Cleveland and Teesside Local History Society*, 30, 1976, pp. 1–20.
Hempstead, C. A. (ed.), *Cleveland Iron and Steel*, Redcar, British Steel Corporation, 1979.
Herschberg, T., 'The Philadelphia Social History Project: A methodological history', unpublished Ph.D. thesis, Stanford University, 1973.
Higgs, E., *Making Sense of the Census: The Manuscript Returns for England and Wales, 1801–1901*, London, 1989.
Higham, J., 'Anti-semitism in the gilded age', *Mississippi Valley Historical Review*, 43, 1957, p. 566.
Higham, J., *Anti-Semitism in British Society 1876–1939*, London, 1979.
Hinde, P. R. A., 'The population of a Wiltshire village in the nineteenth century: a reconstitution study of Berwick St James, 1841–71', *Annals of Human Biology*, 14(6), 1987, pp. 475–85.
Hitchins, F. H., *The Colonial Land and Emigration Commission*, Philadelphia, 1931.
Hobcraft, J. and Rees, P. (eds), *Regional Demographic Development*, London, 1977.
Holahan, A. M., 'St Kilda: Emigrants and Disease', *Scottish Medical Journal*, 31, 1986.
Holmes, C. (ed.), Immigrants and Minorities in British Society, London, 1978.
Holmes, C., *Anti-Semitism in British Society 1876–1939*, London, 1979.
Holmes, C., 'The impact of immigration on British society 1870–1980', in T. Barker and M. Drake (eds), *Population and Society in Britain 1850–1980*, London, 1982.
Holmes, C., *John Bull's Island, Immigration and British Society 1871–1971*, London, 1988.
Holmes, C., *A Tolerant Country? Minorities in British Society*, forthcoming.
Holmes, R. S., 'Ownership and migration from a study of rate books', *Area*, 5, 1973, pp. 242–51.
Holt, S. C., 'Family, kinship, community and friendship ties in assisted emigration from Cambridgeshire to Port Phillip district and Victoria, 1850–67', unpublished MA thesis, La Trobe University, 1987.

Horn, P., 'Agricultural trade unionism and emigration, 1872–1881', *Historical Journal*, 15, 1972, pp. 87–102.

Horn, P., *Labouring Life in the Victorian Countryside*, London, 1976.

Horn, P., *The Rural World 1780–1850: Social Change in the English Countryside*, London, 1980.

Horn, P., 'Victorian villages from census returns', *Local Historian*, 15(1), 1982, pp. 25–32.

Hornsby-Smith, M., *Roman Catholics in England. Studies in Social Structure Since the Second World War,* Cambridge, 1987.

Houston, R. A., *Scottish Literacy and the Scottish Identity: Illiteracy and Society in Scotland and Northern England 1600–1800*, Cambridge, 1985.

Houston, R. A., 'Geographical mobility in Scotland 1682–1811', *Journal of Historical Geography*, 11, 1985, pp. 379–94.

Houston, R. A. and Whyte, I. D. (eds), *Scottish Society 1500–1800*, Cambridge, 1989.

Howell, D., *Land and People in Nineteenth-Century Wales*, London, 1979.

Hudson, P., 'Proto-industrialization: the case of the West Riding wool textile industry in the eighteenth and early nineteenth centuries', *History Workshop Journal*, 12, 1981.

Hufton, O., *The Poor of Eighteenth-Century France*, Oxford, 1974.

Hughes, R., *The Fatal Shore*, London, 1987.

Hunt, E. H., *British Labour History 1815–1914*, London, 1981.

Huttenback, R. A., *Racism and Empire: White Settlers and Colored Immigrants in the British Self-Governing Colonies 1830–1910*, Ithaca and London, 1976.

Jackson, J. A., *The Irish in Britain*, London, 1963.

Jackson, J. A., *Migration*, London, 1986.

Jackson, J. H. and Moch, L. P., 'Migration and the social history of modern Europe', *Historical Methods*, 22(1), 1989, pp. 27–36.

Jackson, J. T., 'Long-distance migrant workers in nineteenth-century Britain: a case study of the St Helens glass makers', *Transactions of the Lancashire and Cheshire Historical Society*, 131, 1982, pp. 113–37.

Jeremy, D. (ed.), *Dictionary of Business Biography*, London, 1983–6.

Johnson, J. H., 'Harvest migration from nineteenth-century Ireland', *Transactions of the Institute of British Geographers*, 41, 1967, pp. 97–112.

Johnston, H. J. M., *British Emigration Policy 1815–1830: Shovelling Out Paupers*, Oxford, 1972.

Jones, E., 'The Welsh in London in the seventeenth and eighteenth centuries', *Welsh History Review*, 10, 1981, pp. 461–79.

Jones, E., 'The Welsh in London in the nineteenth century', *Cambria*, 12, 1985, pp. 149–69.

Jones, H., 'The evolution of Scottish migration patterns: a social relations of production approach', *Scottish Geographical Magazine*, 102, 1986, pp. 151–64.

Jones, J. R., *The Welsh Builder on Merseyside*, Liverpool, 1946.

Jones, R. M., 'Welsh immigrants in the cities of North West England 1890–1930: some oral testimony', *Oral History*, 9, 1981, pp. 33–41.

Jones, R. M. and Rees, D. B., *The Liverpool Welsh and their Religion*, Liverpool, 1984.

Joshua, H. et al., *To Ride the Storm: the 1980 Bristol 'Riot' and the State*, London, 1983.

Jupp, J. (ed.), *The Australian People*, Sydney, 1988.

Kealey, L. (ed.), *A Not Unreasonable Claim: Women and Reform in Canada 1880–1920*, Toronto, 1979.

Kelsall, R. K., *Population*, London, 1979 edition.

Kennedy, D., 'Empire migration in post-war reconstruction: the role of the Oversea Settlement Committee, 1919–22', *Albion*, 20, 1988.

Kiernan, V. G., 'Britons old and new', in C. Holmes (ed.), *Immigrants and Minorities in British Society*, London, 1978.

Krause, J. T., 'The changing adequacy of English registration', in D. V. Glass and D. E. C. Eversley (eds), *Population in History*, London, 1965, pp. 379–93.

Kussmaul, A., *Servants in Husbandry in Early Modern England*, Cambridge, 1981.

Laslett, P., *Family Life and Illicit Love in Earlier Generations*, Cambridge, 1977.

Laslett, P. and Harrison, J., 'Clayworth and Cogenhoe', in H. E. Bell and R. L. Ollard (eds), *Historical Essays, 1600–1750 Presented to David Ogg*, London, 1963, pp. 157–84.

Lawton, R., 'Population movements in the West Midlands 1841–1861', *Geography*, 43, 1958, pp. 164–77.

Lawton, R., 'Irish migration to England and Wales in the mid-nineteenth century', *Irish Geography*, 4, 1959, pp. 35–54.

Lawton, R., 'Population changes in England and Wales in the later nineteenth century', *Transactions, Institute of British Geographers*, 44, 1968, pp. 55–75.

Lawton, R., 'Rural depopulation in nineteenth-century England', in D. R. Mills (ed.), *English Rural Communities*, London, 1973, pp. 195–219.

Lawton, R., 'Regional population trends in England and Wales, 1750–1971', in J. Hobcraft and P. Rees (eds), *Regional Demographic Development*, London, 1977, pp. 29–70.

Lawton, R. (ed.), *The Census and Social Structure: an Interpretive Guide to Nineteenth-century Censuses for England and Wales*, London, 1978.

Lawton, R. and Pooley, C. G., 'David Brindley's Liverpool: an aspect of urban society in the 1880s', *Transactions of the Historic Society of Lancashire and Cheshire*, 126, 1975, pp. 149–68.

Lawton, R. and Pooley, C. G., *The Social Geography of Merseyside in the Nineteenth Century*, Final Report to the SSRC, Department of Geography, University of Liverpool, 1976.

Lawton, R. and Pooley, C. G., 'Problems and potentialities for the study of internal population mobility in nineteenth-century England', *Canadian Studies in Population*, 5, 1978, Special Issue, 1980, pp. 69–84.

Lee, E. S., 'A theory of migration', *Demography*, 3, 1966, pp. 47–57.

Leech, K., '"Diverse Reports" and the Meaning of "Racism"', *Race and Class*, 28, 1986.

Lees, L. H., 'Mid-Victorian migration and the Irish family economy', *Victorian Studies*, 20, 1976, pp. 25–43.

Lees, L. H., *Exiles of Erin: Irish Migrants in Victorian London*, Manchester, 1979.

Le Lohe, M., 'The effects of the presence of immigrants upon the local population in Bradford 1945–77', in R. Miles and A. Phizacklea (eds), *Racism and Political Action*, London, 1979.
Leneman, L. (ed.), *Perspectives in Scottish Social History*, Aberdeen, 1988.
Leonard, J. W., 'Urban development and population growth in Middlesbrough, 1831–71', unpublished Ph.D. thesis, Teesside Polytechnic, 1965.
Light, D., 'Class, ethnicity and urban ecology in a nineteenth-century city: Philadelphia's Irish, 1840–1890, unpublished Ph.D. thesis, University of Pennsylvania, 1979.
Little, K., *Negroes in Britain. A Study of Race Relations in English Society*, London, 1948: re-issued 1972.
Lobban, R. D., 'The Irish community in Greenock in the nineteenth century', *Irish Geography*, 6, 1971, pp. 270–81.
Lockhart, D. G., 'Patterns of migration and movement of labour to the planned villages of north east Scotland', *Scottish Geographical Magazine*, 98, 1982, pp. 35–47.
Loebl, H., 'Government-financed factories and the establishment of industries by refugees in the special areas of the north of England 1937–1961', unpublished M.Phil. thesis, Durham University, 1978.
Longstaffe, G. B., 'Rural depopulation', *Journal of the Royal Statistical Society*, 52, 1893, pp. 380–442.
Lovett, A. A., Whyte, I. D. and Whyte, K. A., 'Poisson regression analysis and migration fields: the example of the apprenticeship records of Edinburgh in the seventeenth and eighteenth centuries', *Transactions of the Institute of British Geographers*, New Series, 10, 1985, pp. 317–32.
Lunn, K., 'Reactions to Lithuanians and Polish immigrants in the Lanarkshire coalfield 1880–1914', in K. Lunn (ed.), *Hosts, Immigrants and Minorities. Historical Responses to Newcomers in British Society 1870–1914*, Folkestone, 1980.
MacDonagh, O., 'The Irish famine emigration to the United States', *Perspectives in American History*, 10, 1976, pp. 418–30.
Macfarlane, A., *The Origins of English Individualism*, Oxford, 1978.
Macfarlane, A., *The Justice and the Mare's Ale*, Oxford, 1981.
Mackay, M., 'Nineteenth-century Tiree emigrant communities in Ontario', *Oral History*, 9, 1981, pp. 42–8.
MacKenzie, J. M., *Propaganda and Empire: the Manipulation of British Public Opinion, 1880–1960*, Manchester, 1984.
MacKenzie, J. M. (ed.), *Imperialism and Popular Culture*, Manchester, 1986.
Macpherson, A. G., 'Migration fields in a traditional Highland community 1350–1850', *Journal of Historical Geography*, 10, 1984, pp. 1–14.
Madgwick, R. D., *Immigration into Eastern Australia 1788–1851*, London, 1937.
Mageean, D., 'Ulster emigration to Philadelphia, 1847–1865: a case study using passenger lists', in P. J. Drudy (ed.), *The Irish in America*, Cambridge, 1985.
Malchow, H. L., 'Trade unions and emigration in late Victorian England: a national lobby for state aid', *Journal of British Studies*, 15, 1976, pp. 92–116.
Malchow, H. L., *Population Pressures: Emigration and Government in Late Nineteenth-Century Britain*, Palo Alto, California, 1979.

Marriott, Sir John A. R., *Empire Settlement*, London, 1927.
Marsh, D. C., *The Changing Social Structure of England and Wales 1871–1961*, London, 1965.
Marsh, J., *Back to the Land: the Pastoral Impulse in England from 1880 to 1914*, London, 1982.
Maxwell, M. P., *The Scottish Migration to Ulster in the Reign of James I*, London, 1973.
May, R. and Cohen, R., 'The interaction between race and colonialism: a case study of the Liverpool race riots of 1919', *Race and Class*, 26, 1974–5, pp. 111–26.
McCleary, G. F., *Peopling the British Commonwealth*, London, 1965.
Mess, H. A., *Voluntary Social Services since 1918*, London, 1948.
Miles, R. and Phizacklea, A. (eds), *Racism and Political Action*, London, 1979.
Mills, D. R. (ed.), *English Rural Communities*, London, 1973.
Mills, D. R., 'The residential propinquity of kin in a Cambridgeshire village, 1841', *Journal of Historical Geography*, 4(3), 1978, pp. 265–76.
Mills, D. R. (ed.), *Victorians on the Move*, Thornborough, 1984.
Mills, D. R. and Pearce, C., *People and Places in the Victorian Census*, Historical Geography Research Series, 23, 1989.
Mitchison, R. M. 'The making of the old Scottish poor law', *Past and Present*, 63, 1974, pp. 58–93.
Mitchison, R. M., *Lordship to Patronage. Scotland 1603–1754*, London, 1983.
Mitchison, R. M., 'North and south; the development of the gulf in poor law practice', in R. A. Houston and I. D. Whyte (eds), *Scottish Society 1500–1800*, Cambridge, 1989.
Monk, Una, *New Horizons: a Hundred Years of Women's Migration*, London, 1963.
Morokvasic, M., 'Women in migration: beyond the reductionist outlook', in A. Phizacklea (ed.), *One Way Ticket*, London, 1983.
Musgrove, F., *The Migratory Elite*, London, 1963.
Newbury, C., 'Labour migration in the imperial phase: an essay in interpretation', *Journal of Imperial and Commonwealth History*, 3, 1975, pp. 234–56.
Nicholas, S. (ed.), *Convict Workers*, Melbourne, 1988.
Nicholas, S. and Shergold, P., 'Internal migration in England 1818–39', *Journal of Historical Geography*, 13, 1987, pp. 155–68.
Nicholas, S. and Shergold, P., 'Inter-county labour mobility during the Industrial Revolution', *Oxford Economic Papers*, December, 1987.
O'Farrell, P., *Letters from Irish Australia, 1825–1929*, Sydney, 1984.
Ogle, W., 'The alleged depopulation of the rural districts of England', *Journal of the Royal Statistical Society*, 52, 1889, 205–40.
Oliver, F. R., 'Notes on the logistic curve for human populations', *Journal of the Royal Statistical Society*, Series A, 145, 1982, pp. 359–63.
Orwin, C. S. and Darke, W. F., *Back to the Land*, London, 1935.
Ostergren, R. C., 'Kinship networks and migration: a nineteenth-century Swedish example', *Social Science History*, 6(3), 1982, pp. 293–320.
O'Tuathaigh, M. A. G., 'The Irish in nineteenth century Britain: problems of

integration', *Transactions of the Royal Historical Society*, 31, 1981, pp. 149–74.
Owen, A. D. K., 'Social consequences of the Industrial Transference Scheme', *Sociological Review*, 29, 1937.
Owen, D., *English Philanthropy 1660–1960*, London, 1964.
Palliser, D. M., 'A regional capital as magnet: immigrants to York, 1477–1566', *Yorkshire Archaeological Journal*, 57, 1985, pp. 111–23.
Palmer, R. C. G., 'The Britalians. An anthropological investigation', unpublished Ph.D. thesis, Sussex University, 1981.
Panayi, P., 'Germans in Britain during the First World War', unpublished Ph.D. thesis, Sheffield University, 1981.
Parker, R. A., 'The emigration of unaccompanied British children to Canada 1867–1917', ESRC End of Grant Report, 1982.
Parr, J., *Labouring Children: British Immigrant Apprentices to Canada, 1869–1924*, London, 1980.
Parry, M. L. and Slater, T. R. (eds), *The Making of the Scottish Countryside*, London, 1980.
Parton, A. G., 'The travels of Joseph Smith, well sinker 1877–1897: a study in personal migration for work', *North Staffordshire Journal of Field Studies*, 20, 1980, pp. 33–40.
Parton, A. G., 'Poor-law settlement certificates and migration to and from Birmingham, 1726–57', *Local Population Studies*, 38, 1987, pp. 23–9.
Patten, J., *Rural–Urban Migration in Pre-industrial England*, Research Papers, No. 6, School of Geography, University of Oxford, 1973.
Patten, J., 'Patterns of migration of labour to three pre-industrial East Anglian towns', *Journal of Historical Geography*, 2, 1976, pp. 111–29.
Patterson, S., 'The Poles: an exile community in Britain', in J. L. Watson (ed.), *Between Two Cultures. Migrants and Minorities in Britain*, Oxford, 1977.
Pearce, C. G. and Mills, D. R., *Census Enumerators' Books: an Annotated Bibliography of Published Work Based Substantially on the Nineteenth Century Census Enumerators' Books*, Milton Keynes, 1982.
Perks, R. B., '"A feeling of not belonging": interviewing European immigrants in Bradford', *Oral History*, 12, 1984.
Perry, P. J., *British Farming in the Great Depression, 1870–1914*, Newton Abbot, 1974.
Phizacklea, A. (ed.), *One Way Ticket*, London, 1983.
Plant, G. F., *A Survey of Voluntary Effort in Women's Empire Migration*, London, Society for the Oversea Settlement of British Women, 1950.
Plant, G. F., *Oversea Settlement: Migration from the United Kingdom to the Dominions*, London, 1951.
Pollins, H., *Economic History of the Jews in England*, London and Toronto, 1982.
Pooley, C. G., 'Migration, mobility and residential areas in nineteenth century Liverpool', unpublished Ph.D. thesis, University of Liverpool, 1978.
Pooley, C. G., 'Welsh migration to England in the mid-nineteenth century' *Journal of Historical Geography*, 9, 1983, pp. 287–305.
Poos, L. R., 'Population turnover in medieval Essex: the evidence of some early fourteenth-century tithing lists', in L. Bonfield, R. M. Smith and K. Wrightson (eds), *The World We Have Gained: Histories of Population and Social Structure*, Oxford, 1986, pp. 1–22.

Pound, J., *Poverty and Vagrancy in Tudor England*, London, 1971.

Pred, A., 'The social becomes the spatial, the spatial becomes the social: enclosures, social change and the becoming of places in Skane', in D. Gregory and J. Urry (eds), *Social Relations and Spatial Structures*, London, 1985, pp. 337-365.

Pritchard, R. M., *Housing and the Spatial Structure of the City*, Cambridge, 1976.

Pryce, W. T. R., 'Migration and the evolution of culture areas; culture and linguistic frontiers in north east Wales 1750–1851', *Transactions of the Institute of British Geographers*, 65, 1975, pp. 79–108.

Pryce, W. T. R., 'Wales as a culture region: patterns of change 1750–1971', *Transactions of the Honourable Society of Cymmrodorian*, 1978, pp. 229–61.

Ravenstein, E. G., 'Census of the British Isles, 1871: Birthplaces and Migration', *Geographical Magazine*, 3 1876, pp. 173–7, 201–6.

Ravenstein, E. G., 'Laws of migration: counties and general', *Geographical Magazine*, 3, 1876, pp. 229–33.

Ravenstein, E. G., 'The laws of migration', *Journal of the Royal Statistical Society*, 48, 1885, pp. 167–227.

Ravenstein, E. G., 'The laws of migration', *Journal of the Royal Statistical Society*, 52, 1889, pp. 214–301.

Razi, Z., *Marriage and Death in a Medieval Parish: Economy, Society and Demography in Halesown 1270–1400*, Cambridge, 1980.

Redford, A., *Labour Migration in England 1800–1850*, Manchester, 3rd edition, 1976.

Rees, A. D., *Life in a Welsh Countryside: a Social Study of Llanfihangel yng Ngwynfa*, Cardiff, 1950.

Reese, T. R., *The History of the Royal Commonwealth Society 1868–1968*, London, 1968.

Report of the Select Committee, Appointed to Enquire into the Expediency of Encouraging Emigration from the United Kingdom, 1826, (404), IV.I.

Rex, J., *Race Relations in Sociological Theory*, London, 1970.

Rex, J., *Race, Colonialism and the City*, London, 1973.

Rham, W. L., *The Dictionary of the Farm*, London, 1850.

Rich, P. B., review of *John Bull's Island* in *History Today*, 39, April 1989.

Richards, E., 'Problems on the Cromartie Estate', *Scottish Historical Review*, 41, 1973.

Richards, E., 'A voice from below: Benjamin Boyce in South Australia 1839–1846', *Labour History*, 27, 1974.

Richards, E., 'The Highland Scots and South Australia in the 1850s', *Journal of the Historical Society of South Australia*, 4, 1978.

Richards, E., 'Immigrant Lives', in E. Richards (ed.), *The Flinders History of South Australia. Social History*, Adelaide, 1986.

Richards, E., 'Australia and the Scottish Diaspora', in J. Hardy, *Stories of Australian Migration*, Sydney, 1988.

Richardson, C., 'Irish Settlement in mid-nineteenth-century Bradford', Yorkshire Bulletin of Economic and Social Research, 20, 1968, pp. 40–57.

Robbins, K., *The Eclipse of a Great Power: Modern Britain 1870–1975*, London, 1983.

Roberts, B., 'A work of Empire: Canadian reformers and British female immigration', in L. Kealey (ed.), *A Not Unreasonable Claim: Women and Reform in Canada 1880-1920*, Toronto, 1979.

Robin, J., *Elmdon: Continuity and Change in a North-West Essex Village 1861-1964*, Cambridge, 1980.

Robin, J., 'Family care of the elderly in a nineteenth-century Devonshire parish', *Ageing and Society*, 4(4), 1984, pp. 505-16.

Rodgers, M., 'The Anglo-Russian military convention and the Lithuanian immigrant community in Lanarkshire, Scotland 1914-20', *Immigrants and Minorities*, 1, 1982, pp. 60-88.

Rogers, A. and Castro, L. J., *Model Migration Schedules*, Luxembourg, 1981.

Roxby, P., 'Rural depopulation in England during the nineteenth century', *Nineteenth Century and After*, 71, 1912, pp. 174-90.

Rushdie, S., 'The Empire writes back with a vengeance', *The Times*, 3 July 1982.

Salaman, R. N., 'The Jewish Fellows of the Royal Society', *Miscellanies of the Jewish Historical Society of England*, part 5, 1948.

Saville, J., *Rural Depopulation in England and Wales, 1851-1951*, London, 1957.

Saxon Mills, J., 'Unemployment and the Empire', *Contemporary Review*, March 1922, p. 317.

Schofield, R. S., 'Age specific mobility in an eighteenth century rural English parish', *Annales de Démographie Historique*, 1971, pp. 261-74.

Schofield, R. S., 'Traffic in corpses: some evidence from Barming, Kent (1788-1912)', *Local Population Studies*, 33, 1984, pp. 49-53.

Scholes, A. G., *Education for Empire Settlement: a Study of Juvenile Migration*, London, 1982.

Schultz, J. A., 'Canadian attitudes towards Empire Settlement, 1919-1930', *Journal of Imperial and Commonwealth History*, 1, 1973, pp. 237-51.

Schultz, J. A., 'Finding homes fit for heroes: the Great War and Empire Settlement', *Canadian Journal of History*, 18, 1983, pp. 99-110.

Schurer, K., 'Historical Demography, Social Structure and the Computer', in P. Denley and D. Watson (eds), *History and Computing*, Manchester, 1987, pp. 33-45.

Schurer, K., 'Migration, population and social structure. A comparative study based in rural Essex, 1850-1900', unpublished Ph.D. thesis, University of London, 1988.

Schurer, K., Oeppen, J. and Schofield, R., 'Theory and methodology: an example from historical demography', in P. Denley, S. Fogelvik and C. Harvey, *History and Computing II*, Manchester, 1989, pp. 130-42.

Sedgwick, T. E., 'Town lads on Imperial farms', London 1935.

Sewell, W. H., *The Men and Women of Marseille, 1820-1870*, Cambridge, 1985.

Shaw, A. G. L., *Convicts and the Colonies*, London, Faber, 1966.

Shaw, F. J., *The Northern and Western Islands of Scotland: Their Economy and Society in the Seventeenth Century*, Edinburgh, 1980.

Shepperson, W. S., *British Emigration to North America*, Oxford, 1957.

Sherington, G., *Australia's Immigrants*, Sydney, 1980.

Shryock, H. S. and Siegel, J. S. et al., *The Methods and Materials of Demography*, New York, 1976.

Shultz, R. J., 'Review article: Immigration into eastern Australia, 1788–1851', *Historical Studies*, 14, 1970, pp. 273–82.
Sidney, S., *The Three Colonies of Australia*, London, 1852.
Smith, C. T., 'The movement of population in England and Wales in 1851 and 1861', *Geographical Journal*, 107, 1951, pp. 200–10.
Smith, D. (ed.), *A People and a Proletariat, Essays in the History of Wales 1780–1980*, London, 1980.
Smith, R. M., 'Kin and neighbours in a thirteenth-century Suffolk community', *Journal of Family History*, 4, 1979, pp. 219–56.
Smout, T. C., *Scottish Trade on the Eve of Union*, Edinburgh, 1963.
Smout, T. C., *A History of the Scottish People 1560–1830*, Glasgow, 1972.
Snell, K. D. M., 'Parish registration and the study of labour mobility', *Local Population Studies*, 33, 1984, pp. 29–43.
Snell, K. D. M., *Annals of the Labouring Poor*, Cambridge, 1985.
South Australian Parliamentary Papers: *Reports of the Select Committee of the Legislative Council of South Australia into the Excessive Female Immigration*, Adelaide, 1856.
Sponza, L., *Italian Immigrants in Nineteenth-Century Britain: Realities and Images*, Leicester, 1988.
Stevenson, J., *British Society 1914–45*, London, 1984.
Swift, R. and Gilley, S. (eds), *The Irish in the Victorian City*, London, Croom Helm, 1985.
Swift, R. and Gilley, S. (eds), *The Irish in Britain 1815–1939*, London, 1989.
Swinerton, E. N., Kuepper, W. G. and Lackey, G. L., *Ugandan Asians in Great Britain*, London, Croom Helm, 1975.
Sword, K. et al., *The Formation of the Polish Community in Great Britain*, London, 1989.
Sykes, A. O., *Tariff Reform in British Politics 1908–1913*, Oxford, 1979.
Tannahill, J. A., *European Volunteer Workers in Britain*, Manchester, 1958.
Taylor, A. J. P., *English History 1914–1945*, Oxford, 1965.
Thane, P., *The Foundations of the Welfare State*, London, 1982.
Thirsk, J., 'Industries in the countryside', in F. J. Fisher (ed.), *Essays in the Economic and Social History of Tudor and Stuart England*, London, 1961, pp. 70–88.
Thirsk, J., *England's Agricultural Regions and Agrarian History 1500–1750*, London, 1987.
Thistlethwaite, F., 'Migration from Europe overseas in the nineteenth and twentieth centuries', *Comité International des Sciences Historique*, XIe Congress, Report, V, 1974, pp. 32–61.
Thomas, B., 'The migration of labour into the Glamorganshire coalfield 1861–1911', *Economica*, 10, 1930, pp. 275–94.
Tillot, P. M., 'Sources of inaccuracy in the 1851 and 1861 censuses', in E. A. Wrigley (ed.), *Nineteenth-Century Society: Essays in the Use of Quantitative Methods for the Study of Social Data*, Cambridge, 1972.
Tilly, C. (ed.), *Historical Studies of Changing Fertility*, Princeton, 1978.
Timperley, L., 'The pattern of landholding in eighteenth-century Scotland', in M. L. Parry and T. R. Slater (eds), *The Making of the Scottish Countryside*, London, 1980, pp. 137–54.
Trinder, B. (ed.), *Victorian Shrewsbury*, Shropshire Libraries, 1984.

Trollope, J., *Britannia's Daughters: Women of the British Empire*, London, 1988.

Tucker, W., 'Patterns of migration of textile workers in Accrington in the early nineteenth century', *Local Population Studies*, 30, 1983, pp. 28–34.

Tupling, G. H., *The Economic History of Rossendale*, Manchester, 1927.

Van Helton, J. J. and Williams, K., 'The crying need of South Africa: the emigration of single British women to the Transvaal, 1901–10', *Journal of Southern African Studies*, 10, 1983, pp. 17–38.

Vincent, D., *Bread, Knowledge and Freedom: A Study of Nineteenth-Century Working Class Autobiography*, London, 1981.

Visram, R., *Ayahs, Lascars and Princes. Indians in Britain 1700–1947*, London, 1986.

Wagner, G., *Children of the Empire*, London, 1982.

Wakefield, E. G., *A View of the Art of Colonization in Letters Between a Statesman and a Colonist*, Oxford, 1914.

Wall, R., 'Work, welfare and the family: an illustration of the adaptive family economy', in L. Bonfield, R. M. Smith, and K. Wrightson (eds), *The World We Have Gained: Histories of Population and Social Structure*, Oxford, 1986, pp. 261–94.

Walton, J. R., 'Agriculture, 1730–1900', in R. A. Dodgshon, and R. A. Butlin (eds), *An Historical Geography of England and Wales*, London, 1978, pp. 239–65.

Walvin, J., *Black and White. The Negro in English Society 1555–1945*, London, 1973, re-issued London, 1988.

Ward, D., 'Environs and neighbours in the "Two Nations": Residential differentiation in mid-nineteenth-century Leeds', *Journal of Historical Geography*, 6, 1980, pp. 133–62.

Wareing, J., 'Changes in the geographical distribution of recruitment of apprentices to the London companies 1486–1750', *Journal of Historical Geography*, 6, 1980, pp. 241–9.

Warner, S. B., *The Private City – Philadelphia in Three Periods of Growth*, Philadelphia, 1968.

Warren, A., 'Citizens of the Empire: Baden-Powell, Scouts and Guides and an imperial ideal, 1900–40', in J. Mackenzie (ed.), *Imperialism and Popular Culture*, Manchester, 1986.

Watson, J. L. (ed.), *Between Two Cultures. Migrants and Minorities in Britain*, Oxford, 1977.

Werly, J., 'The Irish in Manchester', *Irish Historical Studies*, 18, 1973, pp. 345–58.

Wertimer, S., 'Migration from the United Kingdom to the dominions in the inter-war years, with special reference to the Empire Settlement Act of 1922', unpublished Ph.D. thesis, University of London, 1952.

West, A. G. B., 'Empire settlement and unemployment', Georgian Pamphlet 1, sold for the benefit of the St George's Day Fund for Child Migration, 1934.

White, J. D., 'Scottish Lithuanians and the Russian Revolution', *Journal of Baltic Studies*, 6, 1975, pp. 1–8.

White, M. B., 'Family migration in Victorian Britain: the case of Grantham and Scunthorpe', *Local Population Studies*, 41, 1988, pp. 41–50.

White, P. and Woods, R., *The Geographical Impact of Migration*, London, 1980.
Whyte, I. D., 'Written leases and their impact on Scottish agriculture in the seventeenth and eighteenth centuries', *Agricultural History Review*, 27, 1979, pp. 1–9.
Whyte, I. D., *Agriculture and Society in Seventeenth-Century Scotland* Edinburgh, 1979.
Whyte, I D., 'Marriage and mobility in East Lothian in the seventeenth and eighteenth centuries', *Transactions of the East Lothian Antiquarian Society*, 19, 1987, pp. 5–15.
Whyte, I. D., 'Urbanization in early-modern Scotland: a preliminary analysis', *Scottish Economic and Social History*, 9, 1989, pp. 21–37.
Whyte, I. D., 'Population mobility', in R. A. Houston and I. D. Whyte (eds), *Scottish Society 1500–1800*, Cambridge, 1989.
Whyte, I. D. and Whyte, K. A., 'Geographical mobility in a seventeenth-century Scottish rural community', *Local Population Studies*, 32, 1984a, pp. 45–53.
Whyte, I. D. and Whyte, K. A., 'Continuity and change in a seventeenth-century Scottish rural community', *Agricultural History Review*, 32, 1984b, pp. 159–69.
Whyte, I. D. and Whyte, K. A., 'Patterns of migration of apprentices to Aberdeen and Inverness during the seventeenth and eighteenth centuries', *Scottish Geographical Magazine*, 102, 1986, pp. 81–91.
Whyte, I. D. and Whyte, K. A., 'The geographical mobility of women in early-modern Scotland', in L. Leneman (ed.), *Perspectives in Scottish Social History*, Aberdeen, 1988.
Williams, B., *The Making of Manchester Jewry 1740–1875*, Manchester, 1976.
Williams Davies, J., 'Merched y Gerddi: a seasonal migration of women', *Folk Life*, 15, 1977.
Williams, K. I., 'The British State, social imperialism and emigration 1900–1922: the ideology and antecedents of the Empire Settlement Act of 1922', unpublished Ph.D. thesis, University of London, 1985.
Williams, K. I., 'A way out of our troubles: the politics of Empire Settlement 1900–22', in S. Constantine (ed.), *Emigrants and Empire: British Settlement in the Dominions Between the Wars*, Manchester, 1990.
Williams, L. J., *Digest of Welsh Historical Statistics*, Cardiff, Welsh Office, 1985.
Williams, L. J. and Boyns, T., 'Occupations in Wales 1851–1911', *Bulletin of Economic Research*, Aberystwyth, 1977.
Williams, W. M., *A West Country Village: Ashworthy*, London, 1963.
Withers, C., 'Highland migration to Dundee, Perth and Stirling 1753–1891', *Journal of Historical Geography*, 11, 1985, pp. 295–318.
Wojciechowska, B., 'Brenchley: a study of migratory movements in a mid-nineteenth-century rural parish', *Local Population Studies*, 41, 1988, pp. 28–40.
Wojciechowska-Kibble, B., 'Migration and the rural labour market: Kent, 1841–71', unpublished Ph.D. thesis, University of Kent at Canterbury, 1984.
Wolniakowski, E. B., 'Family and population change in a nineteenth-century English village', unpublished Ph.D. thesis, Cornell University, 1976.

Wormald, J., *Court, Kirk and Community. Scotland 1470–1625*, London, 1981.
Wrightson, K., *English Society 1580–1680*, London, 1982.
Wrigley, E. A., *An Introduction to English Historical Demography*, London, 1966.
Wrigley, E. A. (ed.), *Nineteenth-Century Society: Essays in the Use of Quantitative Methods for the Study of Social Data*, Cambridge, 1972.
Wrigley, E. A. (ed.), *Identifying People in the Past*, London, 1973.
Wrigley, E. A., 'Fertility strategy for the individual and the group', in C. Tilly (ed.), *Historical Studies of Changing Fertility*, Princeton, 1978, pp. 135–54.
Wrigley, E. A. and Schofield, R. S., *The Population History of England 1541–1700*, Cambridge, 1981.
Young, K., 'Sex specificity in migration: a case from Mexico', *International Migration Review*, 14(1), 1980.
Youngson, A. J., *After the Forty Five*, Edinburgh, 1973.

Index

For Product Safety Concerns and Information please contact our EU
representative GPSR@taylorandfrancis.com
Taylor & Francis Verlag GmbH, Kaufingerstraße 24, 80331 München, Germany

www.ingramcontent.com/pod-product-compliance
Ingram Content Group UK Ltd.
Pitfield, Milton Keynes, MK11 3LW, UK
UKHW020158200926
475702UK00004B/516

* 9 7 8 1 0 3 2 0 0 0 0 2 2 *